THE BEST YEARS CATALOGUE

A SOURCE BOOK FOR OLDER AMERICANS

SOLVING PROBLEMS & LIVING FULLY

LEONARD BIEGEL

Consulting Editor: Orial A. Redd, Assistant
to the Westchester County Executive for Human Development

Graphics and Design by Roberta Biegel

G. P. PUTNAM'S SONS
New York

Also by Leonard Biegel:
MEDIABILITY: A GUIDE FOR NONPROFITS
(coauthored with Aileen Lubin)

CONTENTS

1
About Aging 12
Know thyself . . . and others/12 Attitudes toward aging/15
Better aging/16 Retirement/20 Fiction/22
Poetry/23 Films/24

2
Food 28
Better and cheaper nutrition/28 Cooking and growing/34
Products and processes/37 Special diets/39

3
Shelter 42
Condominiums and other residences/42 Buying and selling a home/44 Making the move/45 Home improvement and maintenance/46 Nursing homes/49

4
Health 52
Health during retirement/52 Fitness/53 Sex/56 General medical care/58 Special care and conditions/60

5
Safety 80
Protection from crime/80 Product and personal safety/87
Important products for safety/89 Driver improvement/89

6
Creative Leisure 90
Planning for creative leisure/91 Education/91 Gardening/97
Crafts/99 Sewing/107 Pets/109 Sports/110

For Mother, who had a source for everything

Contents

7
Transportation and Travel 112
Travel arrangements/113   Medical emergencies while away/120   Special travel help/122

8
Money 124
Financial preparation for retirement/124   Taxes/127   Social Security and government benefits/128   Getting your money's worth/131   Making money during retirement/141

9
Joining and Sharing 144
Major membership organizations/145   Special programs/153   Volunteering/158   Professional organizations concerned with aging/164

10
Communicating 168
Government publications and resources/168   Magazines/172   To ease handicaps/178   Helping those alone to keep in touch/182   Media resources/184   History/186   Stories for children/187

11
Rights and Legacies 188
Federal and state activities/189   Legal aspects/195   Some final words/198

Index 203

ACKNOWLEDGMENTS

The author is most appreciative to countless people and organizations that have provided inspiration and information. Special thanks are due Orial Redd for her tireless hours reviewing the manuscript and giving hints; to the American Optometric Association for recommendations on the type sizes in which this book has been set; to Jack Ossofsky and Rebecca Eckstein, of the National Council on the Aging, who first raised my awareness of the problems and possibilities of older people; and, for the encouragement and inspiration they provided, to Ed Kaskowitz of the Gerontological Society, to Richard Davis of the Andrus Gerontology Center of the University of Southern California, and to Steve Mehlman of the American Association of Retired Persons.

NOTE ON ABBREVIATIONS

In order to conserve space, certain frequently recurring names are often abbreviated, as follows:

American Medical Association (AMA); American Association of Retired Persons (AARP); Food and Drug Administration (FDA); Health, Education, and Welfare, U. S. Department of (HEW); U.S. Department of Housing and Urban Development (HUD); National Council on the Aging (NCOA); National Institute on Aging (NIA), a constituent part of the National Institutes of Health (NIH); National Retired Teachers Association (NRTA); U.S. Department of Agriculture (USDA); U.S. Government Printing Office (USGPO).

CONTENTS

1
About Aging 12
Know thyself . . . and others/12   Attitudes toward aging/15
Better aging/16   Retirement/20   Fiction/22
Poetry/23   Films/24

2
Food 28
Better and cheaper nutrition/28   Cooking and growing/34
Products and processes/37   Special diets/39

3
Shelter 42
Condominiums and other residences/42   Buying and selling a home/44   Making the move/45   Home improvement and maintenance/46   Nursing homes/49

4
Health 52
Health during retirement/52   Fitness/53   Sex/56   General medical care/58   Special care and conditions/60

5
Safety 80
Protection from crime/80   Product and personal safety/87
Important products for safety/89   Driver improvement/89

6
Creative Leisure 90
Planning for creative leisure/91   Education/91   Gardening/97
Crafts/99   Sewing/107   Pets/109   Sports/110

For Mother, who had a source for everything

THE BEST YEARS CATALOGUE

A SOURCE BOOK FOR OLDER AMERICANS

SOLVING PROBLEMS & LIVING FULLY

LEONARD BIEGEL

Copyright © 1978 by Leonard Biegel

Graphics and design by Roberta Biegel

All rights reserved. This book, or parts thereof, may not be reproduced in any form without permission. Published simultaneously in Canada by Longman Canada Limited, Toronto.

SBN: 399-11898-5 (hard cover)
399-12093-9 (soft cover)

Library of Congress Cataloging in Publication Data

Biegel, Leonard
  The best years catalogue.

  Bibliography
  Includes index.
  1. Aged—United States—Handbooks, Manuals, etc.
2. Aged—Societies and clubs—Directories.
I. Title.
HQ1064.U5B38   1978   301.43′5′0973   77-24196

PRINTED IN THE UNITED STATES OF AMERICA

ACKNOWLEDGMENTS

The author is most appreciative to countless people and organizations that have provided inspiration and information. Special thanks are due Orial Redd for her tireless hours reviewing the manuscript and giving hints; to the American Optometric Association for recommendations on the type sizes in which this book has been set; to Jack Ossofsky and Rebecca Eckstein, of the National Council on the Aging, who first raised my awareness of the problems and possibilities of older people; and, for the encouragement and inspiration they provided, to Ed Kaskowitz of the Gerontological Society, to Richard Davis of the Andrus Gerontology Center of the University of Southern California, and to Steve Mehlman of the American Association of Retired Persons.

NOTE ON ABBREVIATIONS

In order to conserve space, certain frequently recurring names are often abbreviated, as follows:

American Medical Association (AMA); American Association of Retired Persons (AARP); Food and Drug Administration (FDA); Health, Education, and Welfare, U. S. Department of (HEW); U.S. Department of Housing and Urban Development (HUD); National Council on the Aging (NCOA); National Institute on Aging (NIA), a constituent part of the National Institutes of Health (NIH); National Retired Teachers Association (NRTA); U.S. Department of Agriculture (USDA); U.S. Government Printing Office (USGPO).

Contents

7
Transportation and Travel 112
Travel arrangements/113   Medical emergencies while away/120   Special travel help/122

8
Money 124
Financial preparation for retirement/124   Taxes/127   Social Security and government benefits/128   Getting your money's worth/131   Making money during retirement/141

9
Joining and Sharing 144
Major membership organizations/145   Special programs/153   Volunteering/158   Professional organizations concerned with aging/164

10
Communicating 168
Government publications and resources/168   Magazines/172   To ease handicaps/178   Helping those alone to keep in touch/182   Media resources/184   History/186   Stories for children/187

11
Rights and Legacies 188
Federal and state activities/189   Legal aspects/195   Some final words/198

Index 203

INTRODUCTION

Today's more than 22 million Americans 65 and over are healthier, better educated, more vital, and with better prospects for long life than any previous generation. We know, despite some commonly held misconceptions, that older people are as diverse as any other age group. At the same time, they have several things in common:

    The experience and perspective of years
    A potential for many more productive years
    Rights and freedoms
    A potential to share and to act together

Today's older people are finding solutions to problems by standing up and being counted.

Being older means complete or partial retirement for some, continued or new careers and interests for others. And for many it also means specific problems of money, health or searches for interesting ways to spend time.

Many people say that it is possible to grow old gracefully. But growing old today, while it has more years and more potentials, is work too. While it is not the work of the office, the factory or the shop, it is the work of individual and group ingenuity.

In a world that has grown more complex, so have the problems and the solutions. Money is not always the answer—though some of its advantages cannot be denied. While this book cannot press magic buttons, it can give a broad cross section of sources for living more joyously, comfortably and productively in the later years.

Considering the diverse profile and the need to bring together some of the specifics of what to do and where to turn in order to help lead more fulfilling and independent lives, we set about finding and checking out countless sources to form this book. We took the joys, the problems, the challenges and looked for sources. While some are specifically for older people, many sources are appropriate for others as well.

We have made every attempt to check the reliability and accuracy of each source in this book. Inevitably some will change, whether in cost or in nature, and though we cannot accept responsibility, we hope you will let us know of any problems. Please tell us when you are satisfied also.

If anything we have done by way of this book leads you to some of your own sourcery, please let us know that, too. If we find there are enough new sources from time to time, you may be helping to put out a new edition.

What to call this book and—more important—what to call the readers, has consumed a good deal of thought of the author and many others. Time and again, as we listened to our potential readers talk among themselves and to younger people, they seldom referred to themselves as old. When the letters o.l.d. are used, they are part of the word old*er*. For the 65-year-old, he or she is old*er* than the 50-year-old. But the 95-year-old is also simply old*er* than the 85-year-old.

The use of cute or all-encompassing terms seems generally the work of those who feel compelled to fit this very diverse group of older people into some niche. We have heard all sorts of references, such as senior citizen, golden ager, old-timer or senior. For the recent Harris survey, **The Myth and Reality of Aging in America**, people 65 and over were asked the extent to which they have preferences for what they are called.

Approximately one in three were indifferent to which names are used. And of those who expressed some strong likes and dislikes, "mature American" (liked by 55%), "retired person" (53%) and "senior citizen" (50%) seemed to signify used and acceptable terms.

The least popular were "old man" or "old woman" (disliked by 67%), "aged person" (45%) and "golden-ager" (36%).

As you read through this book, you will find older Americans referred to in a wide variety of ways by certain programs or publications listed and recommended. We suggest you not be turned off by the titles to the extent that you do not take advantage of the sources. If the titles of some publications personally offend you, voice that opinion to the group responsible. You may effect a change.

Consider each source as offering a specific and current answer, information for the future, or a door-opener leading to other sources.

Given the wherewithal to find the places with the answers, along with the willingness to utilize them, it is reasonable to expect, as a nation and as individuals, that we can cope with and solve many of our problems. And the problems attendant on growing older *are* solvable. We hope that this book will lead in many directions. The sources are numerous and frequently of immediate use. For some readers and for some problems, they may offer comfort, understanding or inspiration. For the problems that are solvable, we wish you good sourcery.

ABOUT AGING 1

Everyone desires to live long, but no one would be old.

—Jonathan Swift,
1667–1745
Irish satirist

THE COMING OF AGE
By Simone de Beauvoir
Warner Paperback Library,
1973, $2.25

This book is without question *the* monumental work on the subject of aging. In the broad scope of history, it covers how the aging have been revered or mistreated and misunderstood. The author makes a fierce indictment of the ways in which society is indifferent and even cruel to older people who, in their younger times, made society function.

THE AGE OF LONGEVITY

We know more about the physical, emotional and practical aspects of aging than ever before. And the chances of living to the "ripe old age" are greater than ever.

A great deal has been surveyed, researched and written, and we think its a good idea to start by telling you of some of the books, films and other sources for understanding more about age; how we prepare for it; and how we are continuing to define the problems and cope with them.

A lazy day in a rowboat may be fun; but retirement today can be more than "gone fishin'."

GROWING OLD IN THE COUNTRY OF THE YOUNG
By Senator Charles Percy
and Charles Mangel
McGraw-Hill, 1974, $7.95

Senator Percy here not only describes the problems of older people, but offers encouragement and a rationale for the growth of "senior power" to continue to solve some of the problems of coping with the older years. Several specific suggestions are made which can help improve the older years.

Know thyself . . . and others

Age does not depend on years, but upon temperament and health. Some men are born old, and some never grow so.

—Tryon Edwards, 1809–1894
American theologian

KNOW THYSELF . . . AND OTHERS

Age is more than chronology. It is at once a state of mind, years, and a frequently fruitful time past 65. What do you really know about growing older? Try our quiz. If you score less than seven correct, you have a great deal to catch up on.

1. How many people are there over 65 in the United States today?
   a) over 22 million   b) over 15 million   c) 30 million
2. Michelangelo produced some of his greatest works in his later years. He lived to what age?
   a) 67   b) 80   c) 89
3. According to established scientific data, the human body's ability to work begins to decline significantly at which age?
   a) 62   b) 72   c) 65
4. According to a Harris survey, 60% of the general public think they themselves are good at getting things done. What percentage of people over 65 think this of themselves?
   a) 20%   b) 60%   c) 55%
5. The state with the largest population over 65 is:
   a) Hawaii   b) California   c) Florida   d) New York   e) Arizona
6. Colonel Sanders began his famous fried chicken business at what age?
   a) 50   b) 70   c) 66
7. What percentage of people over 65 is in the work force?
   a) 2%   b) 5%   c) 10%   d) 14%   e) 19%
8. The average life expectancy for a person who has reached 65 is:
   a) 72   b) 80   c) 75
9. How many people over 65 are confined to some type of institution?
   a) 20%   b) 5%   c) 2%
10. How old was Noah Webster when he finished writing his dictionary?
    a) 70   b) 66   c) 60

It takes a long time to become young.

—Pablo Picasso at 86

GROWING OLD: AN EXPLORATION OF OUR TREATMENT OF AND RESOURCES FOR THE AGING
By Gordon Moss and Walter Moss
Pocket Books, 1975, $1.50

The glorification of youth and the problems of growing older run throughout this book of essays on aging in this country. A varied, fascinating perspective is offered on how we have regarded age in the past, how we look upon it today, and what the hope is for the future.

ABOUT AGING   1

KNOW THYSELF . . . AND OTHERS

Answers to the quiz:

1. **a** is the correct answer. And that represents over 10% of the total population. Back in 1900, people over 65 were about 4%.
2. **c** is correct.
3. None of the choices is correct. There is no evidence that, with the exception of serious illness, age per se carries with it a declining physical capacity for work.
4. **c** is correct.
5. **d** for New York is correct, with an over-65 population of about 1,998,000. California is next with 1,986,000. Florida, though very popular, has 1,267,000.
6. **c** is correct.
7. **d** is correct.
8. **b** is correct. Actually this is an average of the two sexes, with statistics giving men an expectancy of 78 and women of 82 once 65 is reached.
9. **b** is correct.
10. **a** is correct.

NEW FACTS ABOUT OLDER AMERICANS

How many older Americans are there? Where do older Americans live? Has life expectancy changed? How many older persons work?

The fascinating answers to these questions are found in a small pamphlet prepared by the Administration on Aging.

25¢
Publication #SRS 73-20006
USGPO
Washington, D.C. 20402

A GOOD AGE
By Alex Comfort
Crown, 1976, $9.95

In this beautifully illustrated book Dr. Comfort stresses the strengths of age as well as the indignities which society has forced upon most of us as we grow older. The book calls upon everyone to rise to the cause of the growing over-65 population. It is particularly useful as an inspiration for people in organizations trying to improve the image and conditions of older people.

OLDER AMERICANS ARE A NATIONAL RESOURCE

This booklet, prepared by the Administration on Aging, describes the work of the state agencies on aging, The Federal Government's ACTION, and the Department of Labor.

Free
Publication #OHD/A0A 74-20810
USGPO
Washington, D.C. 20402

WHY SURVIVE? BEING OLD IN AMERICA
By Dr. Robert N. Butler
Harper and Row, 1975, $15

Dr. Butler, the director of the National Institute on Aging, won the Pulitzer Prize for this documentation of the problems of growing older in America today.

The book covers all the social aspects of life and its difficulties for many people and offers concrete proposals for solutions.

Thoroughly documented, it is an important source for anyone trying to understand the problems of growing older—and helping to effect change.

14

Know thyself . . . and others
Attitudes toward aging

FACTS AND MYTHS ABOUT AGING

The National Council on the Aging has been working to dispel the myths in this country about growing old, and this attractive booklet covers a broad spectrum of misconceptions—and truths. It treats physical as well as attitudinal aspects and gives several hints on how to help erase errors. The booklet is published with the Advertising Council as a public service.

Free
NCOA
1828 L St. NW
Washington, D.C. 20036

LOOKING AHEAD: A WOMAN'S GUIDE TO THE PROBLEMS AND JOYS OF GROWING OLDER
Edited by Lillian E. Troll, Joan Israel and Kenneth Israel
Prentice-Hall/Spectrum, 1977, $3.95

THE MYTH AND REALITY OF AGING IN AMERICA

In 1975, Louis Harris and Associates issued, for the National Council on the Aging (NCOA), the most complete survey ever conducted of the attitudes and perceptions of what it is like to grow older in America. The survey, financed by a grant from the Edna McConnell Clark Foundation, conducted in-home interviews with 4,250 Americans, both over and under 65.

The hundreds of fascinating questions and answers contained in the survey fall into the following classifications:

- ☐ Public attitudes toward old age
- ☐ Public expectation of most people over 65
- ☐ Social and economic contributions of people over 65
- ☐ Preparation for old age
- ☐ The experiences of being older
- ☐ Accessibility and use of community facilities by the over-65 public
- ☐ The media and the image of people over 65
- ☐ The politics of old age

The results of the survey have broad implications for further study of the problems of growing old, as evidence of public opinion about aging and as an agenda for the dispelling of baseless myths.

For additional information, contact:
The National Council on the Aging
1828 L St. NW
Washington, D.C. 20036

This collection of essays offers insights into marital, sexual and family problems; jobs; continuing education; and psychotherapy.

OLD IS WHAT YOU GET: DIALOGUES ON AGING BY THE OLD AND THE YOUNG
By Ann Zane Shanks
Viking, 1976, $10

In exploring the fears and secrets of growing older, this book discloses a cross section of attitudes. Interviews were held with 17 elderly people in the U.S. and England and with nine teenagers in New York.

ABOUT AGING

THE NATIONAL INSTITUTE ON AGING

The National Institute on Aging of the National Institutes of Health was established by law on May 31, 1974, to organize a comprehensive national plan for research on aging. The institute, headquartered on the Bethesda campus of NIH, conducts and supports biomedical, social and behavioral research and training related to the aging process and the diseases and other special problems and needs of the aging.

In establishing this Institute, Congress had in mind the following:

- ☐ The study of the aging process—a biological condition common to all—has not received research support commensurate with its effects and importance.
- ☐ In addition to the physical infirmities resulting from advanced age, the associated economic, social and psychological factors operate to exclude millions from the full life and the place in society to which their years of service and experience entitle them.
- ☐ Recent research efforts point the way toward alleviation of the problems of old age by extending the healthy middle years of life.
- ☐ There is no American institution that has undertaken systematic and intensive studies of the biomedical and behavioral aspects of aging and related personnel training. NIA would be such an institution.

NIA began to take on full status in June, 1976, when Dr. Robert N. Butler was appointed its first director. The total NIA research scheme includes work done by:

- ☐ The Laboratory of Behavioral Sciences, which investigates the behavioral effects of age on the processes of learning, memory and cognition, as well as the impact of age on intelligence and personality.
- ☐ The Clinical Physiology Branch, which is conducting the Baltimore Longitudinal Study of Aging. The CPB monitors a control group in terms of cardiac capacity, exercise physiology, etc., as they age.
- ☐ The Laboratory of Cellular and Comparative Physiology, which studies the nature of the age-related deterioration of certain types of cells of the body.
- ☐ The Laboratory of Molecular Aging, which investigates the inability of organisms to maintain throughout later life physiological control systems and the genetic-information-transfer system. Its research

HOW TO LIVE TO BE 100
By Sula Benet
Dial, 1976, $8.95

152-year-old Shirim baba. Gasanov

Among the 17.5 million inhabitants of the Soviet republics of the Caucasus is the largest number of long-lived people in the world—men and women who continue into the 90's and often to 100 and more. They are not inactive in their later years, but are functioning, healthy people who work, make love, and have responsible community roles.

Dr. Benet, professor of anthropology at New York's Hunter College, records in this book her observations after living in Georgia, Abkhasia, Azerbaijan, Armenia and Daghestan. She analyzes various factors, including climate, geography, medical practices and diet. The explanation is not as simple as a fountain of youth, Dr. Benet concludes, and yet there are

Attitudes toward aging
Better aging

lessons we might learn about diet and life patterns.

Several dozen recipes culled from the visit are included in the book.

THE BEST YEARS OF YOUR LIFE
By Dr. Leopold Bellak
Atheneum, 1975, $10.00

Dr. Bellak sets out to be the "Dr. Spock for older people," and succeeds in some ways. Covering the broad spectrum of concerns and characteristics of older people, he gives dozens of hints and instills confidence that life can be better for this generation than for those which came before.

A GUIDE TO THE GOLDEN YEARS
By James Rusk, Jr.
Freeway Press, 1974, $1.50

. . . our basic thesis is that we are letting the game go by default, that exciting and gratifying possibilities are

considers the mechanism of age-dependent changes in metabolism, kidney, heart function, as well as muscle activity.

Additional research will likely center on endocrine change, immunology, cognitive change and the societal aspects of aging.

For further information on the research programs of NIA, write:

National Institute on Aging
National Institutes of Health
Bethesda, Md. 20014

waiting merely for us to recognize them, and that our national "problem" is really one of our richest opportunities.

This small book covers a great deal of ground for both older and younger people concerned with their retirement and aging. The problems are thoughtfully examined, and alternative lifestyles are examined from the emotional and physical points of view.

WHEN YOUR PARENTS GROW OLD
By Jane Otten and Florence Shelley
Funk and Wagnalls, 1976, $8.95

This book is geared toward helping adult sons and daughters help their parents as they grow older. And now when many people in their 60's have parents in the 80's, this is a useful book. It is not only proper reading for helping anticipate the crises, but is a handy reference when crisis strikes.

The authors stress the need for people to maintain independence as long as possible. Above all, the book is not dogmatic but succeeds in raising consciousness about the problems of aging, and gives alternative approaches to the solutions.

EDUCATION OF CHILDREN FOR THE NEW ERA OF AGING

Today's young will be tomorrow's old, and there is clear indication that life will be different for them, as today's old live different lives from those in the past.

The AMA in this booklet addresses the subject of educating the young to increased longevity prospects. The suggestions made for schoolteachers may be adapted by parents and grandparents discussing aging with younger family members.

25¢
Order Department
American Medical Association
535 North Dearborn St.
Chicago, Ill. 60610

ABOUT AGING 1

YOUNG TILL WE DIE
By Doris G. and David J. Jonas
Coward, McCann & Geoghegan, 1973, $6.95

The Jonases, a husband-wife team of social scientists, discuss the challenge of growing older in a youth-oriented society. They trace the history of the phenomenon, its consequences, and the remedies. Approximately half the book is devoted to the actions which older persons can take to lead fuller lives, including maintaining health and vigor. The authors stress that an older person should not voluntarily retire from active work—and if retirement must occur, to substitute employment with some other positive task, to seek new horizons, and not to give up the home.

AFTER 65: RESOURCES FOR SELF-RELIANCE

With increased longevity has come the concern with longer years of self-reliance. No one wants to depend on someone else if it can be avoided. This, another in the thoughtful series of Public Affairs Pamphlets, outlines the scope of services and opportunities for self-reliant living for older people.

50¢
Public Affairs Pamphlets
381 Park Ave. South
New York, N.Y. 10016

POWER OF YEARS: THE WISDOM OF ETHEL PERCY ANDRUS
By Dr. Ethel Percy Andrus
AARP-NRTA, 1968, Price on request

Dr. Andrus, the founder and president of the National Retired Teachers Association and the subsequently formed American Association of Retired Persons, wrote extensively on the philosophy of growing and being older. The overriding tone of all her writings is optimism and love of life. Collected in this volume are 49 of her editorials for AARP-NRTA publications.

AARP-NRTA
P.O. Box 2400
215 Long Beach Blvd.
Long Beach, Calif. 90801

THE WONDERFUL CRISIS OF MIDDLE AGE
By Eda LeShan
Warner Paperback Library, 1974, $1.50

Eda LeShan—educator, family counselor and author—has written a joyous book about aging. If 40 is the midpoint, she says, then one must look at the years in the second half of life as the great opportunity to call upon the experience of the past, to free oneself of the burdens of earlier years, and realize the full potentials of life. Step by step, she offers encouraging proof that "today is the first day of the rest of your life."

GREEN WINTER: CELEBRATIONS OF OLD AGE
By Elise Maclay
Reader's Digest Press, 1977, $7.95

For a lift, read or recommend **Green Winter** with its inspirational reflections on "the spirit of men and women I have known—some over a period of years—some for only an instant of intimacy."

TO THE GOOD LONG LIFE
By Morton Puner
Universe Books, 1974, $7.95

For each of the three major ways we age—biologically, socially and psychologically—the author explains what we know and what we can do to improve the quality of "the last of life, for which the first was made."

Along the way, the book exposes alleged life-prolonging quackery, such as monkey glands, rejuvenation pills and bizarre diets, and proceeds to give dozens of common-sense ways to live the longest life possible. An optimistic testament to the worth of age, it includes extensive proof of the progress being made toward longer lives and shows examples of many who, frequently against difficult odds, have made the "last the best."

Attitudes toward aging
Better aging

SUCCESSFUL AGING
By Dr. Olga Knopf
Viking, 1975, $8.95

Dr. Knopf, born in 1888, has written a clear-eyed view of herself and those around her—with some practical tips for making every day and year count. She talks of young people's dislike for older people and of older people's dislike of themselves. Using her background as a psychiatrist, she offers optimism for older people in a long list of everyday ways.

GETTING OLDER AND STAYING YOUNG
By Dr. D. D. Stonecypher
Norton, 1974, $8.95

And so, it is the business of old age, as of every age, to gain confidence and stimulation from normal living. That is the way we human beings keep able, calm our anxieties, and find happiness.

Dr. Stonecypher's survey of gerontology emphasizes that normal old age is healthy, that the true mental and physical capacities of older people are underrated by younger and older alike, that senility results not from physical decline but from a feeling of boredom and uselessness that may be brought on by retirement or by withdrawal from active life.

The Picassos of the world need not be exceptions, says the author . . . they should be the norm.

AGELESS AGING
By Ruth Winter
Crown, 1973, $5.95

Science writer Ruth Winter devotes this entire book to the discoveries at hand—and those on the horizon—that are aimed toward a longer life: a fascinating, practical handbook and a glimpse into what may be.

GROWING OLD AND HOW TO COPE WITH IT
By Alfons Deeken
Paulist Press, 1972, $1.45

The author, a Catholic priest, has written this book of practical advice and spiritual insight from both a religious point of view and from his observations of Chinese society, where the old are honored. The premise is that there are ways to work out the sorrows and the problems and that age can be a time of joy for those who seek it.

ABOUT AGING 1

NEW WRINKLES ON RETIREMENT

If you are part of a group trying to help other people prepare for retirement, television—in the form of videocassettes—may be of assistance. The Georgia Center for Continuing Education has produced eight television programs that may be purchased or rented for group use. The subjects include:

- ☐ Facing inflation
- ☐ Vigor retained
- ☐ A time to learn and a time to play
- ☐ Marriage and love in the later years
- ☐ Confronting loss
- ☐ Your heritage—avoiding legal problems through proper planning
- ☐ Avoiding quacks and frauds
- ☐ Maintaining happiness

Purchase prices: $50 per program or $350 for the complete series

Rental prices: $12 per program or $96 for the series

Program guides are available at 75¢ per copy for the first 100 and 50¢ per copy thereafter.

Write:
*Independent Study
Georgia Center for Continuing Education
Univ. of Georgia
Athens, Ga. 30602*

THE COMPLETE RETIREMENT PLANNING BOOK
By Peter A. Dickinson
Dutton, 1977, $6.95

Dickinson, a retirement-planning expert, has assembled a complete guide with over 75 charts to help keep track of and evaluate all the details involved in retirement. Topics covered include health, money, legal matters, the home and the wise use of time.

PLANNING FOR YOUR SUCCESSFUL RETIREMENT

This booklet makes a strong case for a productive life at 65. The text takes the reader through the retirement day, looking at the possibilities, and presents a strong case for productivity—and making constructive choices.

$1.50 to magazine subscribers, $2.25 to nonsubscribers

*Retirement Living Magazine
150 East 58th St.
New York, N.Y. 10022*

See COMMUNICATING for more on the magazine and its other publications.

ARE YOU PLANNING ON LIVING . . . THE REST OF YOUR LIFE?

Successful retirement doesn't just happen. And as the number of retired persons increases, they are finding several consistent characteristics of this new stage of life:

- Retirement from your job does not mean retirement from life.
- Retirement can be more than "moving to a warm climate" or "just fishing." Many people don't move. And going fishing, or any single activity, may become tiresome after a while.
- Good planning takes time. There is no set age to begin.

This attractive booklet, prepared by the Chicago Mayor's Commission for Senior Citizens, and reissued for the Administration on Aging, guides people facing retirement through various stages of personal planning, including where to live, finances, health factors, and new interests. The quiz technique used throughout poses probing questions to stimulate planning.

*80¢
USGPO
Washington, D.C. 20402*

Retirement

PREPARING FOR AGING
By Bert Kruger Smith
Hogg Foundation for Mental Health, Free

This condensation of Mr. Smith's sensitive book presents several examples of how diverse people prepared for successful retirement by assessing their goals, attributes and resources. Available from:

Hogg Foundation for Mental Health
Univ. of Texas
Austin, Tex. 78712

PRERETIREMENT PLANNING GUIDE

One of the main objectives of the Preretirement Planning Center is to provide information to help with the retirement years. The center offers a series of short courses covering the changing role of the individual in retirement, finances, health concerns, housing, consumerism, continuing education and leisure activities. The courses are conducted in Des Moines and from time to time elsewhere in the country.

The center also distributes a slide/tape program covering these subjects. It may be bought by organizations for $850 for the eight parts. For further information:

Preretirement Planning Center
3009 Ingersoll Ave.
Des Moines, Iowa 50312

THRESHOLD: THE FIRST DAYS OF RETIREMENT
By Alan H. Olmstead
Harper and Row, 1975, $8.95

This personal memoir of a former newspaper editor's entrance into retirement covers his thoughts, both trivial and major. A delight to share, his attitudes are supportive and thought-provoking for those in retirement. Reading the book is like meeting a new friend.

THE SOCIOLOGY OF RETIREMENT
By Robert C. Atchley
John Wiley and Sons, 1976, $12.50

This is a retirement backgrounder—first defining retirement and then looking at its past. It also examines the sociological implications of retirement. Although not a "how to" for the average person, this book is important for those who wish to lead others in the solution to problems of aging.

THE RETIREMENT BOOK
By Joan Adler
Morrow, 1975, $9.95

Essentially for retirement planning, this book has value as well for those who did not plan so thoroughly and need to catch up. Topics include launching a second career, the retirement living place, and making the best use of time. The book lists several source organizations for further assistance and offers good tips on health and nutrition in retirement.

ABOUT AGING 1

I NEVER TOLD ANYBODY: TEACHING POETRY IN A NURSING HOME
By Kenneth Koch
Random House, 1977,
$8.95

If you and others would like to share your thoughts perhaps in the form of poetry—Kenneth Koch's book is an inspiration.

Koch tells of his direct experiences eliciting thoughts of people old in body but rich in spirit. The experience is at once human, touching, and a testimony to the worth of age.

FICTION CAN REFLECT TRUTH

Novelists have frequently written about the wisdom, the problems and the joys of aging. As you browse among the library shelves, you may want to consider some of their creations:

Mr. Sammler's Planet, by Saul Bellow, Viking, 1970, Fawcett paperback, 1974
An aged Polish Jew, a scholar and philosopher who survived the Nazi camps, moves to New York and speculates on the present and future.

The Amazing Mrs. Pollifax, by Dorothy Gilman, Doubleday, 1970
Mrs. Emily Pollifax, a "nice little old lady," becomes a CIA operative sent to Istanbul to contact a defecting Russian agent. She accomplishes her mission, but not without involving herself with some hostile agents and the Turkish police. A delightful bit of fantasy!

Travels With My Aunt, by Graham Greene, Viking, 1970
This is another "armchair adventure"—the author's tale of a trip around the world with his 75-year-old aunt.

Harry and Tonto, by Josh Greenfield and Paul Mazursky, Saturday Review Press, 1974
This novel, made into a memorable motion picture, tells the story of a 72-year-old widower who, when faced with the demolition of his apartment building, picks up himself and his cat and embarks on an odyssey across the country.

The Two of Us, by Claude Berri, Morrow, 1968
An irascible, vehemently antisemitic old French peasant learns to love a nine-year-old put in his care, unaware at first that the boy is Jewish.

One Dragon Too Many, by Louise Field Cooper, Knopf, 1971
This novel is a good-natured exploration of communications between two mothers-in-law thrown together for two weeks while sharing babysitting chores for their grandchildren.

Fiction
Poetry

Angle of Repose, by Wallace Stegner, Doubleday, 1971
Determined to live independently despite crippling arthritis, an aging historian returns to his ancestral home to write the colorful story of his grandmother's life.

THE WORDS OF POETRY

Poets have frequently expressed their thoughts on growing older—and their words are not only some of the loveliest in the language, they are frequently among the most inspiring. The choices are endless, and the search is enjoyable. We offer some directions for starting on a poetry search:

"Let Me Grow Lovely," by Karle Wilson Baker, in **Best Loved Poems of the American People**, edited by Hazel Felleman, Doubleday, 1936
(This poem, with the lines, "Let me grow lovely, growing old . . . So many fine things to do," is frequently quoted.)

"Rabbi Ben Ezra," by Robert Browning
(This well-known poem centers around the line, "The last of life for which the first was made.")

"Do Not Go Gentle Into That Good Night," by Dylan Thomas, published in **Collected Poems of Dylan Thomas**, James Laughlin, 1953
(In a personal plea to his father, Dylan Thomas implored him to resist death, because "old age should burn and rave at close of day.")

"An Old Man's Winter Night," "Provide, Provide," "The Death of the Hired Man," by Robert Frost, in **Modern American Poetry**, edited by Louis Untermeyer, Harcourt, Brace and World, 1962

"For Age is Opportunity," "My Lost Youth," Henry Wadsworth Longfellow, in **The Book of Home Verse**, edited by Burton Stevenson, various editions.

WHAT THE POEM IS

By Gus Krantz

1
It's all what you take out of your mind,
what has happened to your life.
You think,
a man like myself over seventy . . .

2
You can leave rings and jewelry and all the nice stuff,
you can leave that,
but when you can leave something from your mouth, see,
that hangs in there.

YES, IT'S A PLEASURE

By Hildegarde Swensen

1
It's a pleasure to get away.
I can look here and there.
Many things I wouldn't see or enjoy
if I had a dog
or even another friend with me.

2
The snow is deep and pure clean.
The telephone poles are old and dark.
I see the cornfield's picked.
The weeds are stiff and brown
and I can see the white snow
left on the combine wheel track.

3
Yes, it's a pleasure to drive near dark.
The farmers are almost through with their chores,
I can see the lights yet.
The trees are as ever,
bare, and ready for a long winter.
They are undressed now
and perhaps they are soon resting and quiet.

Courtesy COMPAS, St. Paul-Ramsey Arts and Science Council

ABOUT AGING

FILMS ON AGING

In recent years many films have helped to stimulate group discussion on growing older or have served to highlight problems or suggest solutions to them. Nearly all the films are available for rental or purchase.

Some of the several hundred we have researched and screened are included in this description. The Andrus Gerontology Center of the University of Southern California publishes an annual catalogue of films on aging for $3.50. Some of the 16-mm, color films available are listed on these pages. Entitled **About Aging: A Catalog of Films**, it may be ordered from:

> *Publications Department*
> *Ethel Percy Andrus Gerontology Center*
> *Univ. of Southern California*
> *Los Angeles, Calif. 90007*

The Old Woman
2 minutes, 1973

This short film shows an old woman, apparently living alone, sewing and caring for her home. When Death visits in the form of an animated character, she overwhelms him with her busy schedule. And Death himself dies instead.

For sale:
ACI Films, Inc.
35 West 45th St.
New York, N.Y. 10036

For rental:
ACI Films, Inc.

Central Arizona Film Cooperative
Arizona State Univ.
Tempe, Ariz. 85281

Krasker Memorial Film Library
Boston Univ.
765 Commonwealth Ave.
Boston, Mass. 02215

Weekend
12 minutes, 1973

Not a happy film, but important if you need to highlight the plight of rejection. With little narration, it makes a strong statement. An old man living with his children is taken on a picnic and never brought back home but is left sitting in his rocking chair in a vast field with an endless number of other older people also in their rockers.

For sale:
Mass Media Ministries
2116 North Charles St.
Baltimore, Md. 21218

For rental:
Mass Media Ministries

Audio-visual Education Center
Univ. of Mich.
416 Fourth St.
Ann Arbor, Mich. 48104

Now is Forever
42 minutes, 1972

This film presents a series of portraits of active older men and women in San Francisco. The theme of activity as a weapon against the perils of age is constantly advanced.

For sale:
Film Dynamics
7250 Fair Oaks Blvd.
Carmichael, Calif. 95608

For rental:
Film Dynamics

Extension Media Center
Univ. of California
Berkeley, Calif. 94720

Central Arizona Film Cooperative
Arizona State Univ.
Tempe, Ariz. 85281

Audiovisual Center
Univ. of Wisconsin
1705 State
LaCrosse, Wis. 54601

The Art of Age
27 minutes, 1972

An articulate and positive film portraying four productive retired persons. They are a black mail carrier active as a fisherman and community volunteer, a retired businessman helping schoolchildren learn to read, a sculptress and a writer.

For sale:
ACI Films, Inc.
35 West 45th St.
New York, N.Y. 10036

Films

For rental:
ACI Films

The Violin
25 minutes, 1973

This film deals with the development of a young boy wishing to learn to play the violin and an old man who responds. Both benefit well beyond the actual lessons.

For Sale:
*Learning Corp. of America
1350 Ave. of the Americas
New York, N.Y. 10019*

For rental:
Learning Corp. of America

*Audio-visual Education Center
Univ. of Michigan
416 Fourth St.
Ann Arbor, Mich. 48104*

Picasso is 90
51 minutes

This biography of Picasso, produced as a television program by CBS News, traces the great artist's lifetime, shows his art and articulates his philosophy.

For sale:
*Carousel Films, Inc.
1501 Broadway
New York, N.Y. 10036*

For rental:
Carousel Films

*Audio-Visual Services
Pennsylvania State Univ.
6 Willard Bldg.
University Park, Pa. 16802*

Old Fashioned Woman
40 minutes, 1975

A personal portrait and a statement of the philosophy of 86-year-old Martha Tilton Coolidge, this film, produced by her granddaughter, Martha Coolidge, deals with morals, aging, and women's lib.

For sale or rental:
*Films, Inc.
1144 Wilmette Ave.
Wilmette, Ill. 60091*

Stringbean
17 minutes, 1965

A poetic statement confirming the vitality of even the least significant organism—here a bean plant—this French film is a symbolic and beautiful affirmation of life. It depicts a lonely old woman caring for the plant.

For sale:
*McGraw-Hill Films
Princeton-Hightstown Road
Hightstown, N.J. 08520*

For rental:
McGraw Hill Films

*Gerontological Film Collection
North Texas State Univ.
Main Library
Denton, Tex. 76203*

*Film Library
Oregon Division of Continuing Education
1633 S.W. Park
Portland, Ore. 97207*

The Blessings of Love
9 minutes, 1966

This thoroughly enjoyable film produced in Bulgaria is an animated parable. The main character, a man who ages throughout the film, is always living in hopes of capturing his dream. In youth it is to grow into an intellectual with witty friends. This dream achieved, he aspires to marry the woman of his dreams. He succeeds again, and the process continues until old age, when he dreams of youth as he looks at his wife. She dies, and he lingers in thought about their life together.

For sale or rental:
*MacMillan Audio Brandon
1619 North Cherokee St.
Los Angeles, Calif. 90028*

*Audiovisual Education Center
Univ. of Michigan
416 Fourth St.
Ann Arbor, Mich. 48104*

ABOUT AGING 1

The Joy of Communication
18 minutes, 1975

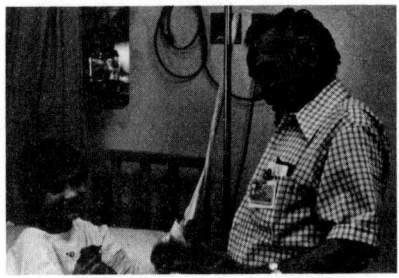

The unique joys of communicating and helping.

Communication between generations is the subject of this film. The joys and problems are revealed without dialogue through the faces and music alone.

For sale or rental:
*Dana Productions
6249 Babcock Ave.
North Hollywood, Calif. 91606*

Peege
28 minutes, 1974

Peege, the nickname for the central character of the grandmother, lives in a nursing home that appears to give her responsible and friendly care. Now blind and incapacitated, she can still murmur a few words. Her family pays an obligatory Christmas visit. Through the stilted, makeshift conversation and a series of flashbacks inspired by the older grandson's remarks, her present vegetable-like existence is contrasted with her exuberance as a young grandmother. The older grandson remains with her in the room after the others leave, and the film concludes with a simple and moving communication between them.

For sale:
*Phoenix Films
470 Park Ave. South
New York, N.Y. 10016*

For rental:
Phoenix Films

*Visual Aids Service
Univ. of Illinois
1352 South Oak St.
Champaign, Ill. 61820*

*Media Resources Center
Iowa State Univ.
121 Pearson Hall
Ames, Iowa 50010*

Antonia: A Portrait of A Woman
58 minutes,
released in 1974

This sensitive portrait of 73-year-old orchestra conductor Antonia Brico is especially interesting in her recollections of experiences as she fought for recognition in the musical world. Her story is one of struggle, activity and accomplishment late in life.

For sale:
*Phoenix Films
470 Park Ave. South
New York, N.Y. 10016*

For rental:
Phoenix Films

*Visual Aids Service
Univ. of Illinois
1352 South Oak St.
Champaign, Ill. 61820*

*Extension Media Center
Univ. of California
Berkeley, Calif. 94720*

Arthur and Lillie
30 minutes, 1976

Arthur and Lillie ... early and later.

Film veteran Arthur Mayer, 89, and his wife Lillie, 86, are portrayed in their lecture touring activities as well as in recollections of the early days of Hollywood.

For sale, or rental:
*Pyramid Films
Box 1048
Santa Monica, Calif. 90406*

26

Films

At My Age
26 minutes, 1966

This film which attempts to promote the employment potentials of older persons includes tips on how employers should deal with the retired returning to work.

For sale:
Sales Branch
National Audiovisual Center
Washington, D.C. 20036

For rental:
Audiovisual Center
Univ. of Iowa
Iowa City, Iowa 52240

The Lost Phoebe
25 minutes, 1974

Henry Reifsnyder longs for his wife, Phoebe, in the film based on Dreiser's short story.

Based on a Theodore Dreiser short story, this drama tells of an old but physically active farmer whose wife has just died. He cannot accept the loss of Phoebe, and he imagines she is still in the house. He wanders the countryside searching for her as his delusions become more acute. In the end, he is found dead at the side of a stream.

For sale:
Esquire Films
488 Madison Ave.
New York, N.Y. 10022

An important film on crime prevention for older people, titled **Senior Power** is described in the SAFETY CHAPTER.

DAYS . . . AND NIGHTS . . . AT THE MOVIES

Of the thousands of feature films that may be rented, many have older people as the stars or as major characters.

Consider, for example, **The Blue Angel, The Autobiography of Miss Jane Pittman, Goodbye Mr. Chips, Harold and Maude, The Last Angry Man, The Shameless Old Lady, Sunset Boulevard** and **The Whisperers**. For details, see **About Aging: A Catalog of Films**, previously described.

Hundreds of other feature films, from the days of the silents to the great musicals, are available for sheer entertainment for groups. We recommend the rental catalogues of:

Blackhawk Films, Inc.
35 Eastin-Phelan Building
Davenport, Iowa 52808

MacMillan Films
34 MacQueston Parkway
South
Mount Vernon, N.Y. 10550

FOOD 2

HEARTY APPETITES!

For many older people eating presents some unique problems. For some it is lonely, as the family with whom one ate and for whom one cooked may have diminished or moved away. Fixed incomes are being used to buy food which increases in price daily, and health concerns are ever present. We know more today about the compositions and the effects of certain foods than ever before, and this knowledge must be part of any special diets and eating adjustments one makes in later years. So while we have the best and most plentiful food available in the world, proper eating still starts with proper information.

In this chapter we present a large number of books which solve not only special dietary problems but also present balanced eating ideas for people living alone or in smaller households on a limited budget.

NUTRITION ALMANAC
By Nutrition Search, Inc.
McGraw-Hill, 1975, $4.95

Good nutrition, this layperson's manual stresses, is essential for normal organ development and functioning; for normal reproduction, growth and maintenance; for optimum activity level and working efficiency; for resistance to infection and disease; and for the ability to repair bodily damage and injury.

Text and charts cover the six nutrients (carbohydrates, fats, protein, vitamins, minerals and water) and their roles in the total diet and their part in prevention and cure of illness. Vegetarianism, food supplements and nutritionally balanced meals are covered fairly and understandably.

YOUR RETIREMENT FOOD GUIDE

Take a positive attitude toward the food you eat. Studies show that proper eating is one of the daily habits we never lose. If you feel that it is too late to change from an inadequate diet, you are wrong. It is not easy to change old habits, but if you put your mind to the task, you will be well rewarded. A desirable diet can result in more energy, a feeling of well-being and improved health.

The important considerations for low-cost meals that are attractive and tasty are the concern of this thorough little booklet offered by AARP-NRTA. Sample recipes are included at the end.

*Free
AARP-NRTA
P.O. Box 2400
215 Long Beach Blvd.
Long Beach, Calif. 90801*

A DIET FOR LIVING
By Dr. Jean Mayer
McKay, 1975, $9.95

Dr. Jean Mayer, considered by many to be the nation's leading nutrition authority, has written a book of sound advice for all ages, giving his outlook on eating right for both pleasure and health; what's wrong with "fad" diets; how what you eat affects your heart; how to avoid obesity; and more.

Better and cheaper nutrition

FROM THE NATIONAL DAIRY COUNCIL

You can only wish good health for another, but you can do something positive about your own health. It is this simple: eat a healthful diet.

While no diet in itself can guarantee a clean bill of health, a nutritionally sound diet can contribute a great deal to a sound body. The National Dairy Council—a nonprofit organization for nutrition research and education in the use of dairy foods—offers two booklets to help toward this:

Can We Eat Well for Less?
This booklet of sound, money-saving ideas includes main dish recipes, shopping tips on all food, including fruits, vegetables, meat and fish, as well as dairy; breakfast suggestions; and ways to control food waste.   20¢

To Your Health . . . In Your Second Fifty Years
This large-type booklet provides guidance in planning, selecting and preparing nutritionally sound meals for older people. Nutrients, basic foods, and the balanced diet are emphasized in the text.   25¢

The booklets are available from any of the 124 local Dairy Council units or from:

*National Dairy Council
6300 North River Road
Rosemont, Ill. 60018*

HANDBOOK OF THE NUTRITIONAL CONTENTS OF FOOD
By Bernice K. Watt and Annabel L. Merrill for USDA Dover, 1975, $4

This book, says the publisher, is the largest, most detailed source of food nutrition information ever prepared. It presents the nutrient values of food, giving data on calories, protein, fat, carbohydrate, calcium and all other essential nutrients.

THE KNOW HOW CATALOG

The Cooperative Extension of the New York State College of Agriculture and Life Sciences and the New York State College of Human Ecology each year issue hundreds of informational booklets, all listed in this publication. In general the most useful for older persons are in the food category. Most booklets are well under $1 and many are free to residents of New York State.

Look for such titles as **Cooking for One in the Senior Years**, **Quick Breads and Cookies**, **Safety in the Kitchen**, **Facts About Organic Gardening** and **Introduction to Home Gardening**.

Free
*Mailing Room
7 Research Park
Cornell Univ.
Ithaca, N.Y. 14853*

YOUR DIET: HEALTH IS IN THE BALANCE

. . . cut down calories as you add on years. The best way to beat the bulges is to begin early. Even in the mid-twenties a subtle slowing-down process begins in the body cells and cuts down energy requirements for most of us. By the time we reach middle age, our caloric requirement is usually reduced by 10 per cent, and this becomes thirty per cent by the seventies. In a nutshell: unless servings grow smaller, waistlines are bound to grow larger.

The Nutrition Foundation, which conducts continuing dietary research, has published this comprehensive booklet outlining all the theories and specifics of a balanced diet. Many diets are included, as well as recommendations for additional reading.

Free
*The Nutrition Foundation
489 Fifth Ave.
New York, N.Y. 10017*

FOOD 2

HEALTH FOODS: FACTS AND FAKES

"Health foods," "organic foods," and "natural foods" all connote something special in shops featuring pesticide-free fruits, grains and special items. Are they the answer to our concerns about chemicals and additives?

In this sober booklet, the facts—pro and con—are carefully developed.

50¢
*Public Affairs Pamphlets
381 Park Ave. South
New York, N.Y. 10016*

HOW TO BUY FOOD FOR ECONOMY AND QUALITY
By U.S.D.A.
Dover, 1975, $1.50

- What are the differences among beef rated prime, choice and good?
- Can cheese be frozen?
- How can you tell the difference between a young and an older chicken?
- Are larger-size eggs the better buy?

Hundreds of questions such as these are answered in this one-volume compilation of 14 USDA booklets giving specific and important food-buying tips. The text is accompanied by many illustrations.

YOUR MONEY'S WORTH IN FOODS

This unique booklet presents some food-buying strategies geared to household income levels and food prices. USDA economists have provided four plans for households that can afford "bare bones," low-cost, moderate-cost and liberal food expenditures, with an eye to maximum nutrition and taste.

50¢
*Home and Garden Bulletin #183
USGPO
Washington, D.C. 20402*

FOOD GUIDE FOR OLDER FOLKS

This U.S. Department of Agriculture booklet presents some advice for the special considerations of older people's eating requirements, emphasizing basic nutritional needs, budget tips and some interesting recipes.

40¢
*Home and Garden Bulletin #17
USGPO
Washington, D.C. 20402*

LUNCH

Lunch can be a lonely meal . . . or quick snack. Or it can be good nutrition with other people in lively conversation.

The federal Administration on Aging's major hot lunch program for older people serves 240,000 meals per day throughout the country, at senior centers and other gathering places. There is no required test of need, though people may make voluntary contributions.

In some locations, the lunch event is so popular that the allotted number of meals is exceeded by the number of people wishing to partake. See your local newspaper or contact the area Agency on Aging for locations and schedules in your community.

FOOD 2

EATING RIGHT FOR LESS
By the editors of Consumer Reports, Consumers Union, 1975, $2.00 apiece (see below for volume discounts)

This 80-page booklet, the first in a projected series for older people, was developed with the help of consultants in food, medicine and nutrition. It dispels some myths about food and health and shows how an older person can eat well on just over $10 per week. The reader is helped to create well-balanced menus based on nutritious and economical foods and provided with useful suggestions about shopping, storing and preparing foods. The booklet is printed in large type.

Quantity discounts are offered as follows:

10–29 copies	$1.75 each
30–49	1.50 each
50–99	1.25 each
100–499	1.20 each
500–999	1.15 each
1,000–4,999	1.10 each
5,000 or more	1.05 each

Copies may be ordered from:
*For Older People
Consumers Union
Orangeburg, N.Y. 10962*

Consumers Union is an independent, nonprofit corporation which provides information and counsel on consumer goods and services. It accepts no advertising, and is not beholden to any commercial interest.

MEALS ON WHEELS

In communities throughout the country **Meals on Wheels** gives home-bound older people the chance for a hot meal and a visit; and for others, young and old, it provides the opportunity to volunteer to deliver the meal.

If you wish to be part of a **Meals on Wheels** program in any way, contact your area agency on aging.

One should eat to live, not live to eat.

*—Benjamin Franklin,
1706–1790
American statesman,
inventor and author*

READ THE LABEL, SET A BETTER TABLE

FDA has recently developed a labeling program to help you identify the nutrient content of the foods you buy. All labels with nutrition information must follow the same format. Any food to which a nutrient is added, or which makes a nutritional claim, must have a proper label. Labeling for other foods is optional.

The labeling, for example, specifies that you must be informed of the number of calories in a serving of food and of the protein, carbohydrate and fat content.

*Free
HEW publication
#FDA 75-4001
FDA
Office of Consumer Inquiries
5600 Fishers Lane
Rockville, Md. 20852*

Nutrients listed are for one serving.

Number of servings per container.

Labels may show amounts of cholesterol & sodium in 100 grams of food and in a serving.

NUTRITION INFORMATION
(per serving)

Serving Size = 1 cup
Servings per Container = 2
Calories 110
Protein . . . . 1 Gram
Carbohydrate . . . . 25 Grams
Fat . . . . 1 Gram
Sodium (970mg/100gm) . . . . . . 275 Milligrams

Percentage of U.S. Recommended Daily Allowances (U.S. RDA)
Protein 2
Vitamin A 25
Vitamin C 25
Thiamine 25
Riboflavin 25
Niacin 25
Calcium 4
Iron 4

Nutrients in metric weight as grams (1 ounce = 28 grams).

Percentages of U.S. Recommended Daily Allowances.

FOOD 2

POULTRY IN FAMILY MEALS

This USDA booklet is an up-to-date guide to buying, storing and cooking poultry. It points out the almost endless possibilities for using this versatile meat in family and company meals. In addition to the basic cooking methods, there is a wide choice of simplified recipes that feature poultry in main dishes, casseroles and salads.

35¢
Home and Garden Bulletin #110
USGPO
Washington, D.C. 20402

MONEY-SAVING MAIN DISHES

In this country the average family spends well over a third of each food dollar for components of main dishes—meat, poultry, fish and other foods such as eggs, cheese, dried beans and dried peas. Thrifty-minded meal planners are always looking for main dishes that will cut the cost of meals while continuing to supply the needed nutrients.

This booklet, prepared and content-tested by USDA, begins by showing how different foods compare as sources of protein, follows with tips on buying foods and time-saving hints on preparation and concludes with a wide assortment of main-dish recipes and suggestions.

60¢
USDA Home and Garden Bulletin #43
USGPO
Washington, D.C. 20402

SOYBEANS IN FAMILY MEALS

Soybeans contribute good quality protein to the diet and may be used together with other foods or as substitutes for meat—with resulting meal variety and economy.

This booklet supplies information on all forms of soybeans, with tips on how to buy, prepare and use them. Recipes are included for main dishes, salads, soups, vegetables, breads, sauces and desserts.

45¢
Booklet #A1.77:208
USGPO
Washington, D.C. 20402

AROUND THE WORLD VEGETARIAN COOKBOOK
By Mary Bayramian
Troubador Press, 1976, $3.95

America's predisposition to eating beef contrasts with dozens of countries' preference for vegetarian cooking. With recent medical theories questioning the consumption of beef to the relative neglect of dairy dishes, this vegetarian cookbook is an attractive and healthy resource. Consider the possibilities of rice with tomatoes, chilies and coconut (*arroz de coco* from Mozambique), cream of carrot soup (*potage crème nivernaise* from France), vegetable stew (*lahanika yahni* from Greece), *labna latkes* (cheese pancakes from Israel) and dozens more.

MAKING COTTAGE CHEESE AT HOME

Cottage cheese can easily be made at home from skim milk or reconstituted instant nonfat dry milk. And most people enjoy doing it. The equipment, ingredients and step-by-step instructions are included in this USDA booklet.

**Better and cheaper nutrition
Cooking and growing**

30¢
*Home and Garden Bulletin
  #129
USGPO
Washington, D.C. 20402*

THE COMPLETE YOGURT COOKBOOK
By Karen Cross Whyte
Troubador Press, 1970,
$3.95

Yogurt, a favorite food in many lands for centuries, is enjoying a new popularity in this country. Some people believe—rightly or wrongly—that, in addition to the economy and good nutritional value of yogurt, there are benefits to the digestive tract.

This large-type book contains introductory material explaining the properties of yogurt and relates its entertaining history and folklore. The cookbook portion gives instructions on how to make your own yogurt from "scratch" and how to use it in virtually every type of recipe imaginable.

A yogurt hint: The Salton Company manufactures an attractive, easy-to-use yogurt maker which sells in most department and appliance stores for under $10. Five cups of yogurt can be made at one time, and you may add your own flavorings upon completion.

THE COMPLETE SPROUTING COOKBOOK
By Karen Cross Whyte
Troubador Press, 1973,
$2.95

It is possible to have a sprout garden in your kitchen with very little time, space or equipment. The beginner needs only a wide-mouthed jar, a bit of cheesecloth and a rubber band. To untreated raw seeds, add moisture and a miniature hothouse is created in which many varieties of seeds will germinate.

This intriguing introduction to seed-sprouting opens up new avenues of inexpensive nutrition—and an interesting avocation as well. The book describes in detail how to sprout many kinds of seeds for edible additions to your menu. Several dozen interesting recipes are included.

COOKING FOR TWO

This USDA publication provides recipes, helpful hints on planning and serving meals, and information on nutrition and the four basic food groups. Most of the recipes are for two servings and would be useful for one and two-person households.

The booklet is conveniently printed in large type.

$1.25
*Publication #0100-03327
USGPO
Washington, D.C. 20402*

A LITTLE FISH . . . GOES A LONG WAY

This pocket-sized booklet, prepared by the U.S. Department of Commerce's National Marine Fisheries Service, presents recipes which can be adapted for most any fish. The ideas are a wealth of economy and good nutrition. All recipes have been tested.

50¢
*Booklet #0320-00074
USGPO
Washington, D.C. 20402*

FOOD 2

MINIGARDENS FOR VEGETABLES

If you have a windowsill, a balcony or a doorstep, you have enough space for a minigarden.

If you have the patience to follow instructions, you do not need the proverbial "green thumb." With the basic materials of containers, synthetic soil and seeds, this booklet will put you on the way to a rewarding vegetable minigarden that will yield low-cost food.

30¢
USDA Home and Garden
 Bulletin #163
USGPO
Washington, D.C. 20402

ORGANIC GARDENING

The environmental movement, the economy, and the general concern over the effects of food additives have made all of us more concerned about our food. Organic gardening is within everyone's reach; the many questions and developments are covered in this new monthly magazine.

Subscription: $6.85 a year
Organic Gardening
Organic Park
Emmaus, Pa. 18049

GROWING VEGETABLES IN THE HOME GARDEN
By Robert E. Wester for USDA, Dover, 1975, $1.35

This book, aimed at fighting the rising costs of food by planting a home garden, incorporates several government publications in a more attractive commercial format.

The excellent text and illustrations give clear answers to hundreds of questions. The sections into which the book is divided include:

> Selecting a site
> Preparing the soil
> Choosing garden tools
> Arranging the garden
> Selecting seed
> Starting the plants
> Planting the garden
> Caring for the garden
> Growing specific vegetables

A list of state agricultural experiment stations is included, and there is an index to the vegetables covered.

Because the book covers the entire country's weather in a general way, local conditions must be taken into account. The author suggests contacting local agricultural experiment stations for answers to specific questions.

Cooking and growing
Products and processes

FROM THE NATIONAL MACARONI INSTITUTE

Pasta products are economical, low in sodium and high in taste and nutrition. Cooking them and combining them with other foods is a particular challenge addressed in two booklets, **Pasta Primer** and **Macaroni is Number One**.

Free
National Macaroni Institute
P.O. Box 336
Palatine, Ill. 60067

HOME CANNING TIPS

Home canning has been enjoying a gradual revival in the past few years. And, considering the advantages of cost and purity of ingredients—to say nothing of the satisfaction—it probably will increase in popularity. Bernardin, one of the manufacturers of lids, offers this very comprehensive booklet of tips and instructions.

An additional, larger booklet giving many recipes is available from the same source for $1. Its title is **Bernardin Home Canning Guide**.

Free
Bernardin, Inc.
Evansville, Indiana 47705

COMPLETE GUIDE TO HOME CANNING, PRESERVING AND FREEZING
By USDA, Dover, 1973, $2.50

When you can foods, they must be heated long enough to destroy the organisms that cause spoilage. The processes are precise and can be fun—and are certainly financially rewarding. This assemblage of USDA booklets, in very graphic and thorough detail, covers the subject of canning fruits, vegetables, meat, poultry, preserves, pickles and relishes.

Freezing, which shares many features of the canning process, is the subject of the second part of the book, dealing with fruits, vegetables, poultry, meat and fish.

HAPPY BABY FOOD GRINDER

Don't be turned away by the name of this product, one of the handiest, easy-to-use one-portion food grinders. It is made of durable plastic and steel and can grind cooked foods right at the table. Available at many natural food stores and supermarkets for under $7.50.

**Products and processes
Special diets**

THE GARDEN WAY HOME FRUIT GRINDER AND CIDER PRESS

Cider and doughnuts make people's old tales and old jokes sound fresh . . . and enchanting, and juggle an evening away before you know what went with the time.
—Mark Twain

If you and other people in your community or group ever wanted to enjoy the fun of pressing your own apple cider and other fruits and vegetables and saving money, the Garden Way Home Fruit Grinder and the Cider Press may be the answer. Patterned along old-fashioned lines but modern in construction and materials, they are available in several forms, as follows:

Home Fruit Grinder and Cider Press	$169.00
Cider Press	119.50
Fruit Grinder	59.50
Home Fruit Grinder and Cider Press, combined kit	64.50
Cider Press kit	44.50
Fruit Grinder kit	29.50

Prices do not include shipping costs.

For further information, write:
*Garden Way Research
Charlotte, Vt. 05445*

COOK TO YOUR HEART'S CONTENT
By Dr. W. Jann Brown,
Dr. Daniel Liebowitz and
Marlene Olness
Van Nostrand Reinhold,
1976, $5.95

Two physicians and a dietician have compiled a wide variety of ideas for the individual or family which must cook low-fat and low-salt meals. Recipes and ideas range from antipasto to picnics, with each recipe indicating the caloric value and sodium level. Two-week model diets are provided.

THE FAT AND SODIUM CONTROL COOKBOOK
By Alma Payne and Dorothy Callahan
Little, Brown, 1975, $8.95

Blood pressure and heart disease are closely linked to the fat and sodium intake. Restrictions are not the end of the world, and this is an example of one of the cookbooks which make eating very pleasant and safe within the limitations of most low fat and sodium diets. Contents include comparative fat values of various cuts of meat; analysis of typical commercial products; sodium content of most alcoholic beverages; lists of food, both high and low in saturated fats; the carbohydrate content of most foods; and a lengthy section of appealing recipes.

THE AMERICAN HEART ASSOCIATION COOKBOOK
Edited by Ruthe Eshleman
and Mary Winston
Ballantine, 1976, $2.25

"Eat—to your heart's delight!" says this book. If you always thought you had to sacrifice eating enjoyment for good health—think again. The editors, nutritionists for the American Heart Association, assembled recipes from volunteer and staff members of AHA chapters across the country, with calorie and fat control prime considerations.

FOOD

They tested and tasted thousands of the recipes to assemble this guide to eating well and wisely. The selections range from the easy-to-make to gourmet meals.

An especially interesting chapter of hints is, "When you eat out." A fat-cholesterol chart of foods is included.

THE ARTHRITIC'S COOKBOOK
By Dr. Collin H. Dong and Jane Banks
Crowell, 1973, $6.95

When the Arthritis Foundation proclaimed that no specific food has anything to do with causing arthritis and that none will cure it, Dr. Dong disagreed. Afflicted with arthritis at age 35, he experimented with the simple Chinese diet of his youth, and within a few weeks he came upon the "right" combination of seafood, vegetables and rice that made his arthritis disappear. Dr. Dong who was 71 in 1973 when he coauthored the book, plays golf each morning and has a busy medical practice.

The theory of the diet is that food additives and preservatives cause rheumatic diseases. Thus, the basis of Dong's diet is a high-protein, low-calorie natural regimen. His coauthor is a former patient of Dr. Dong's.

The recipes cover everything from appetizers to desserts.

A description of Dr. Dong's and Ms. Banks' general book on arthritis, **New Hope for the Arthritic,** can be found in the chapter, HEALTH.

DIETARY CONTROL OF CHOLESTEROL

More and more doctors are recommending that, as a positive health measure, we eat meals lower in saturated fats and cholesterol and higher in polyunsaturated fats. A low-cholesterol diet—as one can discover from reading this booklet—involves only moderate changes in eating habits and can be delicious and easy to follow. Sample menus are provided at three different calorie levels, along with menu-exchange lists which suggest a wide variety of meals. Shopping tips and dozens of recipes are included.

Free
Fleischmann's Margarine
625 Madison Ave.
New York, N.Y. 10022

LOW-SODIUM DIETS CAN BE DELICIOUS

Most of us are accustomed to seasoning food with salt. If it becomes necessary to drastically reduce salt intake, it is often difficult to adjust to the taste. However, subtle techniques can be used to compensate significantly for the lack of salt as a seasoning. This booklet presents salt-restricted, taste-enhancing menus and recipes and includes charts analyzing the sodium contents of foods.

Free
Fleischmann's Margarine,
625 Madison Ave.
New York, N.Y. 10022

Part of the pleasure of dining is not only the food, but the people and surroundings. In this 1920's gathering, Douglas Crockwell has clearly portrayed the warmth of a family gathering.

SHELTER 3

THE CONDOMINIUM BOOK: A GUIDE TO GETTING THE MOST FOR YOUR MONEY
By Lee Butcher
Dow Jones Books, 1975, $4.95

For some people and for some areas of the country, condominium has become synonymous with retirement community. Considering that half of the new residences constructed in the U.S. in 1974 were condominiums, the subject is important. For those who cannot or do not choose to sustain the chores and expenses of single-family homes, "condos" seem to be the answer.

For some people, though, the experience has been less than happy, with the condominium running into financial trouble. Other people, whose former rental properties have been turned into "condos," have had financial trouble themselves, lacking sufficient money to buy.

The book surveys the trends in condominiums, detailing the successes, the disasters and the unpredictables. The author then gives hard, useful information you will need to know if you consider this form of home. Floor plans and a glossary of condominium terms are included.

FROM "CONDOS" TO COMMUNES

The question of one's home is central. Are retirement communities right for some older persons and not others? What of the condominium movement? What of the problems of those faced with living in nursing homes?

Home takes on further challenge when moving is involved. Moves are never to be taken lightly, for it is our whole world we move along with us. Whether or not to move upon retirement—and where and when—are very personal questions with no wholesale answer for all people. To help sort out the choices, we have presented several references in this chapter.

There are sources in this chapter also on the difficult question of nursing homes, where 5% of the people over 65 in this country live. Choosing a nursing home for those close to us is hard; several references giving sound advice on how to make an appropriate selection are included.

For all housing concerns, the answers are diverse. What is good for some is deplorable for others. Consider, for example, the proliferation of entire communities of older people. Some like them, some do not. Others prefer a combination of lifestyles. Consider also the growth in communal-living experiments. There is strong evidence that communal living—wherein several people, unmarried and unrelated, combine finances and chores—can result in a generally higher standard and in a more pleasant atmosphere than is possible in living alone.

Condominiums and other residences

QUESTIONS ABOUT CONDOMINIUMS: WHAT TO ASK BEFORE YOU BUY

This booklet is a "short course" in condominiums. It paints a generally favorable picture, though it is realistic about the problems. To help potential owners buy wisely, it discusses negative factors, which may be the result of something inherent in the building project or the result of an error or lack of understanding by the developer. The more you as a consumer know of these pitfalls, the better your position to avoid and to correct them.

Buying a "condo" is far more demanding than renting an apartment and in some ways more complicated than assessing the purchase of a single-family dwelling. Suddenly the "condo" owner needs to know about the more intricate construction and operation of a huge building. Why? Because he or she owns part of it. Management, a new experience for many, is also explained.

The advantages can be considerable, and the participation in managing the "condo" building as a cooperative effort, many retired people have found, can be very stimulating and rewarding.

Free
Booklet HUD–365–F
Office of Public Affairs/HUD
Washington, D.C. 20410

THE NATIONAL DIRECTORY OF RETIREMENT RESIDENCES: BEST PLACES TO LIVE WHEN YOU RETIRE
By Noverre Musson
Frederick Fell, 1973, $9.95

Whether to retire to a heterogeneous or a homogeneous community is a personal choice and frequently a difficult one. This directory gives some general hints on the homogeneous side and lists, state by state, some communities and multiple dwellings of particular interest. The directory is by no means exhaustive, but is definitive on each entry, including addresses, phone numbers, ownership, transportation, and description of the locale. Though some of the listings are private dwellings such as Leisure World, many are group retirement homes which provide complete room, board and medical care.

GUIDE TO HOUSING SECURITY

This booklet addresses the basic question upon retirement of whether to move, to stay put, or to divide one's time between old and new homes. Financial guidance is stressed, as well as an analysis of climate in various parts of the country.

Free
Action for Independent Maturity
P.O. Box 2400
Long Beach, Calif. 90801

SHELTER   3

YOUR HOME . . . AND YOUR RETIREMENT

The many problems of making the right decision on where to live in retirement require a checklist and questions and answers. This guide covers the pros and cons of moving or staying put and analyzes climates, costs and tips on buying.

$1.50 to current subscribers of the magazine; $2.25 to nonsubscribers

*Retirement Living Magazine
150 East 58th St.
New York, N.Y. 10022*

(See COMMUNICATING for more on the magazine and other publications in the series.)

BUYING AND FINANCING A MOBILE HOME

Mobile homes have come a long way, but their mobility now appears to be more descriptive of their having been transported to home sites for use as permanent residences. Generally sold as completely furnished and equipped units, they are the choice of many people concerned with economy and convenience. This relatively new housing form raises many questions which this pamphlet from HUD can answer to protect the prospective buyer.

Addresses of the regional offices of HUD are listed for further reference.

*Free
Publication #HUD–243–F(4)
Office of Public Affairs
HUD
Washington, D.C. 20410*

MANUFACTURED HOUSING INSTITUTE

The trade association of the manufacturers of mobile homes is ready to answer your general and specific questions. They can be addressed as follows:

*Consumer Education Division
Manufactured Housing
 Institute
14650 Lee Road
P.O. Box 201
Chantilly, Va. 22021*

HOW TO SELL YOUR HOME WITHOUT A REAL ESTATE BROKER
By Karl J. Kosnar
McGraw-Hill, 1975, $10.95

Why pay a broker a commission to sell your property, asks the author, when you can handle it on your own? With broker fees today averaging from 6 to 10%, the saving can be significant.

Kosnar, himself a real estate broker, provides a short course on selling your property. Details include pricing, advertising, showing the property, negotiation, financing, legal and tax aspects. Mortgage interest tables and a glossary of real estate terms are included.

BUYING YOUR HOUSE: A COMPLETE GUIDE TO INSPECTION AND EVALUATION
By Joseph C. Davis and Claxton Walker
Emerson Books, 1975, $8.95

The purchase of a house, old or new, is one of the most important investments, and retirement homes are no exception. Two recognized housing experts take the reader through a systematic inspection tour of prospective purchases, beginning with the exterior and proceeding to the basement and mechanical areas, the attic and the interior rooms.

The tips go beneath the surface, showing, for example, how to detect basements prone to water seepage, poor ventilation and heating, and structural needs versus cosmetic needs.

Davis and Walker are

**Condominiums and other residences
Buying and selling a home
Making the move**

WISE HOME BUYING

Investing in a home—whether for retirement or as a second home—involves no mean feat or small expense. This booklet sets down some of the considerations, pitfalls and checklists even the most experienced can at times forget. It covers the financing and inspection particularly well—and includes a glossary of those special words people are afraid to ask to be defined.

The addresses and phone numbers of all the field offices of HUD are listed.

*Free
Booklet #HUD–267–F(6)
Office of Public Affairs
HUD
Washington, D.C. 20410*

especially thorough, explaining construction and how things work. Other chapters cover: climate-control devices, securing the house against burglary, special types of houses and their specific problems, renovating and remodeling, energy saving and insurance.

Be it ever so humble, there's no place like home.
—John Howard Payne,
1792–1852
American poet

A SHOPPER'S GUIDE TO CHOOSING A MOVER
By Linda S. Yakovich
Consumer News, Inc., 1975, $1

"Don't make a move without reading the fine print," the cover illustration warns. An unusual discussion of moving, this booklet offers no hints on how to pack—but gives straight facts and suggestions on how to choose a moving company. Using previously unavailable data, it outlines the comparative performance of the 25 largest movers and the complaint statistics concerning them, and goes on to explain the rights of a customer with a grievance.

Available from:
*Consumer News, Inc.
813 National Press Building
Washington, D.C. 20045*

TIPS ON MOVING

Twenty-two moving-day tips are included in this small pamphlet. Particular attention is given to those easily forgetten items that can be a nuisance if not handled properly. If any one tip stands out overall in this checklist, it is that planning is the key ingredient—a minimum of four to six weeks is suggested.

*Free
American Movers Conference
Suite 806
1117 North 19th St.
Arlington, Va. 22209*

SHELTER 3

THREE MOVING BOOKLETS

- A Guide to Do-It-Yourself Packing
- It's Your Move
- Tips and Cautions on Self-Moving

These three booklets give some organized and encouraging tips on moving: what to do with the "last-minute" items; how to pack safely; and how to avoid back strain.

25¢ each
Consumer Information Division
Office of the Impartial Chairman
Moving and Storage Industry of New York
10 Columbus Circle
New York, N.Y. 10019

YOUR RETIREMENT MOVING GUIDE

Some people would do anything to avoid moving. But the new home can be a reward if the move is as smooth as possible. Details seem to be the key, and this booklet in the AARP-NRTA series gives hints particularly geared to the retired person. They cover not only the actual move but some of the considerations in finding services at a new location.

Free
AARP-NRTA
P.O. Box 2400
215 Long Beach Blvd.
Long Beach, Calif. 90801

THE COMPLETE HOME OWNER'S GUIDE: FROM MORTGAGE TO MAINTENANCE
By John M. Doyle
Reston Publishing Co. 1975, $9.95

This guide for those purchasing a first home—or a retirement home—is useful in assessing finances, inspecting and negotiating. On maintenance, the author covers air-conditioning, plumbing and electrical systems, and painting. The drawings and explanations are clear and useful, whether one does the job on one's own or needs to be an intelligent consumer.

HOW TO MAKE YOUR HOUSE BEHAVE
By Tom Philbin
Golden Press, 1976 $9.95

Living in the single-family dwelling has its share of maintenance challenges. Indeed, many people agree there is always something to do around the house to repair, redecorate, expand or improve it. This book graphically explains how the parts of the house work, and how to take care of them yourself. If you don't, it tells you enough so that you can get the job done by the right individual.

Contents include:

- How the house works
- Products
- Tools
- Decorating
- How to hang wallpaper, install tiles, etc.
- Common home repairs
- Cleaning and maintenance
- Major home improvements such as a new driveway or bathroom
- Safety

POPULAR MECHANICS COMPLETE APPLIANCE REPAIR MANUAL
By Mort Schultz
Popular Mechanics Books, 1976, $8.95

More and more people are finding they can do simple repairs themselves on large and small appliances such as

Making the move
Home improvement and maintenance

electric can openers, vacuum cleaners, irons, clothes dryers and ranges. Perhaps the most difficult stage of the repair is determining the cause of the malfunction. This manual gives complete diagrams and instructions for simple repairs.

HOME CLEANING TIPS FROM JOHNSON WAX

When you make lots of wax, you ought to know a lot about housecleaning—and the Johnson Wax people have prepared three booklets which share much of this knowledge: **Floor Care**, **Rug and Carpet Care**, **Home Care**.

The booklets describe at considerable length many housecleaning problems and give hints for easy and successful results. They are not advertisements for Johnson products, which, however, are described at the close of each text.

Free
Consumer Education Department—SC
P.O. Box 567
Johnson Wax
1525 Howe St.
Racine, Wis. 53403

SIMPLE HOME REPAIRS . . . INSIDE

This guide to home repairs has been prepared in easy, step-by-step fashion to help even the most inexperienced persons do simple home repair jobs or teach others.

YOUR RETIREMENT HOME REPAIR GUIDE

Do-it-yourself has become more of a necessity for all of us, and, when you add any available extra time, this may be an especially attractive approach to keeping the home up to date. This guide gives 46 pages of tips on repairing and fixing—from the point of view of the older person.

Free
AARP-NRTA
P.O. Box 2400
215 Long Beach Blvd.
Long Beach, Calif. 90801

Though not every repair is covered, some important basics are included in this pamphlet prepared by the U.S. Department of Agriculture: faucets, electric plugs, cracks around the bathtub or shower, tiles, screens, windows, plaster and wallboard, problem doors and drawers, etc. Basic tools and nails, screws and bolts are described.

65¢
Publication #A1.68:1034
USGPO
Washington, D.C. 20402

HOME HANDYMAN'S ELECTRICITY AND ELECTRIC APPLIANCES HANDBOOK
By Jeannette T. Adams
Arco 1975, $10

Electrical repairs in the home baffle many, and the easy—and costly—alternative is expensive professional help when the answers may be simple enough. With ample illustrations, this book answers the problems of electrical repairs for the inexperienced.

SHELTER 3

GOOD HOUSEKEEPING GUIDE TO FIXING THINGS AROUND THE HOUSE
By Marcia D. and Robert M. Liles with Eileen Stukane and the editors of Good Housekeeping Magazine, Good Housekeeping Books, 1976, $7.95

Five hundred specific entries cover repairing everything in the home, using techniques of the professionals. Section 1, itemized alphabetically, indexes over 500 types of repair situations, from baby carriages to roof shingles. Section 2 gives background and professional techniques, including trade jargon, safety rules and pest control.

TIPS ON HOME IMPROVEMENT

This pamphlet, part of the Better Business Bureau's Consumer Information Series, gives a 23-point checklist for concerns you should have when dealing with a home-improvement contractor. Intended to protect you from disreputable contractors, the checklist covers hints on a contractor's reputation, on guarantees and on contracts and materials.

Free
Publication #205
Council of Better Business Bureaus, Inc.
1150 17th St. NW
Washington, D.C. 20036

THE OLD-HOUSE JOURNAL

The joys of an old house are frequently diminished by the difficulties of retaining its original lovely form or restoring it if it has been altered. *The Old-House Journal* is the special publication devoted exclusively to the art and means of preserving houses built before 1914. Each monthly issue includes tips on repairs and products and shares others' experiences with their homes.

The annual **Buyer's Guide** lists sources for hundreds of hard-to-find products and services for old homes. Typical listings include suppliers of ornaments, lighting fixtures, structural materials and inspection services.

The Old-House Journal: Annual subscription $12
The Old-House Journal Buyer's Guide: Annual edition $6.50

Both available from:
The Old-House Journal
199 Berkeley Place
Brooklyn, N.Y. 11217

Home improvement and maintenance
Nursing homes

AMERICAN HEALTH CARE ASSOCIATION

AHCA is the largest federation of nursing homes and long-term health-care facilities for the aged and the convalescent. It is composed of 50 state associations of 7,800 facilities providing over 600,000 beds. The association works to promote high standards and to represent its members' interests in Washington.

It offers a booklet, **Thinking About a Nursing Home?**, which describes the different types of facilities and gives a thorough checklist of what to look for in making choices. Single copies are free and available either through your state health care association or by writing to:

*American Health Care Association
1200 15th St. NW
Washington, D.C. 20005*

WHAT TO LOOK FOR IN A NURSING HOME

A patient and his family know in general what services to expect in a hospital, but lack general knowledge about facilities called nursing homes, which vary tremendously in the services they are prepared to offer.

This AMA pamphlet distinguishes the different types of nursing homes: those which provide personal care, nursing care, extended care, around-the-clock nursing care or residential care. A checklist of key questions is provided.

*25¢
Publication #OP-061
Order Department
American Medical Association
535 North Dearborn St.,
Chicago, Ill. 60610*

POSITIVE APPROACHES TO SELECTING ALTERNATIVE LIVING ARRANGEMENTS FOR THE ELDERLY

What is the best type of home for the elderly patient who needs some nursing supervision but not acute hospital care?

What types of community-care services are available to the elderly person living on his or her own?

When is an adult day-care center an excellent alternative?

This sensitively prepared booklet, while aimed primarily at the medical person who must give advice on alternate living arrangements, is, however, appropriate for the relative or friend guiding another in selection. An appendix lists, state by state, appropriate state nursing-home agencies and state agencies on aging.

*Free
Sandoz Pharmaceuticals
East Hanover, N.J. 07396*

SHELTER

HOW TO CHOOSE A NURSING HOME: A SHOPPING AND RATING GUIDE

A joint publication of Citizens for Better Care (Detroit) and the Institute of Gerontology, University of Michigan this guide outlines the pitfalls, and explains how careful planning can avoid tragic mistakes in selection. Finances, medical care, food and safety are discussed in detail, and the booklet shows how a visitor can probe the qualities of a home through observation and questioning.

The booklet is printed in large type.

$1
*Institute of Gerontology
Univ. of Michigan
543 Church St.
Ann Arbor, Mich. 48104*

NURSING HOMES: CITIZEN'S ACTION GUIDE
By Linda Horn and Elma Griesel
Beacon, 1977, $2.95

In light of the scandals associated with some nursing homes, this book serves as a reference to effect improvements. The authors advocate uniform standards and consistent accountability for all facilities. They give specific recommendations on what to do and list various community consumer activist groups.

LIVING AND DYING AT MURRAY MANOR
By Jaber F. Gubrium
St. Martin's Press, 1975

What is it really like inside a nursing home? We have heard many stories about the horror establishments but few about the responsible institutions.

The author, posing as an ordinary employee, worked in a variety of jobs at a nursing home whose identity is not revealed in the book. Called "Murray Manor," this church-related establishment with 360 beds is considered large.

His jobs having run from the most menial to gerontologist, Gubrium can report on the intricate social patterns and workings of this "home." For anyone contemplating a nursing home for himself or another, the book is important reading.

NURSING HOME CARE

This HEW booklet gives a good overview of nursing homes from a consumer point of view. Standards and types of homes are described, and a thorough checklist gives points to look for when investigating this living alternative.

55¢
*Publication #(SRS)76-24902
USGPO
Washington, D.C. 20402*

AMERICAN ASSOCIATION OF HOMES FOR THE AGING

This association of nonprofit homes for the aging serves its members in the traditional manner and also offers a referral service to homes in various localities. Without making specific recommendations, the association will provide lists of nonprofit member homes in a specified area. Selection is then dependent upon personal visits and needs.

For referral information:

*American Association of Homes for the Aging
374 National Press Building
Washington, D.C. 20045*

Nursing homes

WHEN YOU HAVE A COMPLAINT ABOUT A NURSING HOME . . .

If you have a complaint about a nursing home, you can tell it to:

1. The nursing home administrator.
2. Your local Social Security district office. It functions as a clearing house for complaints about all nursing homes, whether or not they receive government funds.
3. The patient's caseworker or the county welfare office if the patient is covered by Medicaid.
4. The state Medicaid agency if the home is certified for that program.
5. The state health department and the state licensing authority.
6. The nursing-home ombudsman if such an office has been established in your community.
7. Your congressman and senators. (Address congressman at House of Representatives, Washington, D.C. 20515; senators at United States Senate, Washington, D.C. 20510.)
8. Your state and local representatives.
9. The Joint Commission on Accreditation of Hospitals (645 North Michigan Ave., Chicago, Ill. 60611) if the home has a JCAH certificate.
10. The American Association of Homes for the Aging (529 14th St. NW, Washington, D.C. 20004) if the home is a member.
11. The American College of Nursing Home Administrators (4650 East-West Highway, Bethesda, Md. 20014) if the administrator is a member.
12. Your local Better Business Bureau and Chamber of Commerce.
13. Your local hospital association and medical society.
14. An attorney or legal aid society.

If you have difficulties in locating an appropriate state association, you may write for information to the *American Health Care Association (1200 15th St. NW, Washington, D.C. 20036)*.

HEALTH 4

FROM PREVENTION TO UNDERSTANDING

Though age is not a disease, certain ailments and infirmities accompany it more than youth. There is much we can do in terms of prevention, treatment, adjustment and understanding. Early diagnosis and the hope of prevention are clearly within our own control. This chapter's sources present a diversity of publications, services and products. Each in its own way makes sense for our own welfare—or that of someone close to us.

AMERICAN MEDICAL ASSOCIATION

The AMA Committee on Aging is convinced that a sense of purpose and the opportunity to contribute to the well being of others are as vital to an individual's health as are adequate medical care, nutrition or rest. For this reason, the Committee is deeply concerned with policies which call for arbitrary retirement based on chronological age, without regard to individual desires and capabilities.

The above is quoted from the American Medical Association's **Retirement: A Medical Philosophy and Approach** (#OP-421), a booklet which summarizes the health problems that many experience upon mandatory retirement. From the point of view of those already forced into retirement, the problem may be insoluble. For others, the booklet can be val-

YOUR RETIREMENT HEALTH GUIDE

This guide offers a positive outlook and a set of constructive tips on maintenance of good health. The chapters cover such items as the need for adequate rest, proper mental outlook, ear, eye, foot and dental care, choosing a doctor and good nutrition.

Free
AARP-NRTA
P.O. Box 2400
215 Long Beach Blvd.
Long Beach, Calif. 90801

YOUR RETIREMENT PSYCHOLOGY GUIDE

We are in great measure the architects of our added years. It may not be in our power to arrange for ourselves good living quarters or a decent wage; but it is within our power to enrich our later years by maintaining wholesome personal contacts with our fellows and by using our leisure time in some useful activity.

—Ethel Andrus
Founder
AARP-NRTA

This well-organized, thoughtful booklet treats the problems of attitude and adjustment to the aging process in a direct, encouraging way. It covers the anatomy of aging, friends, new marriages and crises. The booklet closes with some "great rules for living":

Health during retirement
Fitness

uable in taking an advocacy position through other organizational structures—to regain or retain employment and to fight for others' rights. A medical evaluation system for determining fitness for continuing work is suggested. A rational health tool for individual and employers alike. The price is 50¢.

Other interesting publications include:

How the Older Person Can Get the Most Out of Living (#OP-312) (45¢)

What to Look for in a Nursing Home (#OP-061) (25¢)

Quantity discounts are offered on orders exceeding 99 copies of one title. A complete catalogue of publications is available.

Write:

*Order Department
American Medical Association
535 North Dearborn St.
Chicago, Ill. 60610*

HEALTH... AND YOUR RETIREMENT

How many more years of vigorous life can you expect, asks this guide? Where do you live? Are you married? These and other questions contribute to the profile of your life expectancy presented in the booklet's opening quiz. The booklet goes on to deal with why we age, and how to maximize the chances for a long life—including good nutrition, exercise, rest, and positive attitudes.

How often have we heard the expression, "You're only as old as you think you are"? Obviously only partly a truth, the truth to the notion that a positive attitude helps, is still unmeasured. The booklet includes a self-scoring quiz on attitudes based on Duke University's study of the aged.

$1.50 to current subscribers of the magazine; $2.25 to nonsubscribers

*Retirement Living Magazine
150 East 58th St.
New York, N.Y. 10022*

(See COMMUNICATING for more on the magazine and the other publications offered in the series)

1. I have a choice
2. I am important
3. I deserve emotional satisfactions
4. I deserve occasional fun

*Free
AARP-NRTA
P.O. Box 2400
215 Long Beach Blvd.
Long Beach, Calif. 90801*

SIXTY-PLUS AND FIT AGAIN: EXERCISES FOR OLDER MEN AND WOMEN
By Magda Rosenberg
M. Evans and Company, 1977, $6.95

This book of medically-approved exercises for older people is worth looking at. Exercise of this type can be fun, stimulating, and contribute to good body tone. If you have any doubts as to the wisdom of your doing an exercise, of course consult your personal physician.

Fitness

TOTAL FITNESS IN THIRTY MINUTES A WEEK
By Lawrence A. Morehouse and Leonard Gross
Simon and Schuster, 1975, $6.95.

With the daring promise that physical fitness is within easy reach "in 30 minutes a week," Morehouse (a Ph.D, not a medical doctor) attacks what he considers the unnecessary and harmful myths of many of the standard diet and exercise plans.

Dr. Morehouse is well regarded in the physical fitness field, having authored a widely popular standard textbook on the subject. His studies of metabolic activity enabled the astronauts to work successfully on the surface of the moon.

His different approach is that there is no need to punish yourself to stay fit. "If I have learned one thing in my years of study," says Morehouse, "it is that the fountain of youth for which Ponce de Leon searched in vain was right inside the body. Exercise is the means to an alert, vigorous and lengthy life. Inactivity will kill you."

Using the principle that fitness is an individual thing—for every person and for every age—Morehouse runs through his theories and recommendations, which are surprisingly simple—and worthwhile. Relax, exercise, and you'll be better. Do what you can, whether it's a walk or a jog . . . but do it!

THE FITNESS CHALLENGE IN THE LATER YEARS: AN EXERCISE PROGRAM FOR OLDER AMERICANS

This book is a joint publication of the President's Council on Physical Fitness and Sports and the Administration on Aging.

One physician, commenting on the phenomenon of aging, has said, "Most of us don't wear out, we rust out." Disuse is the mortal enemy of the human body. We know today that how a person lives, not how long he or she has already lived, is responsible for many of the physical problems normally associated with advanced age. This book has been prepared to help older people take advantage of the longer life which medical science is making possible. It outlines methods for maintaining youthful health and energy, and it suggests ways of enhancing the enjoyment of leisure.

Advancing age does not inevitably mean inactivity or infirmity. Physical fitness, according to the book, can be defined in two main areas:

Organic fitness—Good organic health, that is, a body free of disease or infirmity and well nourished.

Dynamic fitness—Though free of disease, the body may still not be fully fit. Dynamic fitness promotes the efficiency of the heart and lungs, muscular strength and endurance, balance, flexibility, coordination and agility.

The book outlines cautions and stresses the need to take an exercise program step-by-step—namely, three stages called the red, white and blue.

The diagrams and instructions are clear, and the effort to understand them worthwhile.

75¢
Bulletin #HE 17.302: F55
USGPO
Washington D.C. 20402

Do the joggers of the world intimidate you? Then read what Morehouse has to say about the endurance exercisers. Sweat and pain are not the answer for the average person, says he.

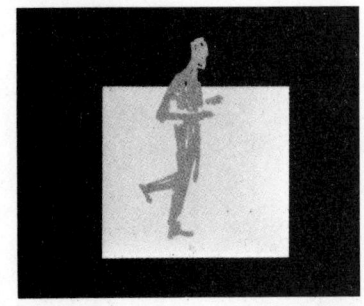

HEALTH

VIGOR IN MATURITY

Another AARP-NRTA service is VIM, an education program designed to provide older persons with an over-all look at health information. The VIM seminars, a group of five sessions which the AARP-NRTA national office helps plan, includes step-by-step instructions, lesson scripts, films, a health-education manual for each participant and an acknowledgment card for all who have attended the sessions.

Areas covered include:
- Safety in everyday living
- Learning about chronic diseases
- Foods, facts and frauds
- Health from head to toe
- Making adjustments in life patterns

A handling fee of 50¢ per participant is required. Sessions are open to members and nonmembers. Groups not affiliated with AARP-NRTA which serve as local organizers are assessed in addition a $10 program fee.

Contact:
Health Education Office
AARP-NRTA
1909 K St. NW
Washington, D.C. 20006

AIMING FOR DYNAMIC FITNESS

What used to be known as middle age has become a growing segment of the life span; it can be a pleasant plateau that lasts for many years. Thanks to medical progress in preventing and controlling diseases, better nutrition, a new understanding of the benefits of activity and exercise, discovery of new drugs and improved medical techniques, the odds are favorable for healthy, rewarding mature years.

This booklet presents a cross section of both practical advice and inspiration. Food is covered in a comprehensive fashion. There are special sections titled "Walk Your Way to Fitness," by Senator William Proxmire, and "Stress: It Can Kill You," by Peter A. Dickinson.

*Free
Action for Independent Maturity
1909 K St. NW
Washington, D.C. 20006*

SEX AFTER SIXTY: A GUIDE FOR MEN AND WOMEN IN THEIR LATER YEARS
By Dr. Robert N. Butler and Myrna Lewis, Harper and Row, 1976, $6.95

Bob Butler, director of the National Institute on Aging, and Myrna Lewis have written a thoughtful book on this aspect of aging we so rarely talk about; or when we do, we marvel at the man of 92 who has just fathered twins. No need to marvel, they say, for the enjoyment of sex can and should continue through the later years, with minor exceptions. They cover thoroughly both the psychological and the physical aspects. The normal relationships and the special problems some people experience with age, such as loneliness, the need to learn new patterns, and the need to communicate about problems and seek solutions, are treated.

The text is realistic and positive, with a glossary of terms and a list of additional readings. Referral sources for help in specific problems are cited throughout.

LOVE IN THE LATER YEARS
By James A. Peterson and Barbara Payne
Association Press, 1975, $7.95

The title concerns more love of life in general in the later years than love as such. Thus it does not connote sex after 60. The book tries to help people as they grow older to become aware of their full potential and covers their emotional, physical, sexual and social potentials. Love plays its role in making the later years the best. The road, as we know, is not smooth, and the authors do not hesitate to document the problems and call on everyone to become his or her own ideal advocate for the best.

HEALTH 4

THE HARVARD MEDICAL SCHOOL HEALTH LETTER

This four-page monthly newsletter, designed to interpret timely health information for the general public, places considerable emphasis on understanding the body and on preventive medicine, including early recognition and diagnosis of illness symptoms.

Individual subscriptions are $10 per year. Bulk subscriptions of at least 100 are encouraged at a cost of $1 per person a year.

Department of Continuing Education
Harvard Medical School
25 Shattuck St.
Boston, Mass. 02115

THE FAMILY MEDICAL ENCYCLOPEDIA
By Justus S. Schifferes
Pocket Books, 1976, $1.95

This is the most comprehensive and lowest-cost medical encyclopedia we have found. While clearly written and understandable, it is responsible and thorough in explaining the body's workings, symptoms of disease, and treatment. Compiled with the help of an advisory board of eight physicians, it is, however, by no means a substitute for treatment by one's own physician.

The author does not hesitate to use slang and popular terms but cross-references them to the more formal or correct terms. Thus, if we know a symptom or a disease as hangover, piles, female troubles, bad blood, etc., we will find it listed as such. The book emphasizes adult health, in effect picking up where Dr. Spock left off.

The appendix lists medical code letters—the abbreviations used by physicians in medical reports, hospital charts, and prescriptions; a directory of national health organizations with their addresses and phone numbers; a chart of desirable weights; and a calorie counter of common foods.

PATHWAYS TO LIVING

This monthly newsletter, "dedicated to a stronger and healthier America," runs four pages each issue and covers a variety of interesting health topics. Recent issues, for example, have detailed some of the ideas of Ben Franklin ("Eat to live, and not live to eat," etc.); a history of American folk remedies, a survey of methods for beating back pain, and the value of some of the basic foods in their natural, fresh states.

Annual subscription (Jan.-Dec.), $3.50

American Health Education Foundation
693 Main St.
Hackensack, N.J. 07601

WHAT YOU SHOULD KNOW ABOUT HEALTH CARE BEFORE YOU CALL A DOCTOR!
By Dr. G. Timothy Johnson
McGraw-Hill, 1975, $8.95

This book has two purposes: (1) To summarize significant health information; (2) To provide a guide to health care where choices may be important.

A sensible look at problem areas by a physician and regular television performer on the Boston TV program "House Call," this book offers a guide to perfecting the indispensable good relationship with one's own physician. It is one of many new books addressing itself to the task of making one a more intelligent and better-served consumer of medical care. The reader is given background information on how to ask questions, make choices and understand the information and implications of what is being done by the medical profession. New developments and what they hold in store for patients are also discussed.

DON'T GIVE UP ON AN AGING PARENT
By Lawrence Galton
Crown, 1975, $6.95

This is a medically oriented book that cites case after case for hope in many areas in which we commonly think

58

General medical care

disease is attributable to age—and therefore we are resigned to it. Galton, a respected medical writer, gives many pointers on being a better consumer of medical services—and thereby helping some older people to lead healthier lives.

TAKE CARE OF YOURSELF: A CONSUMER'S GUIDE TO MEDICAL CARE
By Drs. Donald M. Vickery and James F. Fried
Addison, Wesley, 1976, $5.95

This reference book is a consumer resource for medical services. Through text and graphic layout, the authors discuss symptoms and illnesses, preventive medicine, choosing a doctor, office visits, finding the right medical facility, reducing the high cost of drugs, stocking the home medicine cabinet and awareness of medical frauds.

Easy-to-read charts on 68 of the most common medical problems indicate whether to use home treatment or see a physician. The authors give detailed instructions for home care and explain what to expect if you go to the doctor's office.

There are several blank pages for emergency phone numbers and family medical-history notations.

PHARMACEUTICAL MANUFACTURERS ASSOCIATION

PMA, the trade association of pharmaceutical manufacturers, provides educational materials for individuals and groups. One of the more pertinent is:

The Medicine Your Doctor Prescribes: A Guide for Consumers
This booklet provides information on medicines and gives some important reminders on safe use of prescriptions and on taking medications while traveling.

PMA can furnish speakers on various subjects in the drug field for organizations or community meetings. Its booklet, **The Story of Health: A Catalog of Films and Publications,** lists free material produced and distributed by the member firms. Subjects cover virtually every disease, major and minor.

The pamphlet and catalogue are free. Available from:

Pharmaceutical Manufacturers Association
1155 15th St., NW
Washington, D.C. 20005

THE ESSENTIAL GUIDE TO PRESCRIPTION DRUGS
By Dr. James W. Long
Harper and Row, 1977, $15 (paperback, $5.95)

This consumer-oriented reference work gives the latest data on more than 200 prescription drugs, including guidelines for safe use. With the book the patient is better equipped to discuss medications with his or her personal physician. Included are a glossary, 14 drug information tables, and case histories.

THE BATH BOOK
By Gregory and Beverly Frazier
Troubador Books, 1973, $2.95

This book is fun. Good clean fun at that.

" . . . float away tensions, drown anxieties, relax . . . enjoy," the authors recommend, and they have made the bath into a book. From the history of the bath, they proceed to the analysis of different soaps, the beauty effects, and the various types of baths. Bathroom accessories—both luxury and safety types—and "recipes" for bath-water ingredients are explored.

HEALTH 4

PUBLIC AFFAIRS PAMPHLETS

An unusual effort in public education is the work of the Public Affairs Committee, a nonpartisan, nonprofit organization founded in 1935 "to develop new techniques to educate the American public on vital economic and social problems and to issue concise and interesting pamphlets dealing with such problems."

The pamphlets—averaging some 28 pages—for more than three decades have gained a unique reputation for timeliness, accuracy and readability.

In the health and safety category, the following have been reviewed and are recommended:

MEDIC ALERT FOUNDATION

While driving home from the library, I began to go into insulin shock. I remember that I managed to pull my car over to the side of the road and park it somehow, after which I passed out. I came to in the hospital where I had been taken by the police officers who had stopped to investigate. Because of my Medic Alert bracelet they determined that I was diabetic and not intoxicated, and I was in shock. They were able to send for an ambulance and to start treatment immediately.

—Member #129383, male diabetic, Riverside, Calif.

Nearly a million people are wearing the Medic Alert bracelets and necklaces. Not a piece of costume jewelry, it is a functional daily lifesaver for many. Wearing any of the clear identification pieces, persons with possible medical emergencies are reasonably assured of proper communication.

The Medic Alert Foundation, distributor and coordinator for the system, is a nonprofit organization founded in 1956 to serve persons with specific medical problems that may not be readily apparent. In emergency situations such as a fainting spell or automobile accident in which the individual cannot communicate, the conspicuous bracelet or necklace discloses the condition: diabetes, severe allergies, a heart condition, among more than 200 afflictions of wearers.

The member of Medic Alert has access to the foundation's three-part system:

1. The metallic identification bracelet or necklace, which bears the insignia of the medical profession and the words "Medic Alert" in red. On the reverse side is engraved the medical problem or problems of the wearer, such as "taking anticoagulants" or "wearing contact lenses." The member's name, membership number and the telephone number of the Medic Alert emergency answering service are also included.
2. An annual wallet card which contains additional personal and medical information. Because the card is dated, emergency personnel know how current the information is. Each member also receives an annual report on all data held in his personal record, so that corrections and changes can be made.
3. The Emergency Answering System, which is available to receive calls around the clock from medical person-

General medical care
Special care and conditions

nel. The telephone number is engraved on the bracelet or necklace and printed on the wallet card. Within moments, the emergency operator can retrieve the member's file record and furnish any other stored data. A percentage of the original membership fees is placed in trust to assure the permanent financing of this continuing service.

The foundation is governed by a board of physician trustees. It has the endorsement of many national health-related organizations, including the Allergy Foundation of America, American Hospital Association, American Nurses' Association, and the President's Committee on the Employment of the Handicapped.

One-time fee: $7, tax-deductible

For membership application or further information:
Medic Alert Foundation International
P. O. Box 1009
Turlock, Calif. 95380

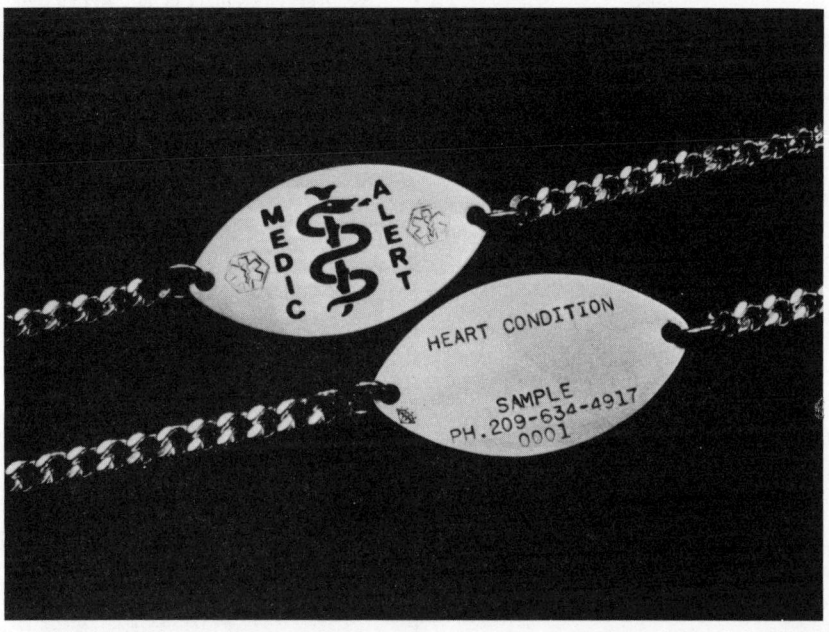

Emblem shown is the bracelet style, front and back.

- **What We Know About Headaches** (pamphlet #502)
- **The Rights of Patients** (#535)
- **Sex After Sixty-Five** (#519)
- **Living with a Heart Ailment** (#521)
- **Depression: Causes and Treatment** (#488)
- **Fads, Myths, Quacks—and Your Health** (#415)
- **Light on Your Feet** (#345A)
- **Watch Your Blood Pressure** (#483)
- **Better Health in Later Years** (#466)
- **How to Cope with Crises** (#464)
- **The Dying Person and the Family** (#485)
- **Male "Menopause" Crisis in the Middle Years** (#526)
- **Protecting Yourself from Prostate Problems** (#532)
- **Making Products Safer: What Consumers Can Do** (#524)

The full scope of the pamphlets covers social problems, family life, health and science. A catalogue of the series is available on request.

Pamphlets are 50¢ apiece. Quantity rates are available for groups.

Public Affairs Pamphlets
381 Park Avenue South
New York, N.Y. 10016

HEALTH 4

MENOPAUSE: THE EXPERTS SPEAK

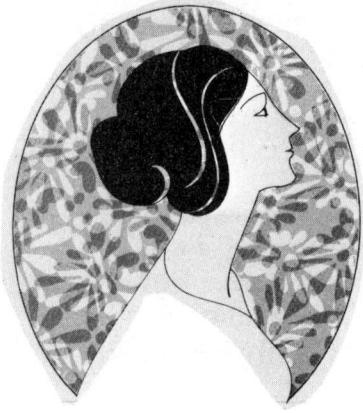

According to the 1970 census, there are about 27 million women in the United States at or beyond the age of menopause—50 years and older. Because the average woman of 50 lives about 28 years more, the menopause and what is known as the climacteric, or change of life, become major factors in the health and well-being of many.

NIA is engaged in studying aging in women during and after menopause; this booklet presents a summary of its findings to date. Topics covered include what is known and not known about menopause and the controversy over the use of estrogens to treat menopausal symptoms.

Free
National Institute of Aging, National Institutes of Health, Bethesda, Md. 20014

SOME BOOKLETS FROM METROPOLITAN LIFE

The Metropolitan Life Insurance Company has prepared several booklets to serve as reminders of some of the things we easily forget or perhaps did not know. The booklets most interesting and applicable to older people are:

Four Steps to Weight Control
The four steps outlined—see your doctor, set a weight goal, retain eating habits, be more active—are simple and often effective. Understanding why weight control is important can motivate us to achieve this goal. The text covers lots of do's and don'ts and has an especially important section on cholesterol levels. Sample menus and calorie tables are included.

Stress—and Your Health
Though stress is part of daily living, we all have levels beyond which we cannot function in a healthy manner. Coping with and recognizing stress and understanding its effects on health are the subjects of this excellent booklet.

Alcoholism
This booklet can be a useful tool for those who have a problem with alcohol or know of someone who does.

You and Your Health
This general view of our bodies and our search for well-being touches on many areas of concern—safety hazards, nutrition, weight control, stress and tension, alcohol, drugs and smoking, and the ways to seek medical help.

Your Health and Your Driving
Many highway accidents can be prevented by more alert, careful drivers. This booklet deals with several areas, from alcohol to correct vision.

Metropolitan Life also makes available a clear first-aid card, printed on heavy paper, suitable for mounting inside family medicine cabinets or other handy places, and a seven-page personal health record in which you can enter dozens of personal medical facts, for convenient reference.

All items are free and are available from:

Health and Welfare Division
Metropolitan Life
One Madison Ave.
New York, N.Y. 10010

The human body, properly cared for, will last a lifetime.

—Traditional joke

Special care and conditions

CLEO LIVING AIDS

People with temporary or long-range physical problems will find many unusual products listed in this diverse catalogue. Products include exercise equipment, walking aids, bathroom safety devices, whirlpools and homemaking aids, among dozens of other items to make daily life more functional.

While many of the products are intended for people with specific handicaps, most anyone will find something useful to ease daily living.

A free catalogue is available from:

*Cleo Living Aids
3957 Mayfield Road
Cleveland, O. 44121*

STOCKING DEVICE

If bending and stretching to put on women's stockings or men's stretch hose is a pain, this device can be a blessing. In a few simple steps it helps in dressing.

The device sells for $7.50 plus a postage charge of $1.75, for a total of $9.25. Discounts of 20% are offered on orders of 6 to 23 and of 25% on orders of 24 or more.

Write:
*Sheltered Workshops for the Disabled, Inc.
200 Court St.
P.O. Box 310
Binghamton, N.Y. 13902*

BE OK SELF-HELP AIDS

This catalogue lists health aids for situations in which mobility is temporarily or permanently impaired. From cooking aids for the person who has use of only one hand to safety devices for the bath, the catalogue seems to have them all. One of the most intriguing products is:

Floating Thermometer
Protect yourself from burns with a floating thermometer that tells at a glance whether your bath water is cool, mild, tepid, warm or hot. Thermometer is mounted on plastic frame. (Page 27 #8K-3466 $1.10)

Many of the homemaking and other everyday items are of use to all people, while the therapeutic aids could be recommended by a physician or physical therapist.

For catalogue write:
*Fred Sammons, Inc.
Box 32
Brookfield, Ill. 60513*

SEARS' HOME HEALTH CARE AND CONVALESCENT PRODUCTS

Specialized products for health care and recuperation can frequently be difficult to find—and they are often required when personal shopping is not convenient or possible. Sears, known for its order-at-home merchandising, has a very complete catalogue entitled Home Health Care and Convalescent Products. Items are fully illustrated and described in detail. There are wheelchairs, walking aids, special beds, toilet facilities, prosthetic undergarments, back supports, portable oxygen kits, blood pressure instruments, bath items and safety devices.

Whirlpool and steambath devices are featured, and special accessories for wheelchairs are offered in profusion.

Merchandise can be ordered by mail, phone, or at a Sears store, and can be picked up or delivered.

Catalogue available from any Sears store, or by writing:

*Sears Roebuck and Co.
925 South Homan Ave.
Chicago, Ill. 60607*

HEALTH 4

HAMMACHER SCHLEMMER

This fascinating "general store" on New York City's 57th Street sells all of its items by mail as well. And many are unique or hard-to-find health and safety aids. Included are extra large nonslip bathtub mats, foot massagers, whirlpool baths, and electronic fever thermometers which display the temperature on a clear dial.

Catalogue on request:
*Hammacher Schlemmer
147 East 57th St.
New York, N.Y. 10022*

WINCO PRODUCTS

Winco Products provides a good range of sitting and standing aids for the convalescent and the ill. Attractive reclining chairs for convalescing patients are featured. Winco offers a good selection of safety bars for the bathroom—which everyone should use.

All items are listed in the free catalogue.

Address:
*Winfield Company, Inc.
3062 46th Ave. North
St. Petersburg, Fla. 33714*

HOMEMAKERS UPJOHN

The Upjohn Company's homemakers division has over 220 offices across the country to provide trained personnel for the home, such as registered or practical nurses, aides, and live-in companions.

You may obtain information on rates and availability by checking your local telephone directory under "Homemakers Upjohn" or write to:

*Homemakers Upjohn
The Upjohn Company
Kalamazoo, Mich. 49001*

THE HOMEMAKER'S GUIDE TO HOME NURSING
By Alice M. Schmidt
Brigham Young Univ. Press, 1976, $3.95

With the costs of medical care rising—and the general concern for good health—this book serves the special purpose of giving the homemaker, male or female, specific guidance and confidence in home nursing. Offering virtually a short course in becoming a para-practical nurse, Alice Schmidt, a nurse and mother of six, tells how she once visited a home where a patient begged her to stay because "you know just how to get me in and out of bed." In a few short minutes, Mrs. Schmidt demonstrated that skill and more to other family members.

Taking care of the sick is not

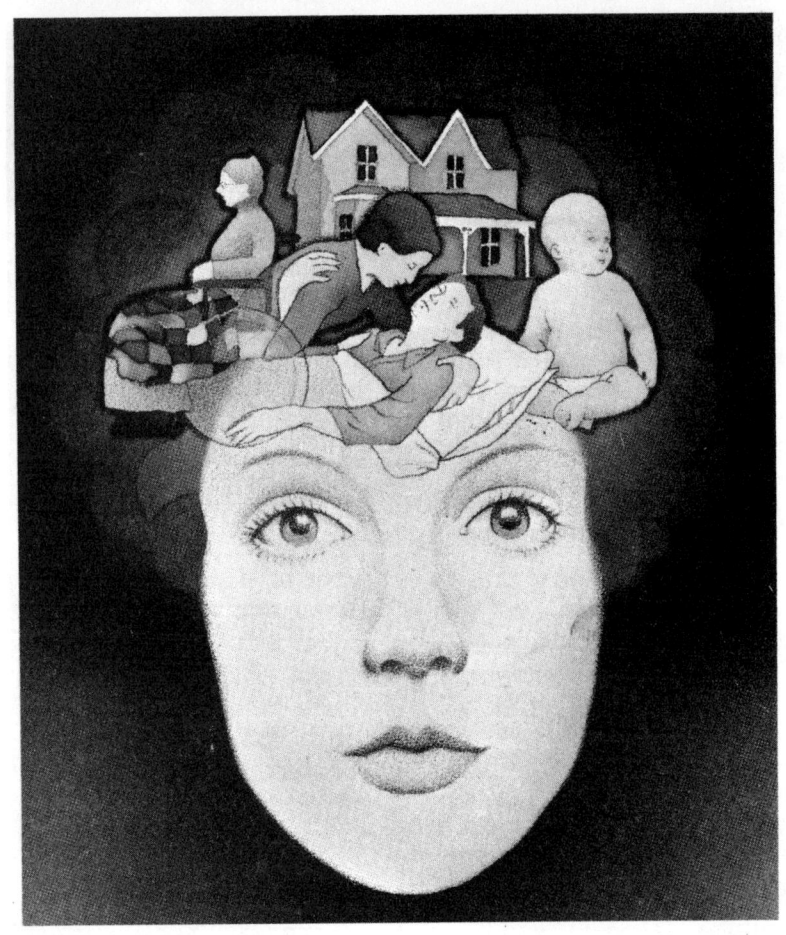

Special care and conditions

the beginning nor the only role for the home nurse, who also assists in prevention of illness. Basic nursing principles in health and illness emphasize safety, comfort, effectiveness, neatness and economy.

FREEDOM FROM BACKACHES
By Dr. Lawrence W. Friedmann and Lawrence Galton
Pocket Books, 1976, $1.95

Dr. Friedmann, who has brought relief to thousands of back sufferers as medical director of the Institute for the Crippled and Disabled Research and Rehabilitation Center in New York City, analyzes why we suffer from backache and what we can do about it. And, happily, he has an apparently successful set of approaches, for he tells more of what we can do by ourselves and by way of prevention than by surgery.

The authors cover exercises, testing for common causes, and coping with acute and lesser pain. A chapter is devoted to the back problems of older persons. Osteoporosis, thinning of the bone structure in women in particular, is given attention, and treatments of the condition through diet and hormones are described.

NATIONAL COUNCIL FOR HOMEMAKER-HOME-HEALTH AIDE SERVICES

Continuing to live at home despite some special needs is a goal of increasing numbers of people. The National Council for Homemaker-Home Health Aide Services is one of the major nonprofit organizations helping to achieve this goal.

The Council operates nationally to set standards and to provide leadership and encouragement for independent living. It also offers an information and referral service which can help you in locating people to meet your needs. Actual aide services are available through affiliated local agencies in most communities, and through visiting nurse associations, public health or social service departments, hospital home-care units or voluntary agencies.

The typical range of services includes:

- ☐ Personal health care services, such as help with bathing, dressing, walking and toileting, changing dressings, exercises, prosthetic equipment and rehabilitation regimens and care of hair, nails, feet and mouth.
- ☐ Homemaking assistance, such as light general cleaning, laundering and mending, washing dishes, making beds, marketing, planning menus, and preparing meals and special diets.
- ☐ Other activities to help the frail or disabled person's daily life run smoothly, such as providing companionship, giving emotional support and encouragement, providing transportation or escort, and taking care of cashing checks, obtaining food stamps, finding needed community services and other personal business.

The council maintains lists of agencies performing services according to its standards. Costs vary according to the type of services and the community. A recent survey of 90 agencies, however, showed an average cost of $5.06 per hour. In some cases insurance policies will reimburse for services.

For information on services in your community, write:
National Council for Homemaker-Home Health Aide Services, Inc.
67 Irving Place
New York, N.Y. 10003

HEALTH 4

MEDOX

Coming home from a hospital—recovering from an illness at home—or seeking an alternative to a nursing home: all require some help. Medox is one of the commercial companies providing per diem personnel—registered nurses, graduate nurses, nurses' aides, physiotherapists, and home economists to assist in recovery and health maintenance at home. Medox screens all personnel and checks references. The nonmedical personnel, called "trained companions," do light housekeeping, prepare simple meals, take patients for walks, or just chat and read aloud.

Also available is **Telecheck**, providing a regular phone call to buoy spirits and to check on any unforeseen setbacks.

Services are available in the following cities:

BOSTON
636 Commonwealth Ave.
262-7010

MIAMI
1150 NW 14th St.
324-4072

OKLAHOMA CITY
6161 North May Ave.
840-1856

PHILADELPHIA
101 South 20th St.
567-7834

PHOENIX
222 West Osbourne Road
277-4411

WASHINGTON, D.C.
1835 K St. NW
872-0977

STROKES AND THEIR PREVENTION
By Dr. Arthur Ancowitz
Van Nostrand Reinhold, 1975, $7.95

A stroke, clarifies the author, is not a heart attack—but like a heart attack, it may also involve the circulatory system and also can be a major medical catastrophe. Stroke results in injury to brain tissue, with subsequent disabilities. The major causes are high blood pressure and hardening of the arteries.

In this practical and comprehensive book, Dr. Ancowitz uses layman's language to tell us how strokes occur and to suggest preventive measures, such as proper diet. What are the warning signs of stroke? Who is likely to have a stroke? Are blacks more stroke-prone? What part do environment and lifestyle play? What about anxiety . . . exercise . . . obesity . . . diet . . . cigarette smoking . . . alcohol?

Dr. Ancowitz discusses degrees of disability and problems of rehabilitation. Recognizing the central connection of blood pressure and stroke, he gives specific guidance and "ten commandments" for sensible habits. Delicious, easy recipes are another feature.

STROKE: A DOCTOR'S PERSONAL STORY OF HIS RECOVERY
By Drs. Charles Clay Dahleberg and Joseph Jaffe
Norton, 1977, $8.95

Dr. Dahleberg suffered a stroke in 1973, and this story of his recovery is an important book for those who have had strokes and for those close to stroke victims. Dr. Dahleberg's most pressing problem was speech, which, together with his inability to write or comprehend writing, was formidable. Not only an important philosophical statement, this is also a book of hope.

THE HEART DOCTORS' HEART BOOK
By Dr. Marshall Franklin, Dr. Martin Krauthamer, Dr. A. Razzak Tai, and Ann Pinchot
Grosset and Dunlap, 1974, $8.95

Heart disease is currently the cause of over half of American deaths.

In this highly readable book, intended to explain recent medical advances, thus helping to allay some fears (and instill caution and cooperation), many actual cases are included, as well as the medical facts. Food charts and suggested exercises are included.

Special care and conditions

LIVE LONGER—CONTROL YOUR BLOOD PRESSURE
By Dr. Max L. Feinman and Joseleen Wilson
Coward, McCann & Geoghegan, 1977, $8.95

High blood pressure is considered a silent killer and cause of many other serious illnesses, including heart disease, kidney ailments and stroke. The problem is easily detected and controlled.

YOUR SECOND LIFE
By Dr. Harold L. Karpman and Sam Locke
J. P. Tarcher, Inc., 1975, $8.95

Concerned with the difficulty heart attack patients encounter in getting clear medical information and their need for an optimistic view of life, Dr. Karpman and playwright Sam Locke have created a patient-oriented book.

Through actual case histories, the reader experiences the fears, hopes and questions of seven of Dr. Karpman's patients. There is Joan Ellen, an executive with hypertension, who finds women often have to pay the same coronary price for success as men. There is the hypochondriac salesman who goes through frightened years of false heart attack symptoms. Bravery and optimism as well as physical conditions are key elements running through the book, which concludes with four easy-reference appendices, in question-and-answer form, covering diet, sex, exercise and smoking, and with a glossary.

AMERICAN HEART ASSOCIATION

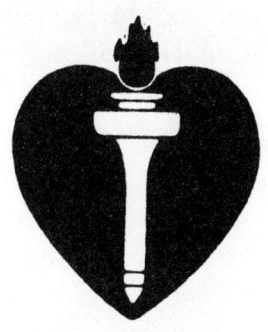

The American Heart Association, engaged in a broad program of research and public education toward the prevention and cure of heart disease, has a number of excellent publications:

- **Fact About Strokes** (order #EM256)
- **Heart Attack** (#EM150) General explanation of an attack and of angina pectoris and coronary artereosclerosis; general rules for the heart patient; what to do in case of a heart attack
- **Heart Quiz** (#EM93)
- **7 Hopeful Facts About Strokes** (#EM344)
- **Cigarette Quiz** (#EM415)
- **Eat Well But Wisely** (#EM478)
- **Heart Attack—How to Reduce Your Risk** (#EM517)
- **How to Stop Smoking** (#EM487)
- **How We Can Reduce the Risks of Heart Attacks** (#EM485)
- **Recipes for Fat-Controlled, Low Cholesterol Meals** (#EM455A)
- **Rescue Breathing to Save a Life** (#EM446)
- **The Way to a Man's Heart, a Fat-Controlled, Low Cholesterol Meal Plan to Reduce the Risk of Heart Attack** (#EM455)
- **Your Blood Pressure** (#EM33)
- **After a Coronary** (#EM365)
- **Do It Yourself Again—Self-Help Devices for the Stroke Patient** (#EM360)
- **If You Have Angina** (#EM448)
- **Up and Around, a Booklet to Aid the Stroke Patient in Activities of Daily Living** (#EM358)
- **Varicose Veins** (#EM181)

A single copy of any of the above publications is free from local chapters of the association or from:

*American Heart Association
44 East 23rd St.
New York, N.Y. 10010*

A full catalogue of publications and other materials, including those which must be requested through physicians, is provided in **A List of Materials for the Public**.

HEALTH 4

NATIONAL SOCIETY FOR THE PREVENTION OF BLINDNESS

The society, founded in 1908, is the oldest national voluntary health agency engaged in the prevention of blindness through a comprehensive program of community services, public and professional education and research.

On the community level, the glaucoma screening program is particularly worthy of note. In cooperation with other agencies, the program coordinates volunteer ophthalmologists to perform the simple procedure for measuring fluid pressure within the eye—excessive pressure usually being associated with glaucoma.

The society has set out to prevent needless blindness, about half of all cases. Its series of booklets is particularly useful in this goal. Offered free of charge to anyone, the following are especially noteworthy:

Your Eyes: For a Lifetime of Sight
This booklet gives a clear explanation of how our eyes function and details a number of eye problems with their symptoms and treatment—including glaucoma, cataract and diabetic retinopathy. Eye safety, contact lenses, eyeglasses, sunglasses and proper lighting are discussed as well.

Sunglasses . . . know what you're getting and what they're really for
Sunglasses have become as much a fashion accessory as a device for screening the sun's rays. This booklet cautions on the proper selection and use of sunglasses, to avoid damage to the eyes.

Television and Your Eyes
Because we all watch television so much, we frequently have questions about its effects on our eyes. This booklet answers the most common questions—putting to rest most of the misconceptions about possible harm, while at the same time making several suggestions for more comfortable viewing conditions.

Glaucoma
Glaucoma, once one of the more dreaded eye diseases, can now be halted in its early stages. This booklet explains the disease and the approaches used by ophthalmologists and also furnishes excellent illustrations approximating the visual symptoms experienced.

PREVENT BLINDNESS.

AIDS AND APPLIANCES FOR THE BLIND AND VISUALLY IMPAIRED

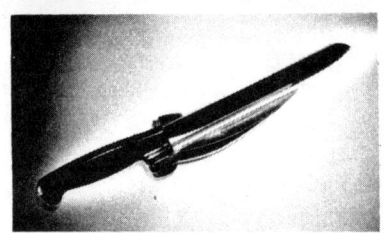

Diverse aids include large playing cards and the Magna Wonder Knife with adjustable slicing guide.

The American Foundation for the Blind publishes a free annual catalogue of its products for the blind and visually handicapped that are available by mail. Included are clocks, watches and timers with raised numerals or Braille markings; tools and instruments with easy-to-read calibrations and other indications to make handling

Special care and conditions

Cataract: What It Is and How It Is Treated
95 out of 100 cataract operations are successful—encouraging news for those affected. The booklet describes symptoms, surgical procedures and changes in sight commonly experienced afterwards.

The Aging Eye: Facts on Eye Care for Older Persons
Although some can maintain good vision throughout life, others will experience vision problems with aging. In fact, eye problems can often be prevented and should not be shrugged off as "the price of aging." Common symptoms and treatments are described. The booklet concludes with a summary of first aid for eye emergencies.

First Aid for Eye Emergencies
An easily displayed sticker for the medicine cabinet or other convenient place.

Single copies of all of the publications listed above are free. Multiple copies are available at modest cost, as listed in the society's **Catalogue of Publications and Films**. Several films listed in the catalogue may be of interest to groups.

Write:
*National Society for the Prevention of Blindness, Inc.
79 Madison Ave.
New York, N.Y. 10016*

> Glaucoma.
> You don't feel a thing.
>
> After a while, you can't see a thing.

easier; and devices for simpler meal preparation. All the products are commercially produced and may be available in some stores. The catalogue groups them conveniently by type. The kitchen devices should be of interest to anyone. Consider, for example, the hot beverage maker that heats water almost instantly, the opener for stubborn jar lids, the separator of egg whites from yolks, and the pressure cooker.

Adult games—such as Scrabble and Monopoly—modified for the visually impaired and large playing cards are available.

One especially useful medical device is the clinical thermometer which shows the temperature on a dial. A large-print telephone dial is designed to fit over the standard phone dial.

Also offered is an accident alert card designed to identify up to six emergency-related health conditions and to provide space for doctors' names and phone numbers and those of the nearest relative. The card is produced in laminated form on the basis of a completed questionnaire.

Write:
*American Foundation for the Blind
15 West 16th St.
New York, N.Y. 10011*

HEALTH

ALLERGY FOUNDATION OF AMERICA

Allergies in one form or another affect perhaps more than 30 million people. While research continues, much can be done in terms of prevention, detection and treatment. Many people in fact do not know that their problems could be allergy-related. The Allergy Foundation can provide some important information.

A basic folder, available free, is called **Questions and Answers to Allergy and Allergic Diseases**.

Additional information is contained in booklets on specific allergies (50¢ each):

- Hay Fever
- Handbook for the Asthmatic
- The Skin and Its Allergies
- Insect Stings Can Be Dangerous
- Mold Allergy
- Food Allergy
- Drug Allergy
- Cosmetic Allergy
- Asthma, Climate and Weather

NATIONAL INSTITUTE OF ALLERGY AND INFECTIOUS DISEASES

Allergic diseases cause few deaths but can make life miserable. The institute, a division of the Public Health Service of the National Institutes of Health, is engaged in research and education on the allergies which afflict many, either constantly or occasionally. It has published several booklets on aspects of allergy and the status of research and treatment. Effective allergy treatment is often possible, and there is clear evidence that the right physician can help the sufferer. The recommended booklets are:

Allergy Research: An Introduction
This overview gives a definition of allergies, their history, relationship to heredity, and current methods leading to successful treatment.
Booklet #NIH 72-281   55¢

Sinusitis
The hollow air spaces called the sinuses cause misery and pain for millions of Americans. Research indicates that help is possible and that proper treatment can avoid more serious complications later—if the sinus pain is looked upon as an indicator of disease, not simply something which will go away by itself or can be deadened by a painkiller.
Booklet #NIH 74-540   30¢

Food Allergy
While experts are not certain how many Americans suffer from food allergy, a conservative estimate is approximately 31 million. The symptoms, the crucial detection process, and the prognosis for cure are discussed thoroughly in this booklet.
Booklet #NIH 74-533   30¢

Dust Allergy
House dust—the plague of the homemaker—is also the source of troublesome allergies for an unknown number of people who are constantly bothered by sneezing and runny noses or by wheezing and shortness of breath. Current and prospective research and the known cures are discussed in detail.
Booklet #NIH 74-490   30¢

Special care and conditions

Drug Allergy
As more medications have become available, the number of adverse drug reactions has increased. The symptoms and the precautions the individual can take once the allergy-causing agent has been discovered are discussed.
Booklet #NIH 75-703   35¢

Order from:

*USGPO
Washington, D.C. 20402*

Address:
*Allergy Foundation of America
801 Second Ave.
New York, N.Y. 10017*

FACTS ABOUT HEARING AIDS

The hearing-aid industry has been subject to a great deal of criticism and scrutiny, and this booklet gives thorough background on how to shop for a hearing aid and to protect your own best interests.

Free
*Council of Better Business Bureaus
1150 17th St. NW
Washington, D.C. 20036*

THE HEARING LOSS HANDBOOK
By Richard Rosenthal
St. Martin's Press, 1975, $8.95

The author, himself affected by a hearing loss, has written a credible consumer's guide to the problem. For many there are happy solutions, while many others follow wrong paths, spend money needlessly, and continue to be frustrated. Rosenthal dissects the hearing-aid world and offers guidelines that reiterate the wisdom of going to the best professionals.

TWO BOOKLETS ON HEARING FROM BELTONE

Hear Better with Your Hearing Aid, by W. F. Carver of the Washington University School of Medicine in St. Louis, is designed to help people use their hearing aids more effectively.

The text includes hints for hearing better on the telephone, while watching television and listening to the radio, and in such group situations as religious services and theatrical performances.
New Hope for the Hard-of-Hearing can be a reassuring and simple introduction to the possibilities for improvement through the use of hearing aids. It describes the general approach to professional diagnosis, advises on better care and safety of the ears, and explains the theories of hearing aids.

The booklets are free and available at many Beltone dealers. Or write:

*Beltone Electronics Corp.
4201 West Victoria St.
Chicago, Ill. 60646*

HEALTH 4

THE ARTHRITIS FOUNDATION

No case is hopeless. Something can be done for arthritis now. Moreover, research for the cause and cure of arthritis is moving forward rapidly. New therapies and many promising new drugs are emerging. Yesterday's discouragement can be replaced by today's optimism.

—**Rheumatoid Arthritis:
A Handbook for Patients,**
The Arthritis Foundation

The Arthritis Foundation is a voluntary health agency working for the answers to the cause, prevention and cure of arthritis—the nation's number-one crippling disease. Patients and physicians receive help through research, information, education and professional training.

Several publications are available for distribution through local chapters, which also provide information and assistance to individuals.

Some recommended pamphlets and booklets:

The Truth About Aspirin for Arthritis
For most people with arthritis, aspirin is the best single medicine, but it is widely misunderstood, misused, and misrepresented. This pamphlet, valuable in setting the record straight on aspirin's advantages as well as side effects, lists do's and dont's.

The Truth About Diet and Arthritis
The foundation, taking the position that food has nothing to do with arthritis, explains its view that medical treatment is the potential cure for many forms of arthritis.

Arthritis Quackery
This pamphlet prepares the reader for dealing with frauds and rackets that apparently run rampant in the arthritis-cure field.

Arthritis: The Basic Facts
This very thorough view of arthritis is aimed both at those with the disease who do not seek help and those who wish to understand more about it in order to lend their support to research and treatment in their communities. Contents: definitions of arthritis; the importance of diagnosis; details on the various forms.

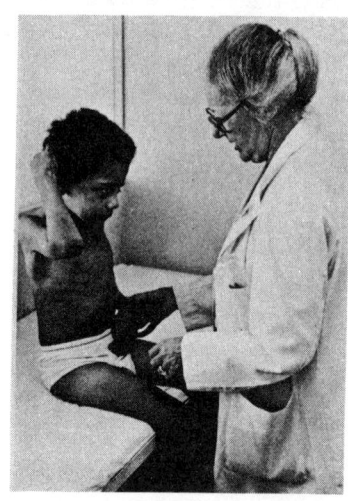

The Arthritis Foundation helps both the young and the old.

Special care and conditions

Osteoarthritis: A Handbook for Patients

Osteoarthritis, often called the "wear and tear" disease, involves the breakdown of cartilage. The chances of this disease increase with years, and women are affected twice as frequently as men. The booklet describes in detail symptoms and physiology and discusses treatment. Though there is no known cure, the booklet explains that symptoms can be alleviated and function of the joints improved. Once again, the foundation cautions against "quack" cures and urges consultation of one's own qualified physician.

Rheumatoid Arthritis: A Handbook for Patients

This, the most serious and painful form of arthritis, is explained thoroughly. It attacks the joints and can also affect the lungs, skin, blood vessels, muscles and other organs. Symptoms and the use of drugs and exercises are covered quite thoroughly, enabling the patient to more fully understand the physician's treatment.

Home Care Programs in Arthritis: A Manual for Patients

This manual for patients with rheumatoid arthritis and similar arthritic diseases offers general instructions on home care. Covered are posture, rest and exercise, hot and cold applications, splints, aids to walking, self-help devices and possible advantageous modifications of the surroundings. Because the manual is general and each patient is an individual, before following any of its suggestions discuss it with your doctor.

Living With Arthritis and Where to Turn for Help

This general booklet handles the problems of adjustment to the disease, from finding a doctor to locating help in the community. The concluding pages list community agencies and tell how to look them up in the phone book.

Individual copies of Arthritis Foundation booklets are free. Requests may be addressed to local chapters, if known, or to:

The Arthritis Foundation
3400 Peachtree Road, NE
Atlanta, Georgia 30326

Mail received at this address is forwarded unopened to the appropriate local chapter, based on your return address, to fill the literature requests. This also helps to establish a line of communication between the individual and the chapter.

NEW HOPE FOR THE ARTHRITIC
By Dr. Collin H. Dong and Jane Banks
Crowell, 1975, $6.95

Dr. Dong, himself a former arthritis sufferer, takes exception to the official position of many specialists that there is no relationship between food and arthritis. By no means a scientific work, the book does relate experiences with patients he has treated and relieved of pain, including himself.

Quoting Victor Hugo, he says, "There is nothing more powerful than an idea whose time has come." In medicine, he says, this idea is nutrition's relation to disease, which requires a massive study to make medicine less an art and more a science.

Based on his findings and experiences with himself and his patients, Dr. Dong claims that he has come to some reasonable conclusions. Foremost, he says: "It isn't what you eat that does it so much as what you do *not* eat." He outlines an extensive roster of do's and don'ts, with major emphasis on the prohibition against meats and dairy products in order to relieve the pain of arthritis. With his collaborator, Jane Banks, he cites menu-planning hints, recipes and an extensive list of permitted foods, with considerable emphasis on fruits, vegetables and fish.

A description of Dr. Dong's and Ms. Banks' cookbook is included in the chapter, FOOD.

HEALTH 4

AMERICAN DENTAL ASSOCIATION

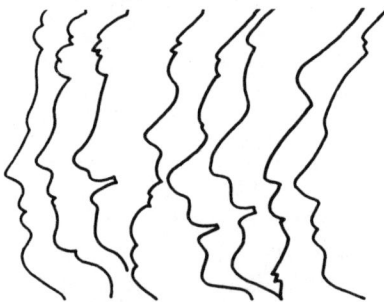

Whatever your age, you can and should have a healthy mouth and a pleasant smile. The American Dental Association, as well as your own dentist and his or her staff, can help. The association has several free booklets:
- **Don't do It Yourself.** This booklet cautions against making your own repairs or adjustments to your dentures.
- **Dentures: What You Don't Know Can Hurt You**
- **Keep Your Teeth All Your Life.** A good general view of prevention for which you can be responsible.
- **They're Your Teeth . . . You Can Keep Them.** Some detailed explanations of the tooth problems that can become more serious.
- **Your New Dentures.** Your dentist will likely give you a long talk on adjustment to new dentures. But for those general concerns and questions after you leave his office—and before the next visit—this handy reference summarizes a good deal of information on speech, facial expressions, chewing, when to remove, and denture care.

*Free
American Dental Association
211 East Chicago Ave.
Chicago, Ill. 60611*

RX FOR SOUND TEETH

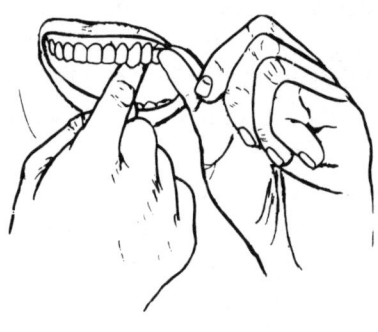

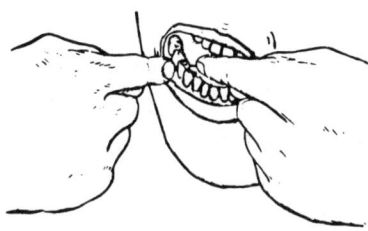

Deplaquing between upper and lower teeth.

Adhesive masses of bacteria are a threat to your health when they invade the teeth and the gums and jawbones that support them. Detection and removal of these masses, commonly called "plaque," is the subject of this highly graphic government folder.

*Free
Publication #NIH 76-793
Public Health Service
National Institutes of Health
National Institute of Dental Research/Office of Public Information
Bethesda, Md. 20014*

SOMEONE CLOSE DRINKS TOO MUCH

Almost two-thirds of adult Americans, it is estimated, know someone who "drinks too much." Over one-third of those polled to obtain that statistic said this drinker is "close to me"—either a friend or relative—and that the drinking problem has existed for at least 10 years. Though a social drink has many positive aspects for friendships, the abuse of alcohol is serious for others.

If alcoholism is closer to you than you think, you might find this pamphlet a constructive beginning toward helping others. It is prepared by the federal government's National Institute on Alcohol Abuse and Alcoholism, and can be ordered for 40¢ from:

*USGPO
Washington, D.C. 20402*

Sources of further information and help in your community are available through two national organizations:

*Alcoholics Anonymous
P.O. Box 459
Grand Central Station
New York, N.Y. 10017*

*Al-Anon Family Groups
115 East 23rd St.
New York, N.Y. 10010*

Local Alcoholics Anonymous chapters are listed in most telephone directories.

Special care and conditions

AMERICA ON THE ROCKS

Alcoholism, America's number-one problem involving an abused "drug," affects nine million drinkers. This film, produced in cooperation with the National Institute on Alcoholism and Drug Abuse, is useful for group discussion. It neither scolds nor preaches, but surveys the American drinking scene in such a way as to stimulate discussion of personal drinking practices and community attitudes. The film is available in 16mm sound versions in either 15- or 28-minute lengths.

Sales:		Rentals:	
28 minutes	$113.50	28 minutes	12.50
15 minutes	72.00	15 minutes	10.00

Available from:
*National Audiovisual Center
Washington, D.C. 20409*

PEACE FROM NERVOUS SUFFERING
By Dr. Claire Weekes
Hawthorn, 1972, $3.95

This confidence-building book by an Australian physician discusses theories on how to cope with feelings of fear and tension. It gives examples of how others have conquered nervous suffering, tells how to understand the meaning of your physical symptoms and how to handle them, and how to free yourself from depression and nervous exhaustion.

AMERICAN PODIATRY ASSOCIATION

The association, the professional society of the specialists treating foot disorders, has published two free short pamphlets worth examining:

- **Foot Health and Aging** provides some insights into aging and foot discomfort, giving general encouragement that much of the pain can be relieved.
- **Podiatrists' Services Under Medicare** reviews the insurance benefits for foot treatment under Medicare.

Free

Write:
*American Podiatry Association
20 Chevy Chase Circle NW
Washington, D.C. 20015*

HEALTH 4

AMERICAN CANCER SOCIETY

Knowledge and experience have shown that cancer can often be cured if treated promptly and properly. According to the American Cancer Society, of every 6 people who get cancer 2 will be saved and 4 will die; and half of those who get cancer could and should be saved.

The American Cancer Society, through its staff, affiliates and volunteers, conducts a massive, continuing program of public and professional education, of service to individuals, and of research. Most immediately of value is the service offered through local chapters, which provide cancer patients with pertinent information and guidance, loans of sickroom equipment, surgical dressings, and transportation to physicians' offices. Most well-known to the public is the massive and continuing publicity campaign urging early detection, by watching for the "7 warning signals," arranged so the first letters spell caution:

Change in bowel or bladder habits.
A sore that does not heal.
Unusual bleeding or discharge.
Thickening or lump in breast or elsewhere.
Indigestion or difficulty in swallowing.
Obvious change in wart or mole.
Nagging cough or hoarseness.

If you have a warning signal, see your doctor.

In the long run, with the support of the society and allied institutions, the goal is the detection of the causes of cancer and its eradication.

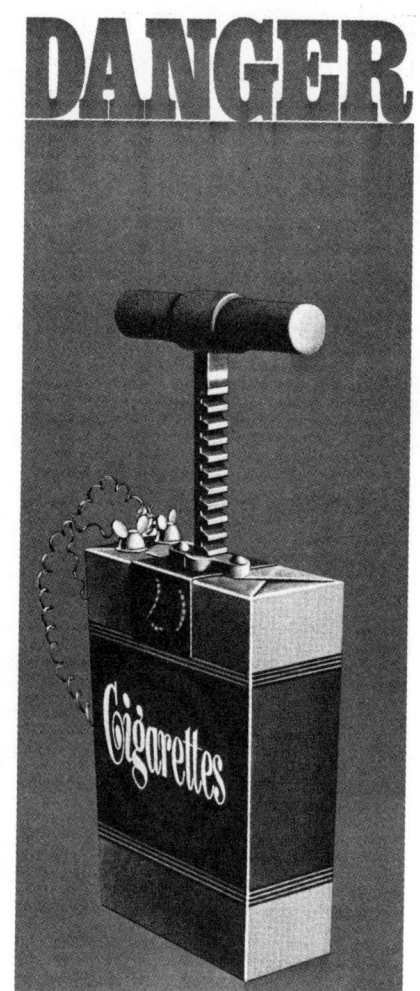

SCORE CARD

Copy this record sheet seven times for seven days. Make a check for each cigarette you smoke, hour by hour, and indicate how much you need it: a mark in the box opposite 1 shows low need, a mark opposite 6 high need; opposite 4, moderate need, etc. Then decide which cigarette you wish to eliminate.

NEED	MORNING HOURS (AM)							AFTERNOON, EVENING HOURS (PM)											
	6	7	8	9	10	11	12	1	2	3	4	5	6	7	8	9	10	11	12	1
1																				
2																				
3																				
4																				
5																				
6																				

Special care and conditions

"Which one is a quack?" asks the provocative booklet I Have a Secret Cure for Cancer. *They rarely can be recognized by appearance alone. But there are some clear, easily detectable guidelines for recognition in this booklet.*

Pamphlets are available free to the general public either through the national headquarters or through local chapters. Some are:

- ☐ **American Cancer Society: What It Is, What It Does, How It Began, Where It is Going**
- ☐ **Stay Healthy! Learn About Uterine Cancer**
- ☐ **I Have a Secret Cure for Cancer!** (this pamphlet warns against "quack" cures)
- ☐ **Open Wide** (about oral cancer)
- ☐ **Sense in the Sun** (about overexposure of the skin)
- ☐ **Danger: Cigarettes**
- ☐ **If You Want to Give Up Cigarettes**
- ☐ **The Hopeful Side of Cancer**
- ☐ **How to Examine Your Breasts**
- ☐ **Answering Your Questions about Cancer**
- ☐ **Cancer Facts for Men**
- ☐ **Cancer Facts for Women**

Write:
*American Cancer Society
219 East 42nd St.
New York, N.Y. 10017*

HEALTH   4

AMERICAN DIGESTIVE DISEASE SOCIETY

Whether your digestive problem has a name or you just hurt when you eat, you have a digestive disease. It's as simple as that—and as common—says the American Digestive Disease Society. The society, committed to the idea that life can be free of digestive disorders, is engaged in research support and public education to that end. The public is offered several free pamphlets giving background data on the symptoms and treatment of various digestive diseases and the current state of research:

- ☐ **Gall bladder**
- ☐ **Peptic/duodenal ulcer**
- ☐ **Diverticulosis**
- ☐ **Esophagitis/hiatal hernia**
- ☐ **Pancreatitis**
- ☐ **Liver disease**
- ☐ **Ileitis and colitis**
- ☐ **Psychological and emotional aspects of digestive disease**
- ☐ **On constipation and diarrhea**
- ☐ **On stomach trouble**
- ☐ **On gas and heartburn**

Through its volunteers in the community, the society will help with referral to a physician specializing in a particular symptom or disease.

Write:
*American Digestive Disease Society
295 Madison Ave.
New York, N.Y. 10017*

A MANUAL FOR PATIENTS WITH PARKINSON'S DISEASE

Considerable strides in understanding the causes of Parkinson's disease—as well as in treatment—have been made in the past 10 years. This attractive and highly graphic booklet explains the symptoms and treatment of the ailment. Also discussed are surgery and the role of physical therapy and other approaches for making the patient more comfortable and functional. A glossary of the relevant medical terms concludes this publication.

*Free
American Parkinson's Disease Foundation
147 East 50th St.
New York, N.Y. 10022*

SAFETY 5

A POUND OF PREVENTION

Several ounces of prevention can be worth several pounds of cure when it comes to safety. At all times—but especially as we grow older—safety is a great concern. Accidents in the home, on the road, in the street; crimes against persons and property; and fire: all are important.

The sources in this chapter afford help with all these matters.

occur are important. This booklet covers tips on crime in the streets, the home, and in commercial transactions.

Free
AARP-NRTA
P. O. Box 2400
215 Long Beach Blvd.
Long Beach, Calif. 90801

TO STOP A THIEF: THE COMPLETE GUIDE TO HOUSE, APARTMENT AND PROPERTY PROTECTION
By George C. Nonte, Jr. Stoeger, 1974, $4.95

This is a somewhat different approach to a book on protecting yourself and your home. The slant is largely psychological, starting with a verbatim transcript of an interview with a burglar who explains his tactics and his view of his victims and how they were victimized. The tips are thorough and very clear. A short, useful directory of recommended products concludes the book.

YOUR RETIREMENT ANTI-CRIME GUIDE

Crimes of violence and crimes against property are genuine fears of everyone, and we have particularly intense reactions as we grow older and find it more difficult to cope with some of the situations.

Prevention and a calm attitude if and when crimes do

Protection from crime

HOW TO PROTECT YOURSELF FROM CRIME
By Ira A. Lipman, Atheneum, 1975, $9.95

Recent FBI reports tell that nearly five of every 10 crimes in this country are against property. Though it may be comforting to realize that such crimes do not involve face-to-face confrontations, the problem is still a large one.

The most important feature of the book is telling how to slow down a criminal or influence him to seek another "mark." Though specific protective products are not indicated by brand name, (since new advances are frequent), types are discussed. Above all, and sadly, says the author, we should recognize that elimination of crime is not around the corner. We need to work at the most important element within our control: methods of prevention by ourselves for ourselves. While not recommending acts of dangerous heroism or vigilante tactics, the book does give sane hints in all areas of security inside and outside the home, as well as during natural disasters or other unusual emergencies.

Checklists and "other gentle reminders" are included. Not happy reading, but essentially useful.

The book is like insurance. Read it and others, and hope you never need to be in a position to use the contents. But be a bit more secure in being prepared.

Dollar for dollar, according to Ira Lipman, the dead bolt is your home's best means of defense.

You can help prevent purse snatchings.

SAFETY 5

GUIDE TO HOME AND PERSONAL SECURITY

Is your home a likely burglary target? This comprehensive booklet discusses your worst enemies—home accidents and fire—along with neighborhood-security plans, and a home-insurance checkup. In today's world of threats and insecurity, this text gives step-by-step plans and advice on achieving the more secure and safe home. And a clear case is made that it is indeed all possible.

Free
Action for Independent Maturity (AIM)
P. O. Box 2400
215 Long Beach Blvd.
Long Beach, Calif. 90801

PREVENTING CRIME THROUGH EDUCATION

The threat of crime is a major concern for all, and there are many things we ourselves can do to help reduce the risks.

Studies indicate that many crimes against older people are committed by opportunists taking advantage of individual thoughtlessness or carelessness. This booklet gives some good hints for the individual and outlines the procedures for organizing a local crime-prevention program.

Free
AARP-NRTA
P. O. Box 2400
215 Long Beach Blvd.
Long Beach, Calif. 90801

Long-established performers Bartine Zane (Buster Keaton's leading lady) and Elisha Cook, Jr. (of **The Maltese Falcon**) *illustrate crime prevention tips in* **Senior Power**.

SENIOR POWER—AND HOW TO USE IT

This 19-minute film is one of the few which directly address the problems of crime prevention among older people. Specific techniques for preventing wallet and purse snatching, burglaries and telephone harassment are presented in dramatic vignettes. A discussion guide and T-shirt promotional materials are available with the film.

For sale and rental:
William Brose Productions, Inc.
10850 Riverside Drive
North Hollywood, Calif. 91602

Actress Marie Miller shows "thumbs up" for crime prevention.

SAFETY 5

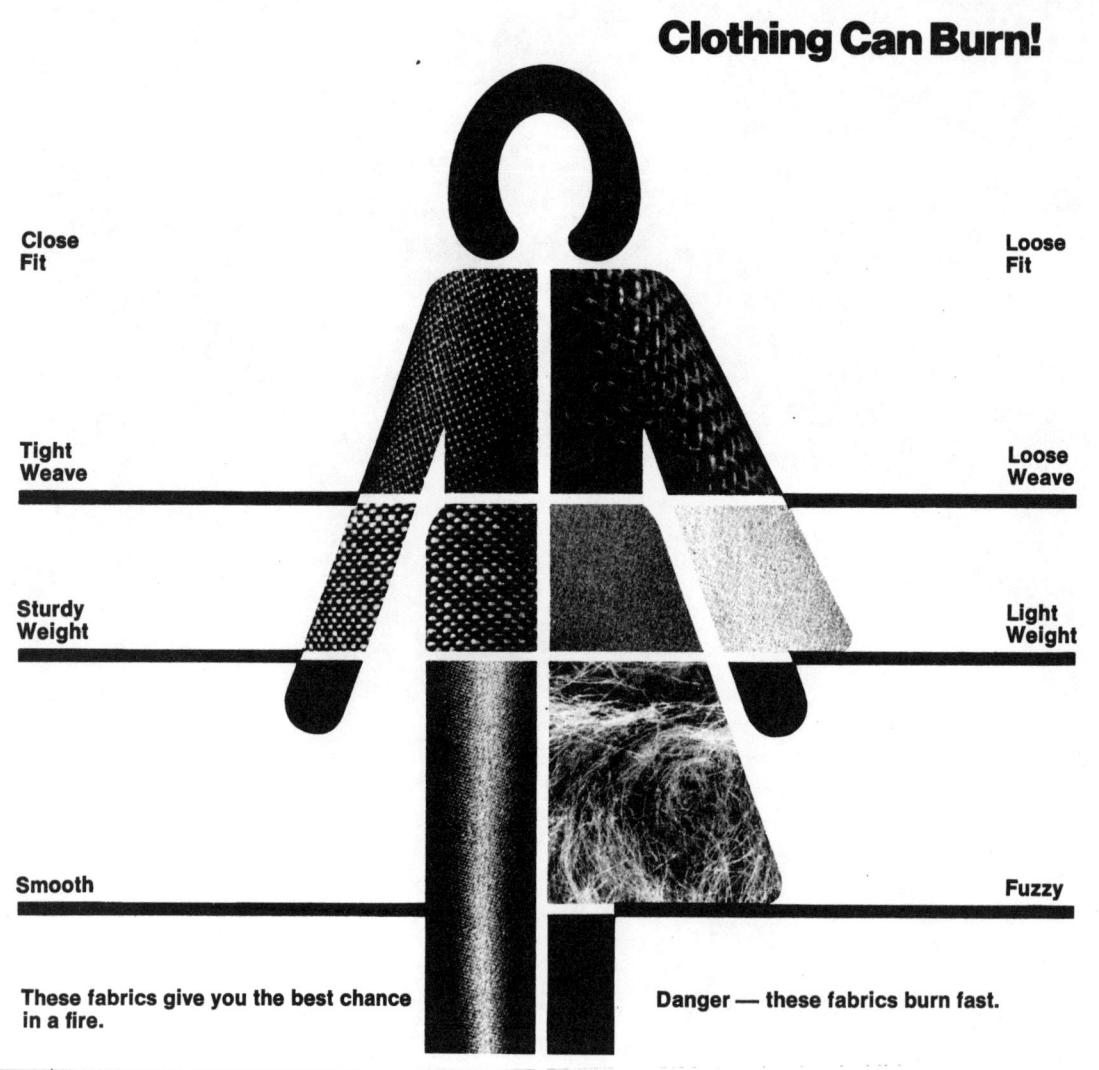

Clothing Can Burn!

Close Fit / Loose Fit
Tight Weave / Loose Weave
Sturdy Weight / Light Weight
Smooth / Fuzzy

These fabrics give you the best chance in a fire.

Danger — these fabrics burn fast.

NATIONAL FIRE PROTECTION ASSOCIATION

Protection against fire—how to prevent fire and what to do when it occurs—is important for all people, and older people are no exception.

The National Fire Protection Association, as part of its public education effort, has several attractive and informative free pamphlets that give good tips and reminders:

- Fire Prevention All Over Your Home
- Home Fire Detection
- Clothing Can Burn!
- Exit: Escape From Fire Wherever You Are

All pamphlets are free. Send stamped, addressed envelope to:

*National Fire Protection Association
470 Atlantic Ave.
Boston, Mass. 02210*

TIPS ON HOME FIRE PROTECTION

This pamphlet summarizes all of the common-sense tips necessary to prevent fires in the home and to know what to do in an emergency.

*Free
Council of Better Business Bureaus
1150 17th St. NW
Washington, D.C. 20036*

Product and personal safety

YOUR RETIREMENT SAFETY GUIDE

This booklet addresses the broad questions of safety for the person over 65, including:

Home, with concerns for safe design, proper lighting, and the special dangers inherent in each room and area of the home.
Traffic, with specific pointers for both drivers and pedestrians.

The booklet concludes with a quiz assessing general chances for accidents—which can be avoided.

Free
AARP-NRTA
P.O. Box 2400
215 Long Beach Blvd.
Long Beach, Calif. 90801

NATIONAL SAFETY COUNCIL

For many, retirement means more hours at home; and at the same time, certain physical changes tend to increase the effects of injuries from accidents. Accidents are preventable.

The National Safety Council has assembled a diverse kit of pamphlets, work sheets, small posters and checklists which can be an important asset in organizing community programs.

Request **Safety of the Elderly Program Kit** ($1.74):

Home Safety Information
National Safety Council
425 North Michigan Ave.
Chicago, Ill. 60611

U.S. CONSUMER PRODUCT SAFETY COMMISSION

Consumer products that may cause injuries or fatalities are the concern of this commission. Its jurisdiction covers the safety of nonfood and nondrug products, such as cleaning materials, flammable fabrics and household appliances, furnishings and toys. The commission can investigate hazards, conduct safety tests and help develop standards. It can ban the sale of products presenting an "imminent hazard."

The commission provides material to educate the consumer in using products safely and in becoming more aware.

The commission's catalogue of publications and audiovisual materials can be useful for individuals or groups. Dozens of fact sheets cover everything from plastics to flammable fabrics to electric irons. The films can help in group projects organized to encourage safety. All are listed in catalogue #CPSC–75–620–9, available from:

U.S. Consumer Product Safety Commission
Washington, D.C. 20207

The commission's work is instigated largely by information reported by people across the country. If you want to report a product hazard, or ask a question, you may write to the commission, though more immediate action will result from the "hotline," which is a toll-free phone number: 800–638–2666. (Maryland residents only, call 800–492–2937.)

SAFETY 5

HANDLE YOURSELF WITH CARE

You are your own most precious possession—handle yourself with care.

As you get older, you get a little more fragile. Your center of balance alters somewhat and you need to step more cautiously, run less frequently. If you fall, you're more apt to break. If you break, you are apt to take considerably longer to mend than when you were younger.

So it is well to take the extra care, the extra time, and to do the extra planning necessary for safety. Often just being aware of danger helps you to avoid it.

This thorough, cheerfully illustrated booklet proves that an ounce of prevention is truly worth a pound of cure, as it covers dozens of hints on avoiding falls, burns, medicine accidents, cuts, bruises and strains, and walking and driving accidents.

Also available from the same source is **Handle Yourself With Care: An Instructor's Guide for an Accident Prevention Course for Older Americans**. This is an especially useful tool for organizing a course perhaps taught by and for older people in a variety of settings—apartment, senior center or school.

Publication #ODH 75-20805   40¢
This and the **Instructor's Guide** available from:
  USGPO
  Washington, D.C. 20402

Product and personal safety
Important products for safety
Driver improvement

NEVER SLIP SAFETY TREADS

These one-piece plastic treads can be slipped quickly over any shoe or boot, insuring sure-footedness on snow or ice. Working on the same principle as studded snow tires, they are equipped with short steel spikes. They fold to pocket size and fit into a plastic draw-string pouch. Sizes small (2–6½), medium (7–8½) and large (9–11½) are $7.95 per pair; extra large (12 and over) are $8.95.

Available from:
American Foundation for the Blind
15 West 16th St.
New York, N.Y. 10011

KICK-STEP STOOL

Many accidents in the home can be prevented by using this stool. As you step on it, the ball casters pop up inside so that the rubber rim grips firmly on the floor and cannot slip. When you remove your weight, the casters pop down so you can kick the light-weight stool where you want it without bending over. The stool sells for $12 and is available from:

Fred Sammons, Inc.
Box 32
Brookfield, Ill. 60513

BATH-SAFETY DEVICES

An extensive selection of bathtub safety railings and seats can be found in the catalogue available from:

IMPORTANT PRODUCTS FOR SAFETY

Several products are available in the safety area. Direct-mail sources are given here, though many of the items are also available through shops. Several other products are also mentioned in HEALTH.

AARP-NRTA DRIVER IMPROVEMENT PLAN

The AARP-NRTA Driver Improvement Plan is offered in cooperation with the National Safety Council to help drivers update skills and prevent traffic accidents. Volunteer instructors who have been certified by the National Safety Council give the programs in two-hour sessions through AARP-NRTA local chapters. Films and other visual aids are used to illustrate safe driving.

A fee of $1 per attendee covers materials and other costs. Upon completion, the participants receive a certificate and card from the National Safety Council.

To enjoy the rewarding experience of serving as a volunteer instructor, you must have:
- ☐ A valid operator's license and drive regularly.
- ☐ A clear voice and the ability to speak in front of groups.
- ☐ Mobility and effective use of hands.
- ☐ The time and ability to keep student records, and, with another instructor, to plan and conduct at least two driving courses in your community each year.

Instructors are trained in two-day development courses. After serving as an assistant instructor in two driving classes, candidates receive a National Safety Council Instructor Card, which is renewable annually.

For information on organizing a course or serving as an instructor, contact:
AARP-NRTA Driver Improvement Program
1909 K St. NW
Washington, D.C. 20006

CLEO Living Aids
3957 Mayfield Road
Cleveland, O. 44121

CREATIVE LEISURE 6

When Franklin D. Roosevelt was inaugurated as President, Oliver Wendell Holmes, Jr., distinguished member of the Supreme Court of the U.S., was unable to attend because of frailty. Noting the absence, Roosevelt decided that courtesy dictated a call on the eminent senior jurist. Hearing no sound as he approached Mr. Holmes' door, Roosevelt assumed that the old man was asleep and entered very quietly. He found, to his surprise, that Mr. Holmes was reading a book in Greek. When asked what he was doing, Justice Holmes replied: "Improving my mind."

—Courtesy American Medical Association
How the Older Person Can Get the Most Out of Living

Planning for creative leisure
Education

TIME FOR SATISFACTION

The leisure of retirement is frequently cherished for years in anticipation. And for many the pleasant dream becomes reality. For others, retirement is idleness and boredom. More and more evidence builds up that active and creative leisure can be not only satisfying to oneself but can also help others—sometimes bring in money—and almost assuredly assist in maintaining the health and vigor of the individual.

Time is an enormous asset. Use it wisely. Explore those things you always wanted to do as well as those you never thought of before. The range of possibilities is endless, from solitary crafts to education to travel. It need not all cost a great deal of money, but it does frequently require creative thinking.

Too late for accomplishments? There are many for whom it is not. Consider a few examples: Pope John XXIII was 77 when he began leading the Roman Catholic Church. Mr. and Mrs. Will Durant have continued their prolific writing into their 90's. Casey Stengel led the New York Mets until he was 76; and many people have even begun new careers . . .

Many people only dream of second careers . . . some plunge in. Harriet Sappington, having spent many busy years raising her family and working in real estate at the same time, never forgot her ambition to be an actress. In 1968, in her late 60's, she was asked on the spur of the moment to pose for a photo which would be used for a record album. From that point on, she sought out modeling and acting experiences. She found a new lease on life with the challenges and eventual successes she has reached—into her 70's—in modeling and acting in commercials for television.

RETIREMENT LIVING MAGAZINE'S GUIDE TO LEISURE . . . AND YOUR RETIREMENT

This Retirement Living guide dissects the life of the retiree and puts it back together. The approach wisely ignores the problems and looks at the positives. And the outstanding positive asset is time. Yes, there now is time. But what to do with it?

The guide starts out with a personal quiz designed to evaluate one's feelings about a particular endeavor. Probably the most persuasive statement for planning, seeking and making the best use of time is the page devoted to the hour-by-hour totally boring day which some imaginary—or real—retiree spends.

The book includes good advice on hobbies, education, television, volunteerism and travel.

$1.50 to current subscribers of **Retirement Living Magazine,** $2.25 to nonsubscribers

Retirement Living Magazine
150 East 58th St.
New York, N.Y. 10022

(See COMMUNICATING for more on the magazine and other publications in the series.)

THE BOUNDLESS RESOURCE
By Willard Wirtz and the National Manpower Institute
New Republic Book Company, 1975, $7.95

There aren't two worlds—education and work—one for youth, the other for maturity. There is one world—life!

This book by a former Secretary of Labor examines our traditional "time traps." Among the wasted groups, he contends, are people over 60, who likely face 15 or more years of idleness but whose lives might instead be enriched by a new period of learning and serving. The solutions are not immediate, but can suggest many approaches for readers engaged in searching, advocating and pressuring for change.

CREATIVE LEISURE 6

NATIONAL HOME STUDY COUNCIL

Home study—or correspondence school—has been a popular educational alternative for many years for people who could not find the time or the transportation to reach schools—or were shut in. As with traditional classroom institutions, accreditation of the school is an important assurance that a legitimate education will be offered by qualified people.

The National Home Study Council is a private organization recognized by the U.S. Office of Education to provide accreditation. Its standards include:
- ☐ A competent faculty
- ☐ Educationally sound and up-to-date courses
- ☐ Careful screening of students for admission
- ☐ Satisfactory educational services
- ☐ Demonstrated ample student success and satisfaction
- ☐ Truthful advertising of courses
- ☐ Financial ability to deliver high-quality educational service

The wide range of accredited courses includes everything from motion-picture-camera repair to real estate.

The council periodically issues a free directory of accredited courses and institutions. Write:

National Home Study Council
1601 18th St. NW
Washington, D.C. 20009

ELDERHOSTEL

Idleness and isolation are poisons to the mind.

With that philosophy, the Elderhostel program has begun providing on-campus summer courses for older people at very low cost. In the summer of 1976, 21 colleges and universities in New England opened their doors to older people, providing comfortable accommodations and a broad series of one-week courses.

The courses, without credit and requiring no outside assignments, offer an enriching range of subjects from creative writing to folk singing.

Campus accommodations average $60 per week, including housing and meals and the use of all facilities. There are no costs for courses as such, provided the individual is at least 65 or already drawing Social Security. Depending on financial factors, those under 65 may be charged tuition.

ADULT EDUCATION ASSOCIATION OF THE USA

Adults are going back to school more than ever before, and older people make up a significant number. Whether for degrees, general enrichment or special skills, adult education is here in a big way. The Adult Education Association of the USA, made up of a large cross section of people in that field, can provide answers to specific questions on where to turn for your special needs in your community, if your own investigations fail. Write:

Adult Education Association of the USA
810 18th St. NW
Washington, D.C. 20006

Education

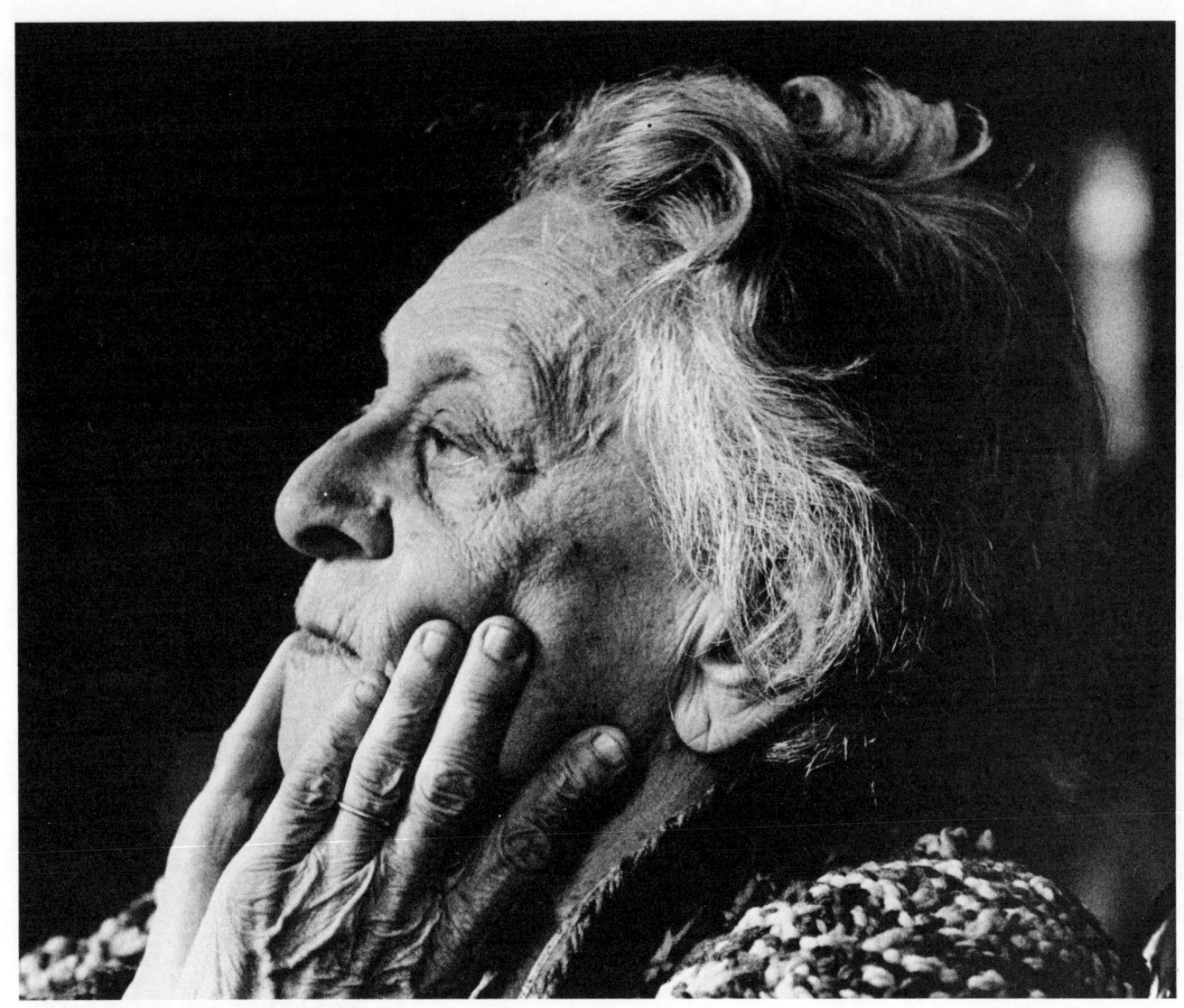

Plans call for several regions to join the original New England group. For further information and referral, write:

Executive Director
Elderhostel
New England Center for Continuing Education
15 Garrison Ave.
Durham, N.H. 03824

CREATIVE LEISURE 6

CORRESPONDENCE COURSES OF THE PENNSYLVANIA STATE UNIVERSITY

Penn State offers an extensive program of correspondence courses in agriculture, family living and community development. The courses are available at very low fees to people throughout the United States.

The lessons, appropriately illustrated, are mailed on 8½" x 11" bound sheets, generally with no additional text required. Students may enroll at any time and are sent the entire course upon receipt of fees. You proceed at your own pace, sending in assignments if you wish. Those assignments submitted are corrected, graded and returned. To receive the Certificate of Accomplishment, the student must submit all assignments in satisfactory form.

If a group of 10 or more enrolls together in a course the fee is reduced by 50¢. Course fees vary, though most are in the $4-to-$5 range. As many as nine individual lessons are included. Some of the more interesting courses are: *Canning and Food Preservation; Care of Clothing; Fabrics—Selection, Sewing, Care; Home Vegetable Gardening; Sharpen Your Consumer Skills.*

For a complete catalogue write:
*Correspondence Courses
The Pennsylvania State University
307 Agricultural Administration Bldg.
University Park, Pa. 16802*

Additional courses, some of which earn credits, are available under the university's independent study program. For the catalogue, write:
*Independent Study by Correspondence
The Pennsylvania State University
3 Shields Bldg.
University Park, Pa. 16802*

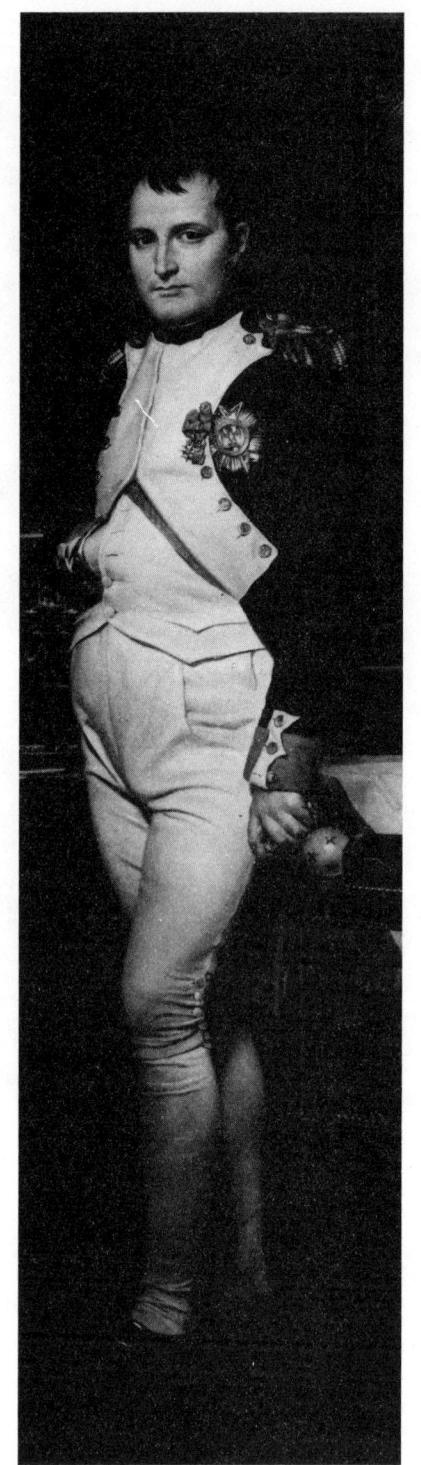

Education

THE NATIONAL GALLERY OF ART

The National Gallery of Art in Washington, D.C., through its Extension Service, has developed a wide range of audiovisual resources for the benefit of the many people across the United States who do not have an opportunity to visit the museum. The programs offered include 16 mm films as well as slide lectures with recordings. Available to community groups and individuals, these materials are lent free of charge except for postage and insurance on return mailings.

The materials cover the history of western art through the 20th century. They are particularly appropriate for senior center and other adult education courses.

A complete catalogue with ordering instructions is available from:

The Extension Service
National Gallery of Art
Washington, D.C. 20565

THE NEW YORK TIMES GUIDE TO CONTINUING EDUCATION IN AMERICA
By Frances Coombs Thompson
Quadrangle Books, 1972, $12.50

This directory lists, by state and by community, the adult education opportunities at hundred of colleges, universities and specialized schools. While not exhaustive, it does more than scratch the surface. A separate section deals with recognized correspondence schools and their offerings.

Gardening

SEED CATALOGUES

Seed catalogues are a joy in themselves, as one browses through the pages of glorious colors. They are also a wealth of information on gardening on small or large scale—for fruits and vegetables as well as flowers. The Sunday papers list all sorts of seed companies offering catalogues, especially in the winter, in anticipation of spring planting. Two of the more popular free seed catalogues you may find interesting are from:

W. Atlee Burpee Co.
Warminster, Pa. 18974

Kelly Brothers Nurseries, Inc.
Dansville, N.Y. 14437

THE GARDENER'S CATALOGUE
By Harvey Rottenberg and Tom Riker
Morrow, $6.95

In an age of catalogues and searches for sources, this work, billed as the "most important gardening tool since the watering can," is a profusely illustrated collection of plant lore, facts, instructions and sources.

GOOD HOUSEKEEPING BASIC GARDENING TECHNIQUES
By the editors of Good Housekeeping Magazine
1976, $8.95

Like a dictionary, this book covers the whole scene—in this case gardening. Chapters include garden design, indoor gardens, greenhouses, and all the "nitty gritty."

CARE AND MAINTENANCE OF COMMON HOUSEHOLD AND OFFICE PLANTS

In 1972, the Green Scene project of the National Capital Parks, the division of the National Park Service responsible for parks in the capital area, established a plant diagnostic center for diseases and other plant problems. This booklet is an outgrowth of that project; and if the Washington area's overwhelmingly green atmosphere is any testimony, the booklet is authoritative.

The first of the booklet's two divisions contains material on buying plants, use of the proper tools, soil and fertilizer, proper location, and watering.

The second division covers 24 specific popular plants.

$1.20
Booklet #24-005-00536-6
USGPO
Washington, D.C. 20402

CREATIVE LEISURE 6

GROWING FLOWERING ANNUALS

A flowering garden is a joy, both in the labor and the results. The secrets to a successful garden become evident if you open yourself to the professionals. In this case, the U.S. Department of Agriculture has set down straight advice on the annuals—those plants that last only a year. Everything is covered, from selection to soil preparation to specific plant care. Careful illustrations help in the description of transplanting.

25¢
Home and Garden #91
USGPO
Washington, D.C. 20402

THE GARDEN WAY CART

If transporting heavy loads around the grounds of your house—as you garden, cart fire wood, or take out the trash—is a burden, then you ought to consider the Garden Way Model 26 cart. Its 26" wheels make the cart easy to manage with the heaviest of loads.

The price is $119.50 plus shipping costs from Vermont. Smaller carts are also available.

For further information, write to:

Garden Way Research
Charlotte, Vt. 05445

98

Gardening Crafts

AMERICAN CRAFTS COUNCIL

The increasing interest in crafts has made this council very active. The annual membership fee of $18 includes special discounts on selected crafts books; a subscription to the attractive and thorough bimonthly **Craft Horizons** magazine; opportunities to participate in conferences, seminars and other crafts events throughout the United States; eligibility for goup insurance; and free admission to the Museum of Contemporary Crafts in New York City.

For additional information or a membership form, address:

*American Crafts Council
44 West 53rd St.
New York, N.Y. 10019*

NATIONAL GUIDE TO CRAFT SUPPLIES
By Judith Glassman
Van Nostrand Reinhold,
1975, $6.95

Buying, making and selling crafts are becoming more popular. Sources for crafts are very diverse, largely because many of the supplying businesses are small and because variety is so great. But the sources exist.

This guide, a "yellow pages" of the craft world, lists every conceivable craft, from bookbinding to quilting, and gives reliable sources by states. The listings of places of instruction, periodicals and organizations are particularly useful.

MOTHER'S BOOKSHELF

The Mother Earth News, a monumental effort toward encouraging self-reliance and sharing know-how, also distributes books on self-sufficient living. This free and ever–growing catalogue of over 500 books lists creative-leisure sources in categories such as gardening, do-it-yourself projects, crafts, music, and camping.

*Mother's Bookshelf
P.O. Box 70
Hendersonville, N.C. 28739*

BOOKBINDING SUPPLIES FROM BASIC CRAFTS COMPANY

The joys and tranquillity of bookbinding are largely left to machines, though a small resurgence in the individual craft has begun. Whether for pleasure or profit, bookbinding can be done by individuals, and Basic Crafts Company has the supplies, equipment and encouragement for the craftsperson.

For a brochure, write:

*Basic Crafts Company
1201 Broadway
New York, N.Y. 10001*

CONTEMPORARY CRAFTS MARKETPLACE

Crafts in themselves can provide great personal satisfaction to the creator. But sharing, selling, and expanding into other craft forms are the sometimes elusive special challenges. **Contemporary Crafts Marketplace** is a book compiled by the American Crafts Council which can help.

This book is organized into several sections:
☐ Buying, selling and exhibiting, arranged by state and city
☐ Finding people and organizations in the world of crafts
☐ The study of particular crafts
☐ Audiovisual materials on crafts
☐ Purchasing craft supplies
☐ Packing, shipping and insuring valuable craft works
☐ Participating in conventions, exhibits, conferences and meetings
☐ Finding other reference books and periodicals on crafts

The price is $13.95 plus 40¢ shipping and handling. Write:

*R. R. Bowker Order Department
P.O. Box 1807
Ann Arbor, Mich. 48106*

CREATIVE LEISURE   6

THE CATALOG OF KITS
By Jeffrey Feinman
Morrow, 1975, $6.95

With today's increasing labor costs and the return to many craft interests, kits are bigger business than ever. The frequent problem, though, is where to turn to find the kit, or to find the kit you never knew existed. This compilation goes far to fill this gap—it describes hundreds of kits and tells where and how to acquire them.

Interested in making your own electronic organ? Yogurt? A rug? A television camera? The right kits are all here, plus extra sources for discovering those not individually described in the catalogue.

THE FIRST NEW ENGLAND CATALOGUE
Edited by Marie S. Hall
Random House, 1973, $4.95 (prepared under the auspices of the Pequot Press, Chester, Conn. 06412)

This book brings together hundreds of creative-leisure and daily-living sources in New England. Since many of them offer books or items through the mail, the compilation is also useful well beyond New England, whose historic character and charm are evident throughout.

Sections include: Earth (sources for gardening and use of plants); Education; Leisure (travel ideas throughout New England and crafts); Habitat, (housing design, repair and furnishings); and Crafts.

BERGEN ARTS AND CRAFTS

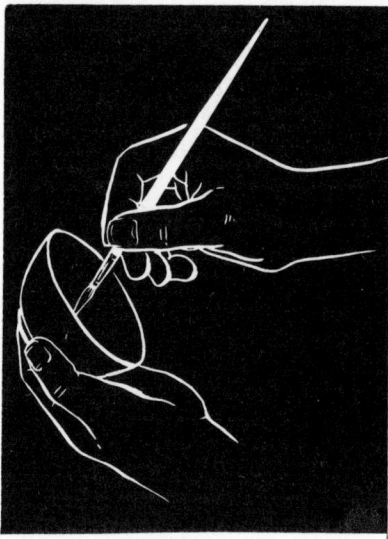

Bergen's catalogue offers a wide range of materials and kits for craft items, such as jewelry, boxes, potting and sculpting, and an extensive selection of craft books.

Write:
Bergen Arts and Crafts
P.O. Box 381
Marblehead, Mass. 01945

CREATIVE CRAFTS

This bimonthly magazine is filled with articles, features and advertisements for the latest in individual craft ideas. The magazine should have appeal to the experienced as well as the curious and untried craftsperson.

Single copies—75¢
A year's subscription—$4.50

Write:
Creative Crafts
P.O. Box 700
Newton, N.J. 07860

PACK-O-FUN

Billed as the "only scrap craft magazine," *Pack-O-Fun*, published 10 times each year, features dozens of craft objects to be made from scraps. The entertainment and economic aspects are numerous, and the results frequently provide good gifts and useful items for yourself. Typical issues include such items as toys, table and holiday decorations, and jewelry.

Subscriptions are available at $6 a year or $13 for three years. **Pack-O-Fun** also publishes several craft manuals; they are generally listed in the magazines or in a separate brochure. Some manuals are:

• More Sock Toys You Can Make $1.50

Crafts

- Make-it With Foam Egg Cartons .75
- Nature Crafts: Over 1500 Uses for Twigs, Leaves, Gourds and More 1.50
- Gifts to Make From Odds 'n Ends 1.50
- 751 Handy Hints .75

For further information and orders:

Pack-O-Fun
14 Main St.
Park Ridge, Ill. 60068

CANING SUPPLIES FROM THE NEWELL WORKSHOP

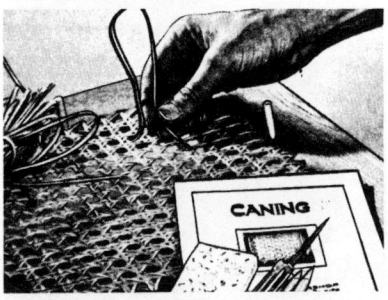

The Newell Workshop supplies genuine cane webbing and related materials for those interested in caning chairs and other items.

A leaflet catalogue is available by writing to:

Newell Workshop
19 Elaine Avenue
Hinsdale, Ill. 60521

CRAFTS 'N THINGS

Published six times yearly, this magazine gives craft news and instructions for beginners as well as advanced craftspeople. Each issue also contains a "swap 'n share" section, dates of current meetings and workshops, and a shopping section.

A one-year subscription is $5.

Write:
Crafts 'n Things
14 Main St.
Park Ridge, Ill. 60068

BASIC BASKETS
By Mara Cary
Houghton Mifflin, 1975, $4.95

This "how-to" book proves that a beginner can actually make baskets for either personal use or income. The author's text is comprised of transcriptions of her classroom lectures, and the illustrations are of beginning students' work in the classes. The book also includes an extensive photo essay of Mrs. Cary's own baskets, which are sold commercially.

SOME BOOKS FROM VAN NOSTRAND REINHOLD

Van Nostrand Reinhold publishes many books on crafts. In four specific categories, descriptive folders are available:
- Graphic Arts
- Needlecraft
- Weaving and Textiles
- Pottery and Ceramics

Write:
Van Nostrand Reinhold Co.
300 Pike St.
Cincinnati, Oh. 45202

SUPPLIES FOR THE AMATEUR WINEMAKER

Did you know that you could make your own wine and beer? Amateur winemakers may manufacture up to 200 gallons of wine a year. They must, however, file a form 1541 with the nearest office of the Federal Alcohol and Tax Department and follow any other rules specified by that office. There is no charge for the application filing.

Making wine at home has become popular in the past few years, and the ingredients and the necessary supplies are all available.

Two of the companies issuing catalogues are:

Semplex of USA
P.O. Box 12276
4805 Lyndale Ave. North
Minneapolis, Minn. 55412

Presque Isle Wine Cellars
9440 Buffalo Road
North East, Pa. 16428

CREATIVE LEISURE   6

WHITTEMORE DURGIN GLASS COMPANY

You've doubtless seen craftspeople sitting at their booths and tables at fairs creating stained glass pieces. While many operations seem almost impossibly intricate and delicate, Whittemore Durgin disputes this. Specializing in stained glass supplies, the firm not only sells all the materials, from glass to tools, but also provides a useful instruction sheet, called **Getting Started in Stained Glass,** for 50¢. The exceptionally clear instructions give the basics for making stained glass ornaments, lampshades, jewelry, even terrariums.

For individual satisfaction or extra income, stained glass appears to have come out of the church window and into the craftsperson's hands.

For an envelope full of free flyers and a full catalogue, write:

*Whittemore Durgin Glass Company
P.O. Box 2065
Hanover, Mass. 02339*

DICK BLICK GRAPHIC ARTS MATERIALS

If you find it inconvenient to reach the art supply store—or if it is not fully equipped for your purposes—mail-order supplies are probably the answer. Dick Blick has one of the most complete catalogues, and pledges prompt filling of orders and shipment by the fastest means.

The catalogue contains everything from pen points to paper and is available by writing:

*Dick Blick
P.O. Box 1267
Galesburg, Ill. 61401*

PATTERNS FOR BETTER LIVING

Yes, leisure is like so many things man yearns after . . . once gained we find the prize loses its luster. But it doesn't have to be if we just learn how to create with our hands instead of sitting on them.

That quote from this 90-page catalogue sums up the vitality of the projects it incorporates. Each listing describes and illustrates a plan available at modest cost. The plans are step-by-step instructions for creating with one's own hands indoor and outdoor furniture and storage space, boating and camping equipment, holiday decorations, handicrafts (such as macramé and leather work), toys and pet shelters.

The catalogue concludes with several pages of good hints.

*$1
U-Build Enterprises
P.O. Box 2383
15241 Stagg St.
Van Nuys, Calif. 91409*

ALBERT CONSTANTINE AND SON, INC.

The Constantine firm, selling woodworking supplies from its Bronx showroom and by catalogue, has been in business since 1812. It offers fine veneers for furniture-making as well as legs, wheels, carvings, furniture plans, kits and accessories. Tools and dozens of instruction books are also listed.

For a copy of the catalogue:
*Albert Constantine and Son, Inc.
2050 Eastchester Road
Bronx, N.Y. 10461*

Crafts

A DOLLHOUSE FROM PLANS ... FROM JOHN EASTMAN MINIATURES

You may now have the time ... and the inclination ... to make that very special gift for a grandchild: a dollhouse.

Bradford House is one of those monumental projects which require time, love and patience. With the plans from Eastman, you can build this authentically detailed dollhouse, which is 36" wide x 27" high x 15" deep. The plans consist of over 30 drawings, photographs and clearly written instructions. Total cost, including the plans, is estimated at $50. The plans are $5.75; write:

*John Eastman Miniatures
9 Johns Road
Setauket, N.Y. 11733*

BROOKSTONE COMPANY: HARD-TO-FIND TOOLS AND OTHER FINE THINGS

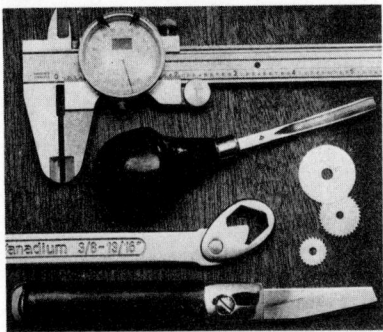

This fascinating free catalogue contains a broad range of unusual and useful items for daily living, hobbies, cooking and auto repairs.

Some of the most intriguing items include a magnifying lamp, real sponges, restaurant-quality cooking implements, an absolutely great jar lid opener, and dozens of woodworking and gardening tools.

Most orders are filled the day they are received.

*Brookstone Company
125 Vose Farm Road
Peterborough, N.H. 03458*

TWO BOOKLETS FROM JOHNSON WAX

A Beginner's Guide to Refinishing Furniture reviews all of the basics and the problems of removing furniture finishes and applying new ones.

A Raft of Craft Ideas contains dozens of gift and decoration ideas using creative hands and scrap items. Not only are the ideas ecologically sound, but they are excellent for gifts, fund-raising items or your own satisfaction.

For both free booklets, write:

*Consumer Education
Department—SC
P.O. Box 567
Johnson Wax
1525 Howe St.
Racine, Wis. 53403*

CREATIVE LEISURE

POTTERY EQUIPMENT FROM SOLDNER POTTERY EQUIPMENT INC.

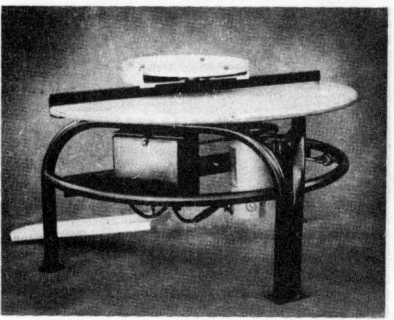

Soldner equipment is particularly well-suited for group art studios, senior centers and other communal situations. The clay-mixing machines and potter's wheels are sturdy and reliable.

Write for catalogue to:
*Soldner Pottery Equipment, Inc.
P.O. Box 428
Silt, Colo. 81652*

STEWART CLAY COMPANY CATALOGUE

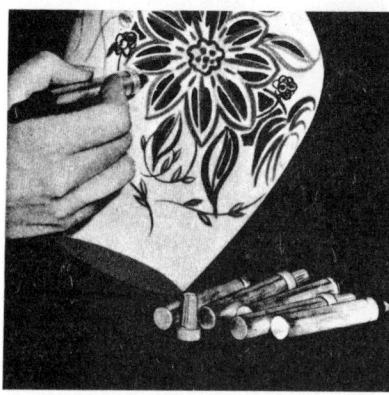

Since 1867, this company has been supplying individuals and manufacturers with basic pottery supplies. From tools to potters' wheels to kilns and books, Stewart's catalogue lists a full range of supplies. Since Stewart's has long years of experience and does its own manufacturing, it is also able and pleased to give advice on special problems.

*Stewart Clay Company
133 Mulberry St.
New York, N.Y. 10013*

PACIFICA POTTER'S WHEELS

Pacifica's small catalogue lists some unusual potting items, including the only portable professional potter's wheel made. In addition, it has a kit for those who want to assemble their own potter's wheel frame.

Write:
*Pacifica Crafts
P.O. Box 1407
Ferndale, Wash. 98248*

ALPINE PRECISION KILNS, POTTERY WHEELS AND CERAMIC EQUIPMENT

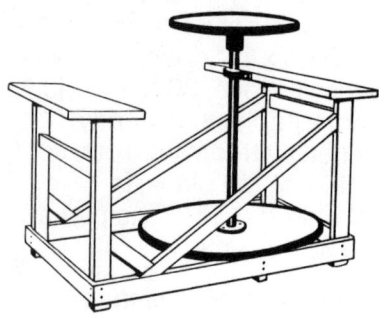

For the serious potter and sculptor, especially in groups such as schools and senior centers, the best equipment will help achieve the best results. Alpine's free catalogue includes the major equipment for this fascinating hobby and craft.

*A. D. Alpine, Inc.
3051 Fujita St.
Torrance, Calif. 90505*

The satisfactions of handicrafts—here shown in this photo of toymaking earlier in the century.

Sewing

CONTESSA YARNS

If you are weaving but cannot get to the shops with the big selections, Contessa Yarns will come to you. It has frequent free mailings of generous samples.

Write:
*Contessa Yarns
P.O. Box 37
Lebanon, Conn. 06249*

MERRIBEE NEEDLECRAFT COMPANY

Merribee's needlecraft catalogue complements the 90 stores selling its merchandise across the country. The free catalogue describes and illustrates all of its products, from afghan kits to yarns, for mail-order customers.

For a copy, write:
*Merribee Needlecraft Company
2904 West Lancaster
P.O. Box 9680
Fort Worth, Tex. 76107*

HAND-WEAVING SUPPLIES

A part of the handcraft renaissance, weaving has come back in a big way. A quality company manufacturing a broad line of looms and supplies for hand weavers is Nilius Leclerc of Canada. Dealers throughout the U.S. carry its items, but you may also order directly from its U.S. office, which has a catalogue. Write:

*Leclerc Corporation
Highway 9 North
P.O. Box 491
Plattsburg, N.Y. 12901*

Residents of California, Oregon and Washington are served by:

*Leclerc West, Inc.
2799-A Del Monte St.
West Sacramento, Calif. 95691*

GOOD HOUSEKEEPING NEW COMPLETE BOOK OF NEEDLECRAFT
By Vera P. Guild
Good Housekeeping Magazine, 1976, $9.95

The book covers the whole world of the needle arts: embroidery, quilting, smocking, needlepoint, rugmaking, knitting, crocheting, weaving, macramé and standard sewing techniques.

MARY MAXIM

Hands and needles can yield many hours of pleasure in the making and many more hours and years in using and wearing the items made. Mary Maxim's fully illustrated free catalogue has complete kits for sweaters, needlepoint, rugs and decorative craft items.

Write:
*Mary Maxim
2001 Holland Ave.
Port Huron, Mich. 48060*

CREATIVE LEISURE

HARRISVILLE DESIGNS

Harrisville has a small, quality selection of hand looms and spinning equipment. In fact, it has a kit for assembling your own loom. Its selection of hand yarns and spinning fleeces is extensive and the color selection beautiful.

For a free catalogue and yarn and fleece samples, write:

*Harrisville Designs
Harrisville, N.H. 03450*

COMPLETE BOOK OF DRESSMAKING
By Ann MacTaggart,
Van Nostrand Reinhold,
1976, $12.95

The high cost of clothing today has sent many women (and some men) to the sewing machine. Department stores, fabric stores, and "dime" stores carry extensive lines of patterns to sew almost everything. Talent and experience help, but the craft can be learned.

This fully illustrated "how-to" book takes much of the guesswork out of sewing. It covers everything from seams and zippers to pockets and collars and details problems you can avoid when you know the pitfalls.

THE MENDER'S MANUAL
By Estelle Foote
Harcourt Brace Jovanovich,
1976, $5.95

Dr. Foote, a general practitioner and medical examiner for the University of Vermont, retired in 1963. In 1976, at the age of 77, she published this book. With "New England attention to thrift and detail," she has perfected hundreds of techniques for patching and saving just about every imaginable garment.

Consider each problem. How much useful wear is in this garment? One general rule is: If six months' wear is in it, it is probably worth mending; for children three months of a winter garment is a good investment of time; and for a baby's rompers, even a shorter period.

Written with wit and clear instructions, the book is a practical manual for fixing one's own garments as well as others'—including some of the very worthy work done with volunteer charities.

CLOTHING REPAIRS

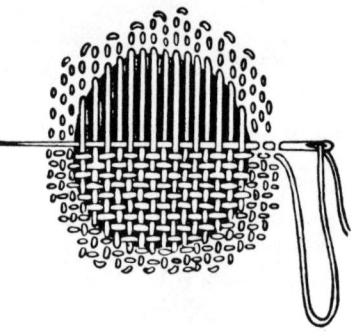

Repairing clothes does pay off in better appearance and savings—and creative use of time. Using up-to-date methods can help cut the size of the mending pile, and extend the life of your wardrobe.

This thorough booklet of the U.S. Department of Agriculture includes sections on:

- Mending equipment and aids
- Basic repair stitches
- Reinforcement of garments before they are worn
- Patches and darns
- Mends for common damages

Sewing
Pets

This publication, Home and Garden Bulletin #107, is available through USDA Extension home economists or by sending 70¢ to:

*USGPO
Washington, D.C. 20402*

SEWING SUPPLIES FROM HOME-SEW, INC.

Thread, ornaments, trimmings, and just about every home-sewing supply imaginable are listed in this free catalogue. For those who are not near a store selling these supplies, or are unable to leave home, this catalogue is a convenient shopper. Home-Sew also offers samples of new laces, eyelets, braids and trims that can be quite useful in making selections. A trial "membership" is available for 25¢. The mailings come three times a year. The front of the mailing contains 12 to 18 actual samples of trimmings, and the reverse describes and illustrates new products.

Write:
*Home-Sew, Inc.
Bethlehem, Pa. 18018*

A FEW IDEAS FROM FRED SAMMONS

Giant Playing Cards
Enlarged faces and print on these playing cards enable those with a visual impairment to enjoy card games.
$1   Catalogue #BK-9419

A CONSUMER HINT:

Sewing machines are indispensable to successful home sewing. Be careful of the unknown brands and the installment deals. Stay with known brands at reliable stores. The more elaborate machines are nice, to be sure, but you can also do a great deal with a basic machine and there are some good buys on rebuilt machines from reliable dealers. And don't forget about grandma's machine which may be gathering dust. For approximately $25 or $30, the original manufacturer can frequently overhaul a machine and make it work like new.

Needle Threader Drop needle in the holder, lay the thread in place, push the lever and the needle is threaded!
99¢   Catalogue #BK-3505

These items and the full **Be OK Self-Help Aids** catalogue, described in HEALTH, available from:

*Fred Sammons, Inc.
Box 32
Brookfield, Ill. 60513*

YOUR RETIREMENT PET GUIDE

There is nothing like a household pet to bring life and love into a home, especially if you are retired. What kind of pet to get? No matter what type you choose, there are a few things that should be kept in mind . . . such as location and size of your home or apartment providing sufficient room for the proposed pet. Also, can you easily afford the pet food that will be required as well as the upkeep such as grooming, shots, etc.? Then, before purchasing that pet, haunt pet shops, consult pet magazines and books, and see if you can find an owner of a similar pet with whom you can talk.

This thorough free booklet in the AARP-NRTA series covers a wide range of advice on dogs, cats, birds, fish, reptiles, wild and exotic pets. Carefully written safety rules and general hints for caring for pets are included.

*AARP-NRTA
P.O. Box 2400
215 Long Beach Blvd.
Long Beach, Calif. 90801*

CREATIVE LEISURE   6

DRESSING FOR THE OCCASION . . . THE L. L. BEAN CATALOG

If your leisure activities require well-made clothing that will serve through long walks or fishing trips or craft projects, you may want to consider the advantages of the garments marketed for the "outdoors." If you are not near one of the stores dealing in such merchandise, L. L. Bean is a fine supplier of mail-order outdoors items. Its catalogue contains clothing, footwear, camping supplies, and an excellent assortment of tote bags.

Write:
*L. L. Bean, Inc.
Freeport, Me. 04032*

SENIOR SPORTS INTERNATIONAL ASSOCIATION

Senior Sports International, a nonprofit corporation, annually sponsors the Senior Olympics. Its goals are:

- To encourage all adults to exercise regularly for better health, greater happiness and higher productivity
- To give recognition to all adult athletes in every sport at every age level
- To broaden the base for international understanding by forming friendships with foreign nationals attending the games and through the Senior Olympics Tour of Champions

The Senior Olympics, first held in 1970, encourages the participation of people of all ages in competitive sports. Many people commonly classified as old are successful participants and competitors.

Annual memberships, which include the quarterly **Senior Sports** magazine and other benefits, are available.
For additional information, contact:

*Senior Sports International Association
5225 Wilshire Blvd.
Suite 302
Los Angeles, Calif. 90036*

Grandma Moses began painting in her later years . . . and lived to 101. Many of her paintings reflect the outdoors.

TRANSPORTATION AND TRAVEL

7

EN TOUR

GETTING AROUND AT HOME AND ABROAD

Isolation is a frequent problem for many older people. Long-distance travel is another concern, for while sometimes the body may not be willing and able, more often the pocket book is insufficient.

Sources of aid in this area are infrequent on the national level. We have presented some we consider exceptional. Many others exist in your community, and we urge you to seek them out. Such local services include discounts on the regular mass transit systems and special volunteer efforts through various organizations. Generally the area Agency on Aging will know of all the programs.

Travel arrangements

HOW TO BEAT THE HIGH COST OF TRAVEL
By the editors of U.S. News and World Report
U.S. News and World Report Books, P.O. Box 951, Hicksville, N.Y. 11802, 1975, $7.95

This is a comprehensive book of economy travel tips, giving pointers on how to take advantage of the most luxurious in transportation and accommodations—at the lowest cost.

VACATIONS FOR THE AGING

Summer camp vacations for older people are increasing. New York City's project has been going on for years, and camps have also begun in Pennsylvania, Michigan and Washington state.

If you would like to hear more about the experience and perhaps to encourage a program in your community, write:

*Vacations for the Aging
225 Park Ave. South
New York, N.Y. 10003*

NOW IT'S YOUR TURN TO TRAVEL
By Rosalind Massow
Macmillan, 1976, $10.95

When traveling long distances, consider the advantages of discounts on restaurants, hotels and fares. Discounts are more and more prevalent for people over 65, and travel is no exception. Many organizations, such as AARP-NRTA, offer good discount packages, but travelers to Europe making their own arrangements may have available some appealing discounts and government-sponsored incentives. In particular, you ought to pay attention to the offers of England, Austria, Canada, France, West Germany, the Scandinavian countries, Holland, Spain and Switzerland. For further information, contact the tourist office of each country; all have offices in New York City and some in other major cities also.

This book is a helpful organizer and confidence-builder for the older person who has time to travel but who may be worried about language barriers, unfamiliar food, strange surroundings, and, above all, fear of health problems far from home. The author eases many of these anxieties by providing practical details on how, when and where to go. Special advantages of being over 65 are detailed in one chapter. Dr. Norton Luger has contributed a separate chapter, "Medically Speaking," which gives a thorough primer on health and traveling for older people.

GOMER'S GUIDE
By Gomer Lewis
Hammond, Inc., 1976, $3.95

Gomer Lewis, himself an older person, perceived the need for and wrote a specialized guide for his age group. The publication, written as he traveled throughout 25 states east of the Mississippi, lists hotels and motels which offer rooms at $15 per night or less for two. Many of the establishments give an additional discount for people 55 or older. While not all cities are included, for those listed the guide is useful for lodgings.

Other features are road maps, state travel office addresses and several discount coupons.

TRANSPORTATION AND TRAVEL 7

VACATION EXCHANGE CLUB

The Vacation Exchange Club publishes a directory of subscribers' descriptions of their homes in the United States and around the world—the reason being to exchange homes for short or long periods. The club does not get people together, but the directory, published each spring, gives members a chance to review available homes and contact individuals in areas which interest them. The advantages are obvious: unusually low cost and the comfort of living in a home in a residential area instead of in a hotel. The directory also includes several hints on arrangements for making the temporary resident feel at home.

The deadline for the main directory is generally in December and for the supplement in February.

For $12 subscribers receive both the directory and supplement and a listing of their home in 15 words or less. For an additional $5 fee, a subscriber may include a photo. Those not desiring to be listed may receive the directory and supplement for $9.

For membership and other information:

*Vacation Exchange Club
350 Broadway
New York, N.Y. 10013*

HOLIDAY HOME EXCHANGE BUREAU, INC.

Imagine being able to settle right down and live for a while in a completely different part of the country and enjoy all the advantages of home. Holiday Home Exchange is the information channel for people who wish to make their own homes available and to live in others'.

The service operates through a directory, published seven times a year, listing the offerings of the persons or families seeking an exchange. Listings remain in the directory for one year. Contacts are made by the individual subscribers.

The bureau of course cannot accept responsibility for the actual exchange, and the subscriber is advised to use good judgment. The annual fee is $15.

Registration and other information may be obtained from:

*Holiday Home Exchange Bureau, Inc.
P.O. Box 555
Grants, N. Mex. 87020*

Styles may differ—but relax and enjoy your travel.

Above, passengers boarding Pan Am's first passenger flight in 1928. They flew from Key West, Florida to Havana, Cuba on a Fokker F-7. Below, refreshments were first introduced on the same airplane in 1929.

Travel arrangements

TRAVELERS' DIRECTORY

Since 1960, this Directory has been a successful but little-known source of an alternative for those who cannot afford or do not care to stay in hotels when they travel.

The publication, issued annually (with quarterly supplements), lists people who enjoy opening their homes to others who have pledged to do likewise. The listings are frequently colorful and certainly descriptive of people who welcome other travelers. The deadline for inclusion in the annual directory is January 15. At last count, there were 595 listees in the United States and 39 foreign countries.

The annual membership fee of $10 includes the directory, the quarterly supplements and the quarterly newsletter, **Links**.

Write:
*Travelers' Directory
6224 Baynton St.
Philadelphia, Pa. 19144*

PEARL'S FREIGHTER TIPS

If you have time and an appetite for travel, try a freighter. The voyages are long—often four, five and more weeks. The atmosphere is relaxing, and the accommodations comfortable. The food is hearty and good. Freighter cruises differ drastically from passenger cruises, however, in that the number of passengers carried is small—generally about 12. The grand salons are not there, and neither is the entertainment. The ships are solid, though, and you can visit the ports you want to see.

Pearl has had many years of experience in freighter travel and acts as travel agent. A letter to Pearl, indicating when you wish to leave, how many people are in the party, and the length of time and preferred destinations will yield a prompt reply.

Write:
*Pearl's Freighter Tips, Inc.
Suite 306
175 Great Neck Road
Great Neck, N.Y. 11021*

THE GOLDEN AGE PASSPORT

Several of the parks administered by the National Park Service charge entrance fees. Persons 62 years of age or over, however, can obtain free a lifetime Golden Age Passport that permits entrance to the parks at no charge and also provides a 50% discount on recreation fees, such as camp-site rentals.

So long as they are in the same private vehicle, those traveling with "passport" holders are admitted under the same conditions. Passports must be applied for in person, and with acceptable proof of age, such as a driver's license or birth certificate.

The "passports" may be obtained at National Park headquarters in Washington, D.C., at regional offices of the park system, at park locations where entry fees are normally charged, and at ranger station offices of the Forest Service.

The rather extensive list of parks ranges from the Shenandoah in Virginia, to FDR's home at Hyde Park, N.Y., to Yosemite National Park.

For a folder titled **Federal Recreation Fee Program** describing the "passport" and listing all of the fee-charging parks, write to:

*Room 1013
National Park Service
U.S. Department of the Interior
18th and C Sts., NW
Washington, D.C. 20240*

TRANSPORTATION AND TRAVEL 7

TIPS ON RENTING A CAR

The instant-auto service of the car-rental companies has become very competitive. The advantages to the consumer who does not require a car all of the time are considerable. But the differences among many of the companies and the quality of service and cars—as well as the risks to the consumer—are considerable. This booklet, prepared by the Car and Truck Renting and Leasing Association and the Better Business Bureau, gives much information to the renter.

Free
Booklet #244 A 100672
Council of Better Business Bureaus, Inc.
1150 17th St. NW
Washington, D.C. 20036

AUTO REPAIR FRAUDS: HOW TO PREVENT YOUR CAR FROM DRIVING YOU TO THE POORHOUSE
By Lyle Kenyon Engle
Arco, 1976, $6.95

This consumer manual evaluates various kinds of repair shops, explains insurance claims and details common repair "tricks." A useful dictionary of automotive terms is included.

TRANSPORTATION AND TRAVEL   7

INTERNATIONAL ASSOCIATION FOR MEDICAL ASSISTANCE TO TRAVELERS

IAMAT is a nonprofit worldwide association of English-speaking doctors ready to aid travelers with their knowledge of North American and British medical techniques and terminology. The association charges no membership fees, though it does encourage donations. Anyone can become a member and receive a pocket-size directory of medical center contacts in 120 cities abroad. Local treatment rates prevail in each case.

Travel is a joy, but a medical emergency can be a nightmare, so IAMAT, in addition to easing the worry of locating medical help in emergencies, has begun preparing a series of eight pamphlets for the traveler. Publications thus far, all included in the membership packet, are:

Traveler Clinical Record, with spaces for organizing personal identification, immunization data and allergy information

World Immunization and Malaria Risk Chart

World Climate Chart

Anyone may join by writing to:
IAMAT
Suite 5620
350 Fifth Ave.
New York, N.Y. 10001

Medical emergencies while away

INTERMEDIC

Intermedic, an international network of English-speaking doctors, assures medical services for travelers in about 200 cities in 100 foreign countries. Personal membership in Intermedic provides the traveler with:

- ☐ Data on each participating physician, covering medical education, experience and hospital affiliation, all on file at the Intermedic office in New York.
- ☐ Assurance that the member physicians speak English. Assurance that the physicians listed will respond to members' calls.
- ☐ An established fee schedule as follows:

Office visit	$15
House or hotel visit (7 a.m.-7p.m.)	20
House or hotel visit (7 p.m.-7 a.m.)	25

    (All fees listed are in U.S. dollars—subsequent service fees are agreed upon between physician and patient)
- ☐ Access to the Intermedic Overseas Health Information Service (each member may request information about health conditions affecting travelers in given countries and information on medications to carry and required immunizations)
- ☐ The **Directory of Participating Physicians**, which also includes a personal section for listing one's own statistics and other data.

Membership fees:
  Personal, $6 per year
  Family,   10 per year

For membership form or additional information, contact:
Intermedic, Inc.
777 Third Ave.
New York, N. Y. 10017

TRANSPORTATION AND TRAVEL   7

SCAMP IS AN EXAMPLE

Across the country one of the most difficult problems for older people is local transportation. Senior citizen discounts on public transportation are of tremendous help. But what if the bus or subway is not readily accessible? Then projects like SCAMP—Senior Citizen Areawide Motor Pool—become important. Volunteers are older persons who take turns transporting other older persons—those without cars—on monthly shopping trips or to other destinations.

If you are interested in participating in this type of service, write:

*SCAMP
Barney Neighborhood House
3118 16th St., NW
Washington, D.C. 20010*

GREYHOUND'S HELPING HAND SERVICE FOR THE HANDICAPPED

Handicapped or infirm persons traveling on Greyhound buses may be accompanied by a companion—such as a friend, nurse, or relative—for the price of the one ticket. A doctor's certificate of eligibility is necessary in advance, with the following statement written on his or her letterhead.

*Greyhound Lines, Inc. allows an attendant to travel with a disabled person when the person is disabled to the extent of requiring the assistance of an attendant to board, alight and travel the bus. _____ is disabled and in my judgment can travel by bus if accompanied by an attendant to assist him or her in boarding, alighting and traveling on a bus.
The disability _____
is ☐ permanent ☐ temporary.*

Date _____
Doctor's Name _____
Address _____

_____
Signature of Doctor

For clearances and additional information:

*Greyhound Bus Lines, Inc.
Greyhound Tower
Phoenix, Ariz. 85077*

FOLDING LUGGAGE CARRIER

With this heavy-duty, chrome-plated, steel-wire-frame dolly, carry your luggage the way airline stewardesses do. The carrier weighs only four pounds, yet enables you to move up to 150 pounds. Folded, it measures 19½" x 9" x 3" for easy storage and carrying. Open, it extends to 34" with a 9½" base. Heavy-duty elastic cord holds the baggage or package against the carrier. The handle adjusts to the height of the user.

$11.98   Catalogue #BK-6511

This and other convenient items are listed in a complete catalogue available from:

*Fred Sammons, Inc.
Box 32
Brookfield, Ill. 60513*

Montgomery County, Maryland's, Elderbus is an example of the special local government services available across the country. With regular schedules between residential areas and shopping centers. Elderbus and its equivalents go and come on routes not serviced by regular public transportation. If you want to know about your local services, check with your city or county government or area agency on aging.

MONEY   8

TIME TO SAVE

Personal money management has many facets, and when one puts one's mind to it there is much that can be done. The sources covered in this chapter are those *directly* concerned with making money and managing it; some of the more *indirect* alternatives are part of the JOINING AND SHARING chapter, while the FOOD chapter has many sources for economizing as well.

Judicious organization, management and imagination can pay off. Maximize what you have, using all that is available, seeking out the greatest number of ways to share—to obtain goods or services at low or no cost, to find new ways of bringing in money, and in doing so to tread new paths when possible. Take advantage of the ever-increasing private and government sources.

And, in this age of the consumer, you have a special opportunity to use your rights and your time to help yourself to better products and services, thereby saving money and helping others as well. The consumer battles are often hard won, and they require everyone's efforts.

YOUR RETIREMENT MONEY GUIDE

"Where does it all go?" is a question we all ask all of our lives, but the question seems more pressing after retirement. This booklet details tips on how to trim costs, how to invest (though modestly in most cases), and how to prepare for possible health care costs.

Free
AARP-NRTA
P.O. Box 2400
215 Long Beach Blvd.
Long Beach, Calif. 90801

THE FAMILY REGISTER OF PERSONAL AND FINANCIAL PAPERS
By the editors of U.S. News and World Report
P.O. Box 951, Hicksville, N.Y. 11802, $7.95

Here's a book that *you* write! This oversize ledger provides ample space for you to put down, in one convenient and permanent place, all the information about you, your family, your home, your possessions and investments. Its big pages allow you to enter records on everything from family medical histories to insurance policies, from a monthly operating budget to a household inventory of valuables.

Financial preparation for retirement

RETIREMENT PLANNING SEMINARS

If you have planned well for retirement—or learned the hard way—you may find that helping others is a productive and satisfying use of your time. Action for Independent Maturity (AIM), a division of AARP-NRTA, provides materials for groups—clubs, religious associations, companies, etc.—to review eight key topics on preretirement planning in eight two-hour sessions. Seminar kits include discussion-leader guides, manuals for participants and audiovisual materials. Subjects covered include:

- ☐ Challenge of retirement
- ☐ Health and safety
- ☐ Housing and location
- ☐ Legal affairs
- ☐ Attitude and role adjustments
- ☐ Meaningful use of time
- ☐ Sources and amounts of income
- ☐ Financial planning

Each participant also receives a one-year membership in AIM. The memberships of those already belonging are extended for one year.

Materials are available as follows:

    Presentation kits for discussion leaders $300

    Participant manuals $10 (available only in multiples of ten)

    Guidebook sets of supplementary readings $2 per set (each set contains 7 guide-books and is available only in multiples of 20)

Further information on materials listed above is available from:

Action for Independent Maturity
1909 K St. NW
Washington, D.C. 20006

MONEY . . . AND YOUR RETIREMENT

This booklet starts out with a surprisingly optimistic approach toward the change in income which takes place in retirement. Instead of simply limiting itself to the reduced income, it also offers a checklist for evaluation of how expenditures will be reduced in many ways.

Some of the more thought-provoking notions have to do with time. How can some cash expenditures be reduced by careful use of the new wealth of time? Can you now be a better consumer? Can you do some of your own home repairs?

The booklet reviews Social Security and gives hints on savings in daily living, medical costs, and shopping. It suggests how to make your savings work for you safely and how to approach that challenging task of earning some extra money.

$1.50 to current subscribers of the magazine; $2.25 to nonsubscribers

Retirement Living Magazine
150 East 58th St.
New York, N.Y. 10022

(See COMMUNICATING for more on **Retirement Living Magazine** and the other publications in the series.)

MONEY   8

SYLVIA PORTER'S MONEY BOOK
By Sylvia Porter
Doubleday, 1975, $14.95
(Avon paperback edition, $3.95)

This book's entire purpose is to prepare you to win in every sphere of your economic life. You may approach its contents in any way you wish, depending on your economic needs or desires at the specific time.

"Winning in the economic sphere" may require more luck—not to mention capital—than this book can possibly give, but it does stand as an encyclopedia of economics for daily living. The well-known financial writer covers earning, spending, saving, investing and borrowing. Practically nothing is left out, from insurance to savings accounts to consumer rights.

YOUR PENSION PLAN

The U.S. Department of Labor has jurisdiction over pension plans. If you have questions about your plan or suspect some abuses, it is authorized to initiate action. For questions or complaints, address your local Department of Labor office if there is one, or:

*The Office of Employee Benefit Security
Department of Labor
Washington, D.C. 20044*

READY OR NOT . . . A STUDY MANUAL FOR RETIREMENT

If you are approaching retirement and have done nothing about it—or if you are already retired and feeling the effects of having done nothing—this manual, a companion to a set of taped television programs, may be the answer to laying out the ground rules.

Presented in workbook fashion, the book is not only easy to follow, intelligent and thorough, but also in a way fun. And before finishing it, you realize you can organize your life past 65. The book is very heavy on information, checklists and questions covering estate planning, income planning and consumerism. Sound advice is provided on employment and business opportunities. Health, and constructive and creative leisure are also covered.

Single copies are $3.50. If two or more are ordered, the price per copy is $2.50. The workbook may also be used in conjunction with the television series of the same title, available either on videotape or 16mm color film. Since rental or purchase prices are scaled according to the size of the groups, information on rates must be requested.

A retirement planning newsletter has been added to the institute's services. It is particularly valuable for corporations or other organizations wishing to disseminate information on retirement to large numbers of people.

Both the booklet and newsletter are available from the Manpower Education Institute which was organized with the support of labor and business to develop education, training and job-advancement programs. It is a nonprofit organization.

*Manpower Education Institute
127 East 35th Street
New York, New York 10016*

Financial preparation for retirement
Taxes

Copies of the complaints should be sent to the Internal Revenue Service as follows:

*Office of Employee Plans and Exempt Organizations
Internal Revenue Service
Washington, D.C. 20224*

TAX FACTS FOR OLDER AMERICANS

This comparative guide to taxes across the country reviews regulations state by state, giving people a basis of comparison, should they consider moving. It also provides a general view of the tax concessions available because of age or fixed income. Income taxes and property taxes both are treated. The reader is reminded that the information is presented for guidance only and that any definitive answers to the latest tax questions should come from local authorities.

*Free
AARP-NRTA
P.O. Box 2400
215 Long Beach Blvd.
Long Beach, Calif. 90801*

TAX-AIDE

In many communities, AARP-NRTA chapters have been able to recruit members as volunteer Tax-Aides. These people, familiar with tax forms or with an aptitude for figures, are sent to a training seminar conducted by the Internal Revenue Service. Working

several hours each week during tax-preparation time, the Tax-Aides explain the different forms and the information necessary to be included. Their role is generally advisory, though those who have the additional time, interest and skills often assist in actual preparation of returns when requested.

The local AARP-NRTA chapter can tell you if there is a Tax-Aide program for the community. If you are interested in becoming a Tax-Aide, write:

*Tax-Aide
AARP-NRTA
1909 K St., NW
Washington, D.C. 20006*

A free booklet, called **Your Retirement Tax Guide**, is also available. The booklet answers some of the more frequent questions, and dissects a 1040 form, explaining, line by line, the reason for each entry and what information is required. Write:

*AARP-NRTA
P.O. Box 2400
215 Long Beach Blvd.
Long Beach, Calif. 90801*

MONEY 8

PUBLICATIONS ON SOCIAL SECURITY

Social Security is all around us and yet it is so large and so complex that questions are often difficult to phrase, ask, *and* answer. In an effort to reply to some of the most common questions, the Social Security Administration has prepared several booklets:

- **Your Social Security Earnings Record** (#SSA 73-10044)
  A general view of the workings of the Social Security system and what the individual earnings record means.
- **Your Social Security** (#SSA 73-10035)
  This booklet gives a comprehensive review of the entire system, including who gets checks, what is Medicare, special rules, and what to do if you work while collecting Social Security or if you go out of the country.
- **A Brief Explanation of Medicare** (#SSA 74-10043)
- **Home Health Care Under Medicare** (#SSA 75-10042)
- **How Medicare Helps During a Hospital Stay** (#SSA 75-10039)
- **Your Right to Question Your Medical Insurance Payment** (#SSA 75-10085)
- **Your Right to Question the Decision on Your Hospital Insurance Claim** (#SSA 75-10085)
- **Right to Appeal Supplemental Security Income** (#SSA 74-10281)
- **Your Social Security Check . . . While You're Outside the United States** (#SSA 74-10137)
- **Your Social Security Rights and Responsibilities** (#SSA 74-10077)
- **A Guide to Supplemental Security Income** (#SSA 75-11015)
  SSI, as distinct from the basic Social Security check, is a federal cash assistance program for the aged, blind or disabled that has replaced former federal assistance programs. This booklet outlines the standards for eligibility and the procedures for applying.
- **Social Security IQ** (#SSA 75-10623)
  This one is a mixture of fun and information, presenting some of the key facts on the Social Security system in the form of a crossword puzzle and other word games.
- **Estimating Your Social Security Retirement Check** (#SSA 74-10047)

YOUR INDIVIDUAL ACCOUNT

If you would like a statement of the funds you have paid into your Social Security account over the years, you may request this simple form from any Social Security office.

Be sure to give your account number exactly as it is shown on your Social Security Card, in order to make sure your account is properly identified. If you have more than one account number, give all of them. It is not necessary to pay anyone to aid you in securing this information. There is no charge for this service.

Mail to:
*Social Security Administration
P.O. Box 57
Baltimore, Md. 21203*

VETERANS' BENEFITS

Veterans' benefits for older Americans are frequently an important part of income to meet living expenses. A good free reference to the sometimes complicated subject is:

Summary of Benefits for Veterans with Military Service Before February 1, 1955, and Their Dependents (VA pamphlet # 20-72-2), 1975

Available from Veterans Administration regional offices or from:

*Veterans Administration
810 Vermont Ave. NW
Washington, D.C. 20420*

Social Security and government benefits

- **A Woman's Guide to Social Security** (#SSA 75-10127)
- **Your Duties as Representative Payee** (#SSA 74-10076)
  This booklet covers your responsibility in handling checks for a person incapable of attending to business affairs.
- **A Citizen's Handbook: Program Options and Public Participation Under Title 20 of the Social Security Act** (#SSA 75-23038)
- **You Can Still Work and Get Social Security Checks** (#SSA 74-10092)
- **Medicare Benefits in a Skilled Nursing Facility** (#SSA 75-10041)
- **Supplemental Security Income for the Aged, Blind, and Disabled** (#SSA 75-11000)

Several of the booklets are available with Spanish translations.

All booklets are free and may be obtained from your local Social Security office or from:

*Office of Public Affairs
Social Security Administration
6401 Security Blvd.
Baltimore, Md. 21235*

The federal government is so vast and so diverse that it is frequently providing services —at no cost—in ways we are not always aware of. In this guide, six basic areas— business; education; employment; environment and the home; health; and leisure—are covered. Many services are direct financial aids for those qualifying, while others listed are feasts of leisure, such as our National Parks. Some are fairly well known, while others are a surprise. The appendix lists the addresses of the local and regional offices of major federal bureaus involved in these areas.

EVERYTHING YOU CAN GET FROM THE GOVERNMENT FOR FREE . . . OR ALMOST FOR FREE
By Craig and Peter Norback
Van Nostrand Reinhold, 1975, $7.95

This is probably the most comprehensive attempt at listing the free (or almost free) services the federal government provides in a host of departments. From the National Parks to Agriculture Extension courses, the book is an index to the scope of government offerings. It may be able to show how to obtain either financial support for volunteer group projects or opportunities for research or model grants in a community service.

WHAT UNCLE SAM OWES YOU
By Jeffrey Feinman
Playboy Press, 1976, $1.95

And there's something for everyone—people with high incomes, low incomes, or no incomes.

MONEY 8

FOOD STAMPS

The U.S. Department of Agriculture's Food Stamp Program enables persons in low-income households to buy more food of greater variety and thus improve their diets. To purchase food stamps, participants pay a sum of money based on family size and net monthly income. They then receive food stamps of a larger face value than the amount they paid and can spend them like money at authorized stores.

To qualify for food stamps, households must meet certain nationwide eligibility standards. Except in special circumstances, food stamp households must have a place to cook meals.

The head of a household applying for food stamps must provide papers to a local office indicating:
- ☐ Location of the household
- ☐ How many are in the household
- ☐ How much money it receives monthly
- ☐ How much it is paying for doctors' bills and rent

Anyone in the household can take the stamps to an authorized food store and use them like money to buy almost any food or seeds and plants to grow food for the recipient's own use. Stamps cannot be used to buy liquor, beer, cigarettes, soap or other nonfood items. And recipients cannot sell the stamps. Most food stores are authorized to accept food stamps.

For additional information, including specific eligibility requirements, your area Agency on Aging should be able to direct you to the proper local government body, or write:

Food and Nutrition Service
U.S. Department of Agriculture
Washington, D.C. 20250

Social Security and government benefits
Getting your money's worth

HELP YOURSELF . . . AND OTHERS . . . TO BETTER PRODUCTS AND SERVICES

We are heading toward the age of the consumer. It will not, however, progress without more and more people becoming better consumers, and complaining is a large part of the process. If the information on a deficiency or danger does not get to the right people in private industry or in government, nothing will be done. There are various places to go with complaints. Most every state and many local governments have a consumer complaint or advocacy office. Get to know and use them for questions and complaints. Various private organizations exist, too—some local, others national. We list here some of the major public sources for consumerism:

CONSUMER ACTION PANELS (CAPS)

In response to consumer complaints about products, service and warranties, complaint-handling mechanisms have been set up by four major industries. Called Consumer Action Panels (CAPS), they constitute a major step forward for both consumers and the industries. They (a) receive comments and complaints from consumers after initial contacts with the merchants and manufacturers have failed; (b) study industry practices; (c) advise the respective manufacturers of ways to improve their consumer services; and (d) provide consumer information materials. The CAPS are

Carpet and Rug Industry
Consumer Action Panel
Box 1568
Dalton, Ga. 30720

Furniture Industry Consumer
Action Panel
Box 951
High Point, N.C. 27261

Major Appliance Consumer
Action Panel
20 North Wacker Drive
Chicago, Ill. 60606

Auto Consumer Action Panel
c/o National Automobile
Dealers Association
2000 K St., NW
Washington, D.C. 20006

The major appliance panel also publishes two interesting booklets:
- ☐ **MACAP Handbook for the Informed Consumer,** which suggests various approaches toward selection and care of major appliances, price, 50¢;
- ☐ **MACAP . . . Representing Consumers at the Highest Levels of Industry,** free.

MONEY 8

WHAT TRUTH IN LENDING MEANS TO YOU

This pamphlet explains clearly the rights you as a consumer and citizen have to full disclosure of all terms in loans or installment buying.

Free
Board of Governors
of the Federal Reserve System
Washington, D.C. 20551

QUESTIONS AND ANSWERS CONCERNING YOUR INSURED SAVINGS

The bank failures of the Depression are part of history, but a very important memory for many. Insurance of deposits improved the safety of the savings you have in the bank drastically. And you may be curious to know what it all means. This booklet asks and answers the most common questions.

Free
Federal Savings and Loan
Insurance Corporation
320 First St. NW
Washington, D.C. 20552

TIPS FOR ENERGY SAVERS

Saving energy can contribute to the solution of the energy problem, and it surely can save money—particularly if one is on a fixed income. This booklet gives dozens of tips for energy saving in the home, on the road and in the marketplace.

SOME MAJOR FEDERAL GOVERNMENT OFFICES

Federal Trade Commission
The FTC has jurisdiction over restraint of trade and unfair business practices, false and deceptive advertising, product labeling and flammable fabrics.

FTC
Washington, D.C. 20580

Food and Drug Administration
The FDA has jurisdiction over distribution and labeling of foods, drugs, medical devices, cosmetics, products which emit radiation and veterinary products. FDA acts through legal processes to control unsafe and misleading practices in the marketing of these products and accepts consumer complaints, which are frequently useful in charting trends.

FDA issues a vast number of consumer protection educational pamphlets; some of the more noteworthy include:
- **We Want You to Know About Impact-Resistant Eye-glass Lenses** (#FDA 75-4002)
- **We Want You to Know About Labels on Medicines** (#FDA 76-3006)
- **Read the Label, Set a Better Table** (#FDA 76-2049)
- **We Want You to Know About Adverse Reactions to Medicines** (#FDA 74-3005)
- **We Want You to Know About Prescription Drugs** (#FDA 74-3011)
- **We Want You to Know About Television Radiation** (#FDA 76-8041)
- **We Want You to Know About Microwave Oven Radiation** (#FDA 73-8049)

For single free copies or for a complete listing of currently available publications, write:

FDA
Office of Consumer Affairs
5600 Fishers Lane
Rockville, Md. 20852

U.S. Postal Inspection Service
This is the oldest, perhaps least known law-enforcement agency in the United States. The Chief Inspector's office receives more than 100,000 complaints of fraudulent use of the mails each year, and conducts more than 10,000 full investigations.

Getting your money's worth

U.S. Postal Inspection Service
Washington, D.C. 20260

The Consumer Product Safety Commission, which is described in the SAFETY chapter, is engaged in the investigation of product safety and in banning from sale any product when imminent danger has been determined.

CONSUMER INFORMATION CENTER

The U.S. Government's General Services Administration has formed the Consumer Information Center for distribution of government publications of particular consumer interest. The center is administered by the U.S. Government Printing Office. You may from time to time find that some of the publications are available from USGPO and the originating government office as well.

The center, located in Pueblo, Colo., periodically issues catalogues listing available publications. Categories are:

- Automobiles
- Children
- Employment and education
- Food, diet and nutrition
- Health
- Housing
- Landscaping, gardening and pest control
- Money management
- Older Americans
- Recreation, travel and leisure activities

Many of the publications are free and most others are quite reasonably priced.

For a copy of the latest catalogue, requests may be sent to:

Consumer Information Center
Pueblo, Colo. 81009

How much can we save through the use of storm doors and windows? Are fluorescent bulbs more economical than incandescent? Are some pans more efficient for cooking than others? How can we save at the gas station? These questions, and many more, are the subject of this timely, necessary booklet.

Free
Office of Public Affairs
Federal Energy Administration
Washington, D.C. 20461

INVESTIGATE BEFORE YOU INVEST

Stocks and bonds are a popular source of speculation—and income—for many people. Besides inherent risks, additional hazards are present when you do not know the possibilities of fraud or deception. This useful booklet is good reading for the new investor.

Free
Office of Public Information
U.S. Securities and Exchange Commission
Washington, D.C. 20549

MONEY 8

U.S. DEPARTMENT OF AGRICULTURE SHOPPER'S GUIDE
USDA, Barron's *Educational Series*, 1975, $2.95

This reissue of a USDA yearbook assembles a wealth of ideas and tips for saving money in daily living. The book is divided into several major headings, including:

- *How to Be a Smart Food Shopper:* Explanations of dietary allowances, what the food-grading symbols mean, nutrition labeling, unit pricing, organic food, tips on home freezing and canning, and many hints on stretching food dollars without sacrificing taste.
- *How to Improve Your Home:* Dozens of do-it-yourself instructions, and explanations. Important pointers are given to help assess what the average person can do and what requires the professional craftsperson.
- *How to Choose Household Equipment to Fit Your Needs:* Tips on shopping for everything from kitchen appliances to lighting fixtures, new furniture and tools. While brand names are not given, this section does give details on what to look for and expect.
- *How to Make Your Garden Bloom:* Advice that will convince you that "green thumbs" are made, not born. This section covers everything on gardening from buying seeds and plants to landscaping.
- *How to Shop Wisely for Services:* How to shop for repairs, how to be a successful complainer, how to use many of the federal government's assistance programs (including those of the Administration on Aging).
- *How to Make the Most of Your Leisure Time:* Some glorious reading on the great outdoors and especially what our National Parks offer.

The book is profusely illustrated with diagrams, charts and photos and offers many recommendations for additional readings and sources.

CONSUMER COMPLAINT GUIDE
By Joseph Rosenbloom
Macmillan, 1976, $4.95

Industry is listening to consumers more than ever. The difficulty, though, is that the consumer often does not know to whom to address the complaint. Government, consumer-action groups and the private or trade groups are frequently the answer, but many complaints can be solved quite well by direct contact. Many manufacturers, however, do not give full identification of their locations on labels and packages. And others are part of very large corporations, making it impossible to locate them in the phone books or know which cities they are in.

This book—updated annually—gives the corporate and trade names and addresses, but also goes a step beyond, providing names and addresses—including the chief executives' names—of hundreds of manufacturers of consumer items.

CONSUMER SURVIVAL KIT
By John Dorfman
Praeger, 1975, $3.95

Consumerism has come to network television with *Consumer Survival Kit*, a weekly series produced for public television at the Maryland Center for Public Broadcasting. The programs, tackling one consumer problem at a time, take a thorough and clear approach toward giving the consumer information to help himself or herself. This book presents in text form many of the programs: subjects such as your rights as a tenant, buying a new car, toys for grandchildren and many more.

Addresses of state consumer affairs offices are listed at the close of the book.

Consumers have always sought value, whether in the store or through mail order. In this nostalgic Norman Rockwell cover from the 1927 Sears Roebuck catalogue, a young couple is shown shopping for an engagement ring.

MONEY 8

YOUR RETIREMENT CONSUMER GUIDE

Older people, perhaps with more time and a reduced income, are in a perfect position to act as better consumers—and make their dollars go farther. This booklet reviews and answers questions on supermarkets, automobiles, clothing, health insurance, funerals, moving, mobile homes and borrowing. A section on how to complain concludes the book with several good hints, including use of AARP-NRTA's own Washington Consumer Referral Desk, which claims a remarkable record for effectiveness. The desk can receive complaints as follows:

*Consumer Information Program Coordinator
AARP-NRTA
1909 K St. NW
Washington, D.C. 20006*

The booklet is free, and may be ordered from:

*AARP-NRTA
P.O. Box 2400
215 Long Beach Blvd.
Long Beach, Calif. 90801*

S.O.S. (SAVE ON SHOPPING)

If you travel across the country or move to a new community, this is a handy directory of discount sources. The book lists places where you can find everything from brand-name clothing, shoes, housewares and even food at discounts

ranging from 30 to as high as 75%.

The directory is available by mail and sells for $6.95 plus $1 for handling and mailing.

Address your inquiries or orders to:

*S.O.S. Directory
P.O. Box 10482
Jacksonville, Fla. 32207*

FOR THE PEOPLE: A CONSUMER ACTION HANDBOOK
By Joanne Anderson
Addison, Wesley, 1977, $6.95

More than 15 actual consumer projects from Ralph Nader's associates are detailed in this handbook. From how to compile a doctors' directory to how to eliminate energy waste, the text is a useful aid for those trying to organize projects in their own community.

THE ANGRY BUYER'S COMPLAINT DIRECTORY
By Jack White, Gary Yanker and Harry Steinberg
Peter H. Wyden Publishers, 1974, $3.95

This "combat manual" for complaining—successfully—gives the information and guidance in order to turn the anger of consumer dissatisfaction into results. Taking the philosophy that if one way won't win the battle another will, the authors first review the rights of the consumer and then proceed to devote the heart of the book to a directory of where to go with complaints, whether concerning federal, state or local government, or specific industries or businesses. How to take someone to court and suggested forms of letters for successful complaining are treated as well.

Getting your money's worth

CONSUMER REPORTS

When Americans think of consumer questions, from safety to durability to price, the basic publication has always been the monthly **Consumer Reports** and the annual buying guide summary. Both are published by Consumers Union, an independent nonprofit testing organization established in 1936. It has no connection with any manufacturer or other commercial interest, does not permit its reports to be used for commercial purposes, accepts no advertising, buys all products to be tested on the open market and receives all income from sale of its publications.

Whether you receive *Consumer Reports* in your home or read it in the library, it is the basic reference source for product information *before* you buy. The magazine is published monthly and sells on the newsstands for $1 per copy. An annual subscription is $11.

*Consumer Reports
Ramland and Blaisdell Roads
Orangeburg, N.Y. 10962*

HELP: THE USEFUL ALMANAC
Edited by Arthur A. Rowse
Acropolis Books, 1976, $4.95

This almanac won't tell you when the tide will come in, the names of the 10 most famous redheads, the tallest brick building, or any of the other thousands of facts and trivia the traditional almanac puts at one's fingertips.

It will tell you, though, what cities have the best water and air and the lowest tax burdens; how to qualify for Social Security, Medicare, Medicaid, and food stamps; how to remove stains from fabrics; your rights as a buyer, seller, tenant, patient, worker and woman—among thousands of other useful facts and tips.

THE CONSUMER SURVIVAL BOOK: HOW TO FIGHT INFLATION
By Marvin L. Bittinger
Barron's Educational Series, 1975, $2.75

This book, presented in highly graphic format, is a virtual primer on consumerism. Tips are given on food, clothing, money management, housing, home maintenance, furnishings, cars, insurance, wills, health and taxes. Your rights under the law are clearly explained, and many of the tips are the candid type you will not learn from the labels. You will learn them only from experience or sharing of information such as this book gives.

CONSUMER FEDERATION OF AMERICA

In addition to its lobbying efforts for more effective consumer rights, the federation publishes a number of useful booklets. A current listing will be sent on request. Some worth noting are:

- **Prescription Drug Pricing: An Almost Total Absence of Competition $1.00**
- **Eleven Principles of Effective, Organized Consumer Action .25**
- **Directory of State and Local Consumer Groups** [non-government] **2.00**
- **How to Challenge Your Local Electric Utility 1.00**
- **How to Form a Consumer Complaint Group .50**

A monthly publication on consumer issues is offered by the federation at a subscription price of $20 per year.

Write:
*Consumer Federation of America
1012 14th St. NW
Washington, D.C. 20005*

MONEY   8

CREDIT UNION NATIONAL ASSOCIATION

"What is a credit union?" many ask. It is a cooperative bank organized by a group of people with some common bond. They may belong to the same labor union, church or fraternal order, or live in the same community. Many regular banking services, such as savings accounts and loans, are provided, and the owners are the customers.

If you would like to be part of a credit union—or organize one for your group or community—the association can help by putting you in touch with a state representative. Write:

Credit Union National Association, Inc.
P.O. Box 431
Madison, Wis. 53701

The association also issues several consumer information publications that are available to the general public as well as members:

Everybody's Money
The association claims this is the largest circulation consumer magazine in the world, and it is worth looking at. Issued quarterly, the magazine covers shopping tips, gimmicks and frauds to avoid, and news of consumer legislation. The magazine is sold by subscription for $1.25 per year for four issues. Bulk subscriptions of 50 or more are available for the low annual cost of 40¢ per person.

Using Credit Wisely
"Used prudently, consumer credit can be one of the most productive tools consumers can use to obtain a more comfortable standard of living. Used unwisely, consumer credit can be as devastating as a savage tornado wrecking home after home."

This comprehensive booklet reviews the credit system, the consumers' and the lenders' rights, and gives some sound advice on the wise use of credit. 90¢ each; 10 or more copies, 75¢ each.

EM Complaint Directory for Consumers
You want to complain but don't know where to write. The most common problem solved in this directory is the identification and location by address of corporate manufacturers of products. Names and addresses of hundreds of manufacturers, government agencies and consumer groups are supplied. Price, $1.

Publications may be ordered from:

Everybody's Money
P.O. Box 431
Madison, Wis. 53701

THE BETTER BUSINESS BUREAU

Your local Better Business Bureau, acting on behalf of responsible businesses in your community, helps the consumer cause by:

- Providing information about a company before you do business with it
- Helping to resolve a complaint you might have against a firm
- Providing you with consumer information to aid in buying decisions
- Offering consumer arbitration to resolve disputes between buyer and seller

Most of the contacts with consumers are actually inquiries, not complaints. Complaints are requested in writing, prior to the bureau's

Getting your money's worth

follow-through with the business.

Consumer information is generally in the form of specific inquiries about companies by name. In such cases a record of business reliability is provided from the files. Of the free general information booklets available, those of particular interest include:

- **Tips on Work-at-Home Schemes**
- **Tips on Refunds and Exchanges**
- **If You Have a Complaint About Advertising**
- **Consumer Tips on Bait and Switch**
- **Consumer Tips on Buying by Mail**
- **Consumer Tips on Guarantees and Warranties**
- **Facts About Health Insurance**

Order from:
Council of Better Business Bureaus
1150 17th St. NW
Washington, D.C. 20036

THE COUPON WAY TO LOWER FOOD PRICES
By Carole Katz and Albert Lee
Workman Publishing Co.
1973, $1.95

Any consumer, say the authors, can save 10 to 15% on the weekly food shopping bill with little effort. And, for the "professional refunder," the stakes, they say, are much higher.

Samples, cents-off coupons, trial offers, trading stamps and dozens of approaches to saving money are described in this unusual book, which also includes sections on subscribing to one of the many newsletters for the "pros."

For information on contests and "freebie" sources, newsletter and information exchanges are listed. Believe it or not, there are places to write to for lists of "freebies"!

COMMUNITY CONCERN FOR SENIOR CITIZENS

This organization dates back to 1971, when Maria A. Redo began an effort to encourage local stores to provide discounts to people over 65. It has now spread to more than 2,500 establishments in New York City. The broad variety of retail establishments approached includes everything from supermarkets to movie theaters. Each participant business is provided with an attractive window sticker. The eligible older people are required to identify themselves with either a New York City Reduced Fare Card or a Medicare card.

Ms. Redo would be happy to share her experience with other community groups; you may write to her:

Maria A. Redo, Executive Director
Community Concern for Senior Citizens, Inc.
415 Madison Ave.
New York, N.Y. 10017

MONEY   8

THE SHOPPER'S GUIDEBOOK
By Herbert S. Dennenberg
Consumer News, Inc., 813 National Press Building, Washington, D.C. 20045, 1975, $3.50

With detailed comparisons of insurance costs, this book presents an armchair shopping trip to the premiums you can expect to pay. Covering homeowner's insurance, health, life, and special types, the book also includes Medicare and Medicaid. The author is a former Pennsylvania Insurance Commissioner. Other important areas treated from the consumer point of view are surgery, patient rights in hospitals, dentistry and lawyers.

INSURANCE FOR THE HOME

You don't have to be an insurance expert to understand the free pamphlet material offered by the Insurance Information Institute. It explains in brief, simple terms the coverage offered by most homeowner policies, including provisions for liability if a guest in the home is hurt or a storm causes damage. Tips are offered on what you can do to avoid needing to make a claim on your policy.

The following titles are available:

- **How to Keep Your Family Burglar Unhappy**
- **Is Your Home Insured for Today's Values?**
- **What's Your IPQ (Insurance Protection Quotient)?**
- **Insurance for the Home**
- **Every Ten Seconds** [relates to auto insurance]

Available from:
*Educational Division
Insurance Information Institute
110 William St.
New York, N.Y. 10038*

HOW TO HAVE A GARAGE SALE

This pamphlet covers some of the important points in planning a garage sale, which is a popular sport and money-maker.

25¢
*Consumer Affairs Division
Office of the Impartial Chairman
Moving and Storage Industry of New York
10 Columbus Circle
New York, N.Y. 10019*

THE GARAGE SALE MANUAL
By Jean Young and Jim Young
Praeger, 1973, $3.95

Garage sales have become a way of life in even the most affluent communities in the country. The events are both good economy—you *can* make some money—and lots of fun. The variations are many, from the single-family operation to the community or joint effort.

A sale often stimulates other more regular or ambitious money-making ventures. This book, which covers the how and the fun of it all, is charmingly illustrated by the authors' son.

HOW TO BUY AND SELL REAL ESTATE FOR FINANCIAL SECURITY
By Robert Irwin
McGraw-Hill, 1975

Extra money and/or time, combined with an interest in real estate, can frequently lead to extra income—and investing does not involve mandatory retirement rules, provided you have some capital.

This guide shows how to become your own business manager, how to choose property, how to renovate and how to sell through a broker while protecting your own best interests.

Getting your money's worth
Making money during retirement

The book emphasizes the business advantages of real estate investing and selling, and, while it does not give pointers on becoming the person on the other end—the broker—it could well inspire some people in that direction as well.

YOUR RETIREMENT JOB GUIDE

Finding a job after 65 is not easy, but the encouraging news is that three million Americans over 65 have landed places in the labor force today in a variety of ways.

Whether the need to work is financial, morale-building, or both, the problem needs an organized approach. This booklet details the looking process, with hints on résumés, letters of application and the conduct of the interview. To avoid the "blind alleys," specific approaches in such fields as retailing, real estate and special projects are given. Hobbies, consulting and small businesses are also explored in this thorough booklet.

Free
AARP-NRTA
P.O. Box 2400
215 Long Beach Blvd.
Long Beach, Calif. 90801

EMPLOYMENT OF OLDER PEOPLE

Mandatory retirement at 65 and earlier is the concern of many people and organizations. In this pamphlet the American Medical Association addresses the problem with a full array of facts and statistics. It details the possible effects of forced retirement on the health of the individual. For many retirement may come as a welcome, hard-earned reward. Others who regard it as long-term unemployment may suffer health problems.

The pamphlet outlines reasons why the older person frequently is the more desirable employee; among the more convincing are:
- ☐ Better attendance
- ☐ Less likelihood of changing jobs
- ☐ High motivation
- ☐ Output generally the same as younger people's
- ☐ No evidence of inability to learn

The booklet can be particularly good material for the person organizing a local advocacy group—or trying to convince an employer to hire him or her.

Write:
Committee on Aging
Council on Medical Science
American Medical
 Association
535 North Dearborn St.
Chicago, Ill. 60610

Prices:
Single copies	15¢ each
2-49	14¢
100-499	12¢
500-999	10¢
1,000 or more	8¢

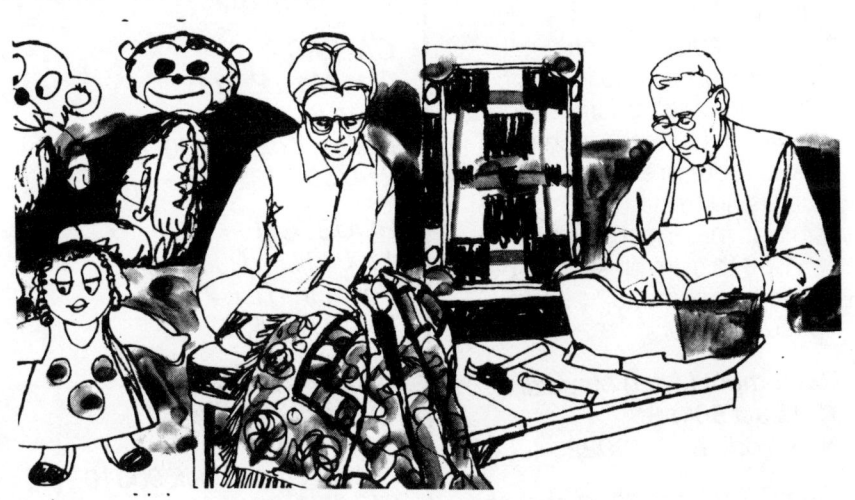

MONEY 8

WORKING IN RETIREMENT

This thoughtful booklet offers encouragement on working in retirement. It opens by detailing several case histories of ordinary people: Bill Martin, a retired sales manager for a large department store, who found some part-time employment as a caretaker at a winter resort; Paul Cipolla, who works as a commission salesman; May Muller, once a dressmaker and now manager of a boutique.

The penalties under the Social Security system for excessive earnings are explained. A comprehensive list of job suggestions, specifics on how to look for jobs, and small business ideas are laid out in clear fashion.

And there are details on an increasing trend: turning hobbies into income.

$1.50 to current subscribers of the magazine, $2.25 to nonsubscribers

Retirement Living Magazine
150 East 58th St.
New York, N.Y. 10022

(See COMMUNICATING chapter for more on the magazine and the other publications offered in the series.)

MATURE TEMPS

Mature Temps, an affiliated service of AARP-NRTA, offers temporary and part-time employment referral service for older people in several cities. Salaries, both for skilled and unskilled positions, are paid by the service, which then bills the temporary employers.

Mature Temps offices are in:

BOSTON
47 Winter St.
Boston, Mass. 02108
617/482-7628

BALTIMORE
10 East Baltimore St.
Baltimore, Md. 21202
301/837-2444

CHICAGO
17 North State St.
Suite 814
Chicago, Ill. 60602
312/368-0266

DALLAS
One Main Plaza
Suite 846
Dallas, Tex. 75250
214/651-9321

HOUSTON
1100 Milam Building
Houston, Tex. 77002
713/237-8552

LOS ANGELES
3660 Wilshire Blvd.
Suite 1130
Los Angeles, Calif. 90010
213/380-6515

NEW YORK
1114 Ave. of the Americas
New York, N.Y. 10036
212/869-0740

PHILADELPHIA
1700 Market St.
Philadelphia, Pa. 19103
215/665-1150

PLYMOUTH MEETING
One Plymouth Meeting Mall
Plymouth Meeting, Pa. 19462
215/825-4400

SAN FRANCISCO
44 Montgomery St.
Suite 2716
San Francisco, Calif. 94104
415/986-7787

WASHINGTON
1750 K St. NW
Washington, D.C. 20006
202/833-8888

GREEN THUMB

Green Thumb, a project of the National Farmers Union, is a special service for older people living in rural areas who require not only additional income but training and specific referral for employment. The people running the program, financed by the U.S. Department of Labor, are very much aware of the gains to be made in self-worth and self-respect as well.

Making money during retirement

The projects Green Thumb carries out are related to community improvement, conservation and the strengthening of existing community services, such as those aiding shut-ins or the handicapped. To qualify for participation, one must be at least 55 years old, of a farming or rural background, with an annual income below the currently designated poverty level, and must pass a medical examination.

Green Thumb projects are coordinated through field offices in selected rural areas of the country.

ARKANSAS
1922 W. 6th St.
P.O. Box 311
Little Rock, Ark. 72203
501/376-6221

CALIFORNIA
3000 Fruitridge Road
Sacramento, Calif. 95820
916/392-2012

FLORIDA
4567 Atlantic Blvd.
Suite 105
Jacksonville, Fla. 32207
904/396-3208

ILLINOIS
407 Iles Park Place
Springfield, Ill. 62703
217/522-6521

INDIANA
3rd & Chestnut Sts.
Seymour, Ind. 47274
812/522-7930

KANSAS
Professional Building
P.O. Box 246
McPherson, Kan. 67460
316/241-0820

KENTUCKY
P.O. Box A
Main Street
Beattyville, Ky. 41311
606/464-8611

MICHIGAN
Municipal Airport Building
801 Airport Drive
Ann Arbor, Mich. 48104
313/761-5335

MINNESOTA
P. O. Box 310
Wadena, Minn. 56482
218/631-3483

MISSOURI
P.O. Box 296
Jefferson City, Mo. 65101
314/635-9019

MONTANA
Civic Center, Room 9B
Great Falls, Mont. 59401
406/761-4821

NEBRASKA
620 North 48 Street
Lincoln, Neb. 68504
402/466-2206

NEW JERSEY
900 South Broad St.
Trenton, N.J. 08611
609/393-8958

NEW YORK
23 Main Street
Cobleskill, N.Y. 12043
518/234-3581

NORTH DAKOTA
318 First Ave. NW
Minot, N.D. 58701
701/839-5408

OHIO
1604 East Main St.
Ottawa, O. 45875
419/523-4305

OKLAHOMA
P.O. Box 25795
Oklahoma City, Okla. 73125
405/232-2044

OREGON
215 Front St. NE
Salem, Ore. 97301
503/585-2433

PENNSYLVANIA
240 North 3rd St., Room 1106
Payne & Shoemaker Bldg.
Harrisburg, Pa. 17101
717/233-7056

SOUTH DAKOTA
513 South Main Ave.
National Reserve Life Bldg.
Sioux Falls, S.Dak. 57102
605/332-7991

TEXAS
800 Lake Air Drive
Waco, Tex. 76710
817/772-7220

UTAH
2520 S. State St., Room 170
Salt Lake City, Utah 84115
801/484-2724

VIRGINIA
Marshall Bldg., Main St.
Blackstone, Va. 23824
703/292-3698

WISCONSIN
Clark County Courthouse
Room 209
Neillsville, Wis. 54456
715/743-3036

PUERTO RICO
P.O. Box 13066
Santurce, P.R. 00907
809/725-2941

JOINING AND SHARING 9

Foster Grandparent Rachel Shibles of Laconia, New Hampshire with one of the 40 retarded "grandchildren" she helps

Friendship improves happiness, and abates misery, by doubling our joy, and dividing our grief.

—Joseph Addison
1672–1719
English essayist

God helps those that help themselves.

—Benjamin Franklin
1706–1790
American statesman, inventor and author

YOU ARE NOT ALONE

We are a country of joiners. Throughout life we have all known the special joys and benefits of sharing hundreds and thousands of experiences and opportunities for countless reasons—professional, fraternal, local, national.

Though many of the joinings and sharings continue as we age, being over 55 or 65 brings some diverse, special opportunities; for example:

- ☐ Learning how others view increasing age and approach their problems
- ☐ Keeping up to date on news as it affects older people
- ☐ Helping others—and being helped
- ☐ Sharing in a wide range of human contacts—meeting other people
- ☐ Learning about everything under the sun

Major membership organizations

☐ Standing up and being counted in advocating better living for older people
☐ Receiving some shared economic benefits

Standing up and being counted in particular is becoming more common. And whether you wish to share experiences, help others, help yourself, or take a stand for improved living for older people, chances are you can find—or start—an organization to suit your interests.

The organizations listed in this section are all nationally coordinated—many with local chapters. In addition to those whose membership is basically older people as such, we have also listed several organizations of professionals in fields concerned with the aging, so that you may be made familiar with their work and know how to contact them for information or assistance.

NATIONAL ASSOCIATION OF RETIRED FEDERAL EMPLOYEES

The membership of NARFE consists of retired federal employees and their families and of some federal employees over 50 who are still employed. The association speaks out on the special issues pertaining to retired civil service employees, particularly questions relating to pensions. Chapters located throughout the country serve generally as social focal points.

Membership dues of $5 per year are separate from local dues, which usually are less. The association's monthly general interest magazine, **Retirement Life**, includes features on retirement, state and chapter news, and national news of older people's interests. Current NARFE membership is approximately 200,000.

For information, write:
National Association of Retired Federal Employees
1533 New Hampshire Ave. NW
Washington, D.C. 20036

NATIONAL COUNCIL OF SENIOR CITIZENS

NCSC, a membership organization of over three million people, is heavily concerned with fighting for benefits for older Americans. This is evidenced, as its membership materials state, in the organizational work which helped pass the Medicare bill, Social Security increases and other benefits.

Other current and pressing legislative efforts include national health insurance and employment rights and tax concessions for older people.

NCSC is affiliated with approximately 3,000 clubs across the country—clubs based in housing complexes, churches and synagogues, civic associations, etc. Many of the members are retired union workers.

Membership benefits include:
- A health insurance plan to supplement Medicare
- Discounts on prescription drugs
- Group travel
- Subscription to **Senior Citizen News**, a monthly newspaper with legislative news and area features.

Annual membership dues:
- $3.50 if a member of a participating club or a supporting trade union
- $4.00 if not already affiliated with a club or union
- $5.00 for family membership
- $100.00 for a lifetime membership for either an individual or family

· For further information and membership forms, write:

National Council of Senior Citizens
1511 K St. NW
Washington, D.C. 20005

JOINING AND SHARING 9

AMERICAN ASSOCIATION OF RETIRED PERSONS-NATIONAL RETIRED TEACHERS ASSOCIATION

AARP-NRTA, operating in close association and proximity, are together the giants of the organizations of older Americans. AARP's membership is over 10 million and NRTA's approximately 500,000 (two out of every three retired teachers). The stated purpose of both organizations is helping older Americans achieve retirement lives of independence, dignity and purpose. The associations share common administrative staffs in large part. And, while some of their publications and programs are separate, others are joint efforts. A broad range of benefits and activities is available for modest annual dues:

Publications: **Modern Maturity** (AARP) and **NRTA Journal**, both issued bimonthly, include a number of articles on the quality of life and news of interest to older people. **News Bulletins**, published monthly, cover timely topics. A large number of booklets are available at all times on a variety of subjects, from hobbies to finance. (Several are described in appropriate chapters of this book.)

Legislative Representation: Staff specialists of AARP-NRTA represent the interests of older Americans, advocating better conditions and recognition for them. In addition to this staff work, which is done on the national level, AARP-NRTA joint state legislative committees are active in every state.

Pharmacy Service: Prescription medicines, medical appliances, sick room supplies, and health aids can be delivered by mail directly to the home at reduced prices. Both brand-name and generic drugs are stocked. Pharmacies are located in St. Petersburg, Florida; Long Beach, Calif.; Kansas City, Mo.; Indianapolis, Ind.; Hartford, Conn.; Portland, Ore.; and Washington, DC.

Retirement Preparation: NRTA's retirement education program and AARP's Action for Independent Maturity (AIM) both offer counseling programs and publications to help people aged 50–64 plan for retirement while they are still in the work force.

Continuing Education: The Institutes of Lifetime Learning in Washington, D.C. and in Long Beach, Calif.—both administrative centers for the organization—and in certain other cities, offer adult education classes in a variety of subjects. They continually urge educational institutions to offer

Major membership organizations

college and university courses to retired people on a free or reduced-tuition basis.

The associations coordinate approximately 2,500 AARP and 2,000 NRTA local groups and encourage the formation of additional units. The national leaders come from the membership. Modest chapter dues are levied. The associations provide a broad support program for local units to conduct seminars and other programs dealing directly with some of the problems people face in retirement. Essentially, the associations give the local groups tools for carrying out their programs. Some of them are:

Health Education Program: Called VIM (Vigor in Maturity), this program is designed to help members maintain their health. The program consists of five sessions dealing with (a) health in general, (b) safety, (c) chronic diseases, (d) food facts and frauds, (e) adjustments in lifetime patterns. Single-session programs on arthritis, diabetes and mental health also are offered.

Driver Improvement Program: Offered in cooperation with the National Safety Council, this program helps drivers through review of driving skills and encouragement of defensive driving.

Crime Prevention Program: This program, conducted with chapter leaders and local police, covers such areas as burglary, fraud, street crime, and community-police relations.

Church and Synagogue Programs: This program works closely with religious bodies of all denominations, helping them explore ways to expand their services to the older members of congregations. Each May material is specially provided to clergymen for use in sermons and other programs during Older Americans Month.

Consumer Information Program: The AARP-NRTA Consumer Office in Washington, D.C. maintains a clearinghouse for consumer assistance. Members may write or call with problems or questions.

Widowed Persons Service Program: The counseling staff of this program encourages and assists groups within chapters to support and advise those newly widowed.

Tax-Aide Program: Help in understanding and preparing tax forms is available through this effort which brings older people together with IRS-trained AARP and NRTA counselors, who explain taxes and answer questions on filing forms.

AARP-NRTA also offers members travel services, with fre-

INTERNATIONAL SENIOR CITIZENS ASSOCIATION

ISCA is an international organization of older people, established in 1963 to:

- Provide coordination on an international level to safeguard the interests and needs of senior citizens around the world.
- Establish means of friendly communication between older persons throughout the world for educational and cultural purposes.
- Enhance the prestige of older persons in world affairs through utilization of their wisdom and experience.

ISCA is affiliated with several organizations in other countries. It publishes a quarterly newsletter, **ISCA News**, which is included with membership.

Membership dues are as follows:

- Organizations or groups of persons 50 years of age or older: Dues to be determined upon application
- Life members: $100
- Individual members: $2 per year
- Professional groups: Dues to be determined upon application

For additional information and membership application, contact:

International Senior Citizens Association
11753 Wilshire Blvd.
Los Angeles, Calif. 90025

JOINING AND SHARING   9

The Institute for Retired Professionals: An Example

Consider the story of the Institute for Retired Professionals (IRP) in New York City: In 1968, a number of retirees enrolled in the New School (an institution of higher learning widely regarded for its imaginative adult education programs), joined together to form the group. For a fixed annual fee of $225, a member is entitled to enroll in one course in the New School's adult division as well as to participate in IRP activities. The group, open to retired professionals and executives, averages about 650 members, with hundreds on the waiting list.

Forming a university within a university, IRP members organize and run their own intellectual and social programs, including discussion groups on public affairs, book reviewing and poetry and play readings. Language, art and music groups function as well. IRP publishes a regular newsletter and literary magazine.

The idea is already spreading to other parts of the country. The University of California in San Francisco and Temple University in Philadelphia have started similar operations, and the Harvard University version is getting under way.

If you would like additional information, perhaps to consider organizing a similar undertaking in your community, write:

quent group arrangements at reduced prices. Insurance is also available.

New services continually appear, many serving the general public as well as members. **Prime Time**, a weekly 15-minute program produced and distributed to radio stations in dozens of cities, provides older people with good, straightforward information on problems concerning their daily lives. Mature Temps, covered in the MONEY chapter of this book, is another example of a service that helps people directly—here in finding temporary employment. A library at the Washington, D.C. office contains an extensive collection of books, pamphlets, and periodicals of interest to older people.

The National Retired Teachers Association was founded in 1947 by Dr. Ethel Percy Andrus, a retired teacher dedicated to helping other retired people improve the quality of their lives. The American Association of Retired Persons was formed as a "sister" organization in 1958. In honor of the late Dr. Andrus, AARP-NRTA members contributed more than $2 million to help build the Andrus Gerontology Center at the University of Southern California. This facility, the home of the country's first undergraduate gerontology school, also conducts extensive research and training in the field of aging.

Since 1973, the AARP-NRTA Andrus Foundation, supported by continuing contributions from members, has provided research grants to USC and a number of other colleges and universities throughout the country.

Membership in either of the associations is $3 for a year and $8 for three years. One membership entitles both husband and wife to full privileges.

For additional information or membership applications, write to:

AARP-NRTA　　　　　　　or　　　　*AARP-NRTA*
1909 K St. NW　　　　　　　　　　*P.O. Box 2400*
Washington, D.C. 20049　　　　　*215 Long Beach Blvd.*
　　　　　　　　　　　　　　　　　Long Beach, Calif. 90801

Hyman Hirsch, Director
Institute for Retired
Professionals
New School for Social
Research
66 West 12th St.
New York, N.Y. 10011

148

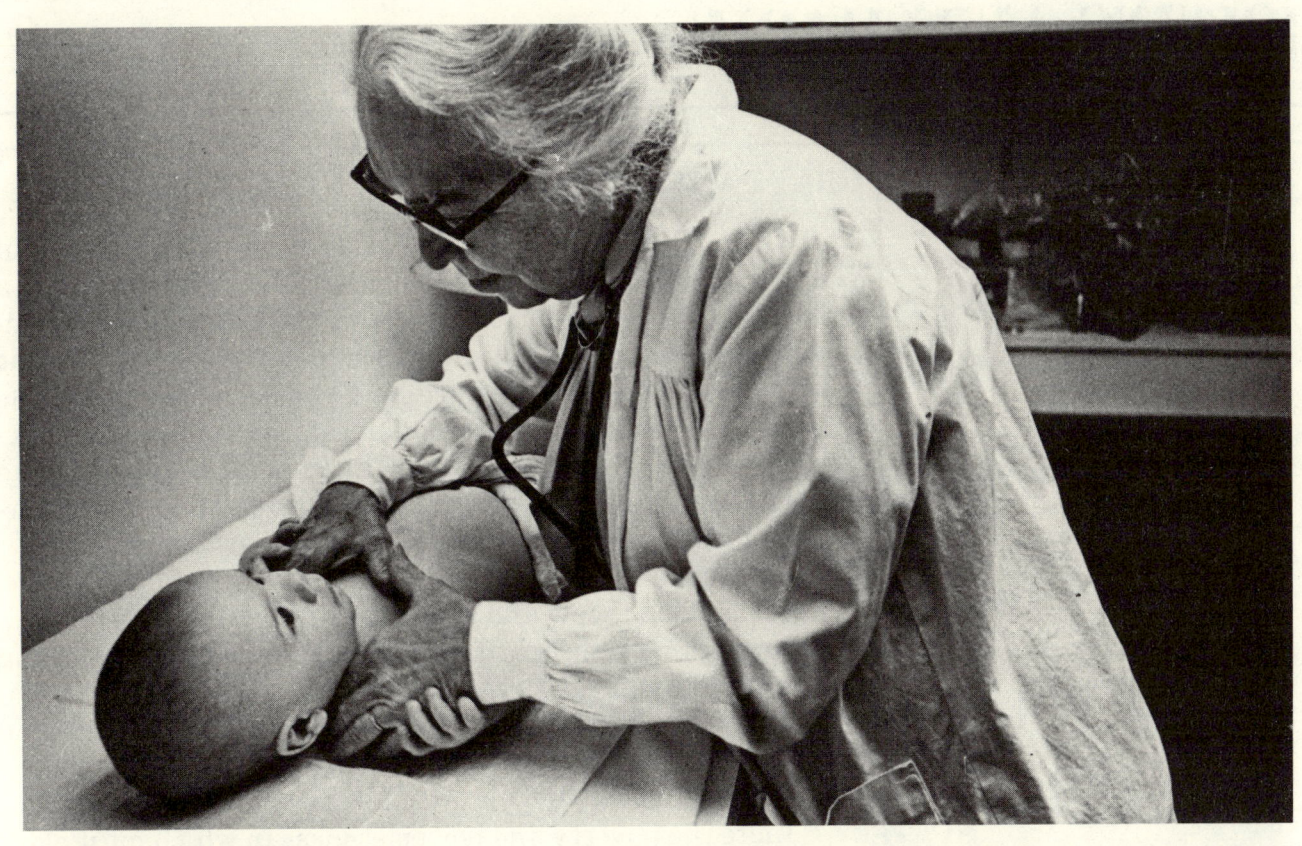

JOINING AND SHARING 9

GRAY PANTHERS

The Gray Panthers, a rapidly emerging, vocal group of younger and older people, is the result of a 1973 merger of a small group of Panther activists with the Retired Professional Action Group, a project supported by Ralph Nader's Public Citizen, Inc. The Panthers are an issues-oriented group. Its concerns are declared as cross-generational, though in practice the focus is on older people. Its general and overriding goal is the elimination of agism—discrimination and determination of status by age in our society's institutions.

The stated broad goals are:
- To develop a new and positive self-awareness in our culture which can regard the total life span as a continuing process in maturity and fulfillment.
- To strive for new options for lifestyles for older and younger people that will challenge the present paternalism in our institutions and culture and will help to eliminate the poverty and powerlessness in which most older and younger people are forced to live, and to change society's destructive attitudes about aging.
- To make responsible use of our freedom to bring about social change, to develop a list of priorities among social issues, and to struggle nonviolently for social change which will bring greater human freedom, justice, dignity and peace.
- To build a new power base in our society, uniting presently disenfranchised and oppressed groups and realizing the common qualities and concerns of age and youth working in coalition with other movements with similar goals and principles.
- To reinforce and support each other in our quest for liberation and to celebrate shared humanity.

Some of the Panthers' specific programs to accomplish these goals include advocacy and persuasion in the following areas:
- Adequate governmental and private support of mass transportation with minimal or no cost to consumers.
- Enactment of a national health care program, through a public corporation rather than commercial insurance companies; an improved (service) delivery system; and preventive care (including home care, institutional care, and alternatives to institutional care).
- Abolition of arbitrary and compulsory retirement and

age discrimination in employment. Adequate job training and career possibilities.
- [ ] Systematic approach toward the abolition of poverty with such measures as adequate universal guaranteed income, radical tax reforms, guaranteed employment opportunities, and adoption of national compulsory standards for private pension systems and adequate supervision of the standards.
- [ ] Renewed effort by the government and industry to encourage and support a national program of housing with a thorough cultural mix of all age groups, income levels and racial backgrounds.
- [ ] Reform of our educational system to include programs and opportunities for people of all age groups to participate at minimal or no cost.

The Gray Panthers, though small in number (approximately 7,000) have attracted considerable press attention, with their strong, outspoken quality.

Membership, technically called affiliation, requires agreement with the organization's purposes. There are no specific membership dues, though contributions are encouraged. Local chapters are active in several cities.

Panther publications are available on request for a nominal cost:

The Network: A newsletter, produced several times a year. A sample copy is available at no cost. Annual subscription $2.

Basic Bibliography: A selection of recommended readings pertaining to agism, political action, positive aspects of aging, important statistics and facts, organization for social change, and personal small group growth and development. 25¢

Selected Bibliography on Politics, Social Action and Advocacy. 25¢

History of the Gray Panthers Movement. 25¢

Liberation from Agism; Two Essays. 50¢

Gray Panthers Brochure. 5¢

Buttons proclaiming, "Gray Panthers, Age and Youth in Action," are also available at $1.

Write:
*Gray Panthers
3700 Chestnut St.
Philadelphia, Pa. 19104*

NATIONAL FEDERATION OF GRANDMOTHER CLUBS OF AMERICA

The federation is a conglomeration of approximately 700 local grandmother clubs across the country. Its goal is simple: to honor grandmotherhood.

One of the major legislative goals is to have the second Sunday of every October declared National Grandmother's Day. Other membership activities include financial support for research on children's diseases and publication of a membership periodical, **Autumn Leaves.**

A group of 10 grandmothers may apply for a charter as a member club. The organization's bylaws state that a member must be a grandmother through motherhood, marriage or legal adoption and must be sponsored by a member when applying.

For additional information:
*National Federation of Grandmother Clubs of America
203 North Wabash Ave.
Chicago, Ill. 60601*

JOINING AND SHARING 9

Family gatherings have always been fun, as illustrated in this 1920's painting, **Family Musicale** by Mead Schaeffer. While families have grown apart by distance, there are many ways to find new friends—even families, in a way—and senior centers are but one of those ways.

Major membership organizations

SENIOR CENTERS

In thousands of communities across the country, the senior center is a focal point—a "community living room" for older people.

In storefronts or in lavish buildings of their own, they are gathering places for people with age in common—and with their diversity as an asset.

The senior center has a combination of characteristics—at once a club, a dining room, a classroom, a meeting room, a ballroom and a place to share problems and solutions.

Senior centers are sponsored and administered most frequently by one of three types of groups:
1. Local government agencies
2. Private social welfare agencies, such as community centers or "Y"s
3. Voluntary citizens' committees or groups, such as religious organizations and clubs

While the centers are usually administered by professional or volunteer staffs, the programs are often planned and carried out by the members themselves.

The Administration of Aging's hot-lunch program for older Americans is a frequent midday feature at senior centers.

To find out about the senior centers in your community, contact the state or area agency on aging as listed in RIGHTS AND LEGACIES chapter or most other local specialized aging information and referral offices. The National Institute of Senior Centers (NISC) publishes a national directory. If there is no senior center in your community—or if you want to encourage establishment of an additional one—you ought to know about NISC. A division of the National Council on the Aging, it serves as a central resource to help develop, improve and expand the services of senior centers throughout the country by providing:
- ☐ Information on all aspects of center operation
- ☐ Consultation to established centers and to communities seeking to establish centers
- ☐ Formation of operating standards for centers
- ☐ Establishment of regional and national conferences and seminars
- ☐ Cooperation with national organizations and governmental agencies
- ☐ Stimulation of research projects to improve center services

JOINING AND SHARING 9

□ Encouragement of student training for work with the aging

Write:
National Institute of Senior Centers
National Council on the Aging
1828 L St. NW
Washington, D.C. 20036

It is great to have friends when one is young, but indeed it is still more so when you are getting old. When we are young, friends are, like everything else, a matter of course. In the old days we know what it means to have them.

—Edvard Grieg, 1843–1907
Norwegian composer

**Major membership organizations
Specialized programs**

ALTRUSA INTERNATIONAL

You may be the recipient—or the organizer and giver—of time and services provided by one of the 565 community-based Altrusa Clubs. Each is a cross section of the community's business and professional women. Though they all make their own choices for community projects, programs for older people are quite prominent on the agendas.

Some of the more typical programs for older people include meals on wheels, telephone reassurance services, senior centers and nutrition programs. The chamber of commerce can usually provide information on your local Altrusa Club, or write:

*Altrusa International
332 South Michigan Ave.
Chicago, Ill. 60604*

THE PAID NEIGHBOR SERVICE

Your community might learn from this activity. Westchester County's Paid Neighbor Service utilizes people over 60 to assist in caring for other older people—home-bound and thus less fortunate—with marketing, light housekeeping and companionship. The Paid Neighbors, who serve temporarily from a week to several months at a time, are paid $3 an hour plus carfare.

For additional information to help you organize a similar project in your community, write:

*Senior Personnel Employment Committee
158 Westchester Ave.
White Plains, N.Y. 10601*

COMMUNAL LIVING IS IN . . . AND THE WORD IS SPREADING

Communal living—sharing the same home, problems and joys—has worked for the sorority, fraternity, kibbutz, and for many young people in this country. Despite differences in geography or age, communes are springing up in Illinois, Maryland, Florida, New York . . .

Members of the household pool their finances to pay the bills, eat together, help each other, provide companionship and maintain a spirit which might otherwise be lost in loneliness or an institution. Usually they have separate rooms. Thus far most of the experiments are working, with an average of five or less people in each sharing situation.

Most area agencies on aging should be able to give data on any communes forming locally . . . or help to put you in touch with an agency or person organizing one.

SYNAGOGUE COUNCIL OF AMERICA

The council offers **A Guide to Aging Programs for Synagogues** in its efforts to help older people in their communities. This work says what it has to say with such clarity, that we recommend it as a guide for organizing to help others whether or not they are part of a synagogue framework. The guide is thoughtful and the suggestions for helping others are very detailed, ranging from meals on wheels to adult education. Though you may be 65, you can help those in their 80's and 90's with the suggestions included in this book. $1.50

Available from:
*SCA Projects on Aging
c/o Institute for Jewish Policy Planning and Research
1776 Massachusetts Ave. NW
Washington, D.C. 20036*

Look well into thyself; there is a source of strength which will always spring up if thou wilt always look there.

—Marcus Aurelius
121–180
Roman emperor
and philosopher

JOINING AND SHARING 9

THE COOPERATIVE EXTENSION SERVICE OF THE U.S. DEPARTMENT OF AGRICULTURE

Since 1914, the Cooperative Extension Service has been working with state and county governments and universities to conduct adult education classes in farming, home economics, personal finance and related subjects. Each of the 50 states has an outlet, generally at a land-grant college, for this special educational effort. The extension activities may take the form of traditional classrooms or media campaigns, seminars or demonstrations. In addition to professional staffs, it utilizes many volunteers.

Extension Service may be a worthwhile contact for many older people, both for information and for volunteer opportunities to help others.

For a complete list of the state offices of the Extension Service, write:

Extension Service
U.S. Department of Agriculture
Washington, D.C. 20250

I shall pass through this world but once. Any good therefore that I can do or any kindness that I can show to any human being, let me do it now. Let me not defer or neglect it, for I shall not pass this way again.

—Henry Drummond, 1851–1897
English scientist and author

He alone has lost the art to live who cannot win new friends.

—S. Weir Mitchell
1829–1914
American neurologist and author

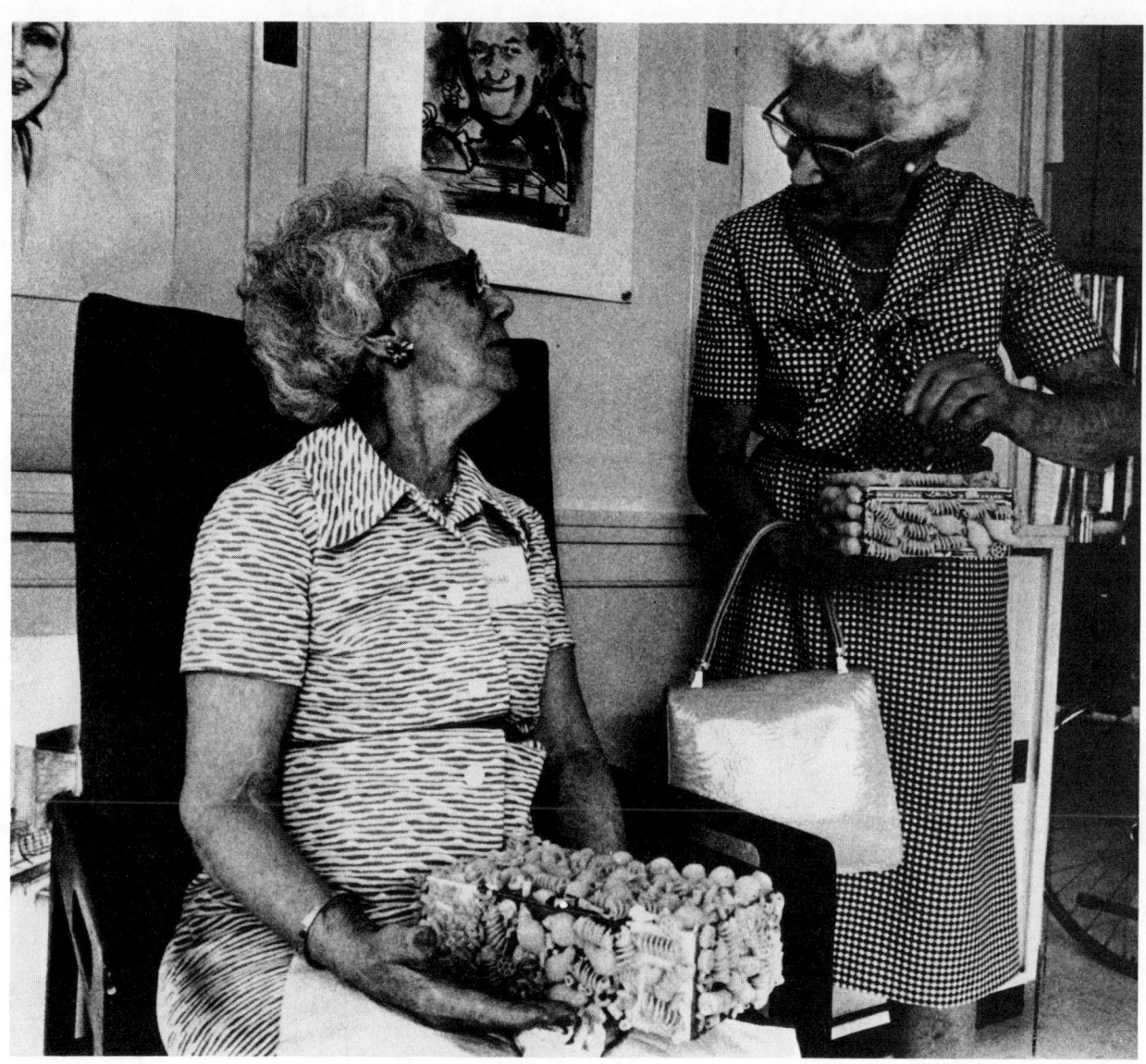

JOINING AND SHARING

NATIONAL CENTER FOR VOLUNTARY ACTION

You can help someone . . . and yourself . . . when you volunteer. The National Center for Voluntary Action is designed to encourage, give ideas and help people to find volunteer opportunities.

In the idea area, it has hundreds of suggestions; consider a few:

- Like to cheer the sick? Short-staffed hospitals and clinics are waiting for your help.
- Prevent suicides by answering a "hot line."
- Join the fight against pollution by gathering data for a local organization.
- Coach a team.
- Register voters.

Matching your skills and interests with opportunities is frequently difficult. So, hundreds of communities have Voluntary Action Centers, all affiliates of the National Center. Check your local phone directory to see if there is a VAC in your community, for it can be effective in matching you with an opportunity. If you cannot locate it easily, perhaps the local VAC is using a slightly different name. Do not give up, but contact NCVA, which will refer you to the proper party.

NCVA has several pamphlets and an information clearing-house that can give hundreds of ideas and examples for volunteering. It publishes a regular quarterly magazine for volunteer leaders, **Voluntary Action Leadership**; each issue features several articles on the art of volunteering and leading.

looking into volunteering?

Write:
National Center for Voluntary Action
1216 16th St. NW
Washington, D.C. 20036

Volunteering

ACTION

ACTION, a federal agency born in 1971 out of President Kennedy's Peace Corps concept, provides many opportunities for older people to act as volunteers. It unites several federal volunteer activities:

>Volunteers in Service to America (VISTA)
>Peace Corps
>Retired Senior Volunteer Program (RSVP)
>Service Corps of Retired Executives (SCORE)
>Active Executives (ACE)
>University Year for Action
>Senior Companion Program
>Foster Grandparent Program

These are the activities of special interest to older people:

VISTA (Volunteers in Service to America)

At any one time VISTA generally has 300 volunteers who are 60 or over. Coming from varying backgrounds, they bring their years of special experience to community projects.

Anna Aicardi, 72, is a team leader for the South Boston project where she and others answer telephones in a mobile city hall referring people to services.

Rolland and Florence Aylesworth left their Florida retirement home to join VISTA. The first year they spent in Anadarko, Okla., working with ghetto residents. Rolland had been a building contractor before retiring and put his knowledge to use helping people repair their homes. The couple then moved on to Smith Station, Ala. from where they have been traveling about 1,200 miles each month assisting others to obtain home-improvement loans and find building contractors.

Frances Hollenbeck and Mary Feerlick were widowed and retired. They left their home in San Diego to enter a three-week training period at the University of Oregon, after which they became teacher aides helping young people catch up with their education.

VISTA services are requested by local nonprofit organizations, such as community action groups, churches or synagogues, schools or government agencies.

VISTA volunteers must be U.S. citizens or permanent residents, have abilities, skills or education required by the community organization requesting volunteers, and be medically qualified. VISTA provides transportation to and from train-

---

ACTION Recruiting Offices

NORTHEASTERN REGION

John W. McCormack P.O. & Courthouse Bldg.
Room 1405
Boston, Mass. 02109

26 Federal Plaza
Room 1605
New York, N.Y. 10007

1405 Locust St.
Philadelphia, Pa. 19102

Federal Bldg.
100 State St.
Room 317
Rochester, N.Y. 14614

SOUTHERN REGION

730 Peachtree St. NE
Suite 900
Atlanta, Ga. 30308

Wesley Foundation
Univ. of North Carolina
214 Pittsboro St.
Chapel Hill, N.C. 27514

212 N. St. Paul St.
Room 1622
Dallas, Tex. 75201

812 Connecticut Ave. NW
Washington, D.C. 20525

WESTERN REGION

100 McAllister St.
Room 2204
San Francisco, Calif. 94102

Prudential Plaza, Suite 524
1050 17th St.
Denver, Colo. 80202

VISTA volunteer Constance Williams shown here working with Citizens Housing and Planning Association of Metropolitan Boston.

ing sites and assignments. Food, lodging and limited medical care are supplied during training. There is a monthly allowance, which varies according to the cost of living in the locality, and a $50 per month stipend. The length of service runs for one year.

Peace Corps

The Peace Corps, perhaps the most famous of the volunteer efforts, welcomes older people in projects in other countries.

Mrs. Toni Maxwell, a grandmother, decided she was not ready to "sit and knit" when she retired from her teaching job. She joined the Peace Corps to teach French at the Collège Moderne in Adzoje, Ivory Coast.

According to another volunteer, Bea Alford, "We've been working all our lives for our children and all of a sudden they were raised. We couldn't see going to work collecting material things, so we decided to work collecting experiences instead by living in another culture. So many people hesitate because they don't have anything to offer. They don't realize that the experience and skill they've gathered all their lives is the best thing they could take with them."

Volunteering with her husband for service in British Honduras, Mrs. Alford relates, "The first thing I did was start a chicken project. When we arrived, the people's diet consisted mainly of rice and beans, beans and rice. Their protein intake was practically nil. We started with 1,400 baby chicks and formed a cooperative. Now they not only have enough to feed themselves but to export as well."

Peace Corps volunteers must be U.S. citizens; if married, preferably able to volunteer together; possess skills or education that will qualify them to work in available projects; and be medically qualified.

Transportation to and from the country in which you will be volunteering is provided, and you get 12 to 15 weeks training there. A monthly allowance covers daily living. Upon return, a readjustment stipend based on $75 for each month served is paid. The length of service is 24 to 27 months.

RSVP (Retired Senior Volunteer Program)

RSVP offers retired people 60 and over opportunities to serve in their communities. Using operating funds provided by the federal government, it refers volunteers to several hundred community service programs throughout the country. Volunteers are provided with transportation and meals or reim-

---

ACTION Recruiting Offices

WESTERN REGION
(continued)

1333 Westward Blvd.
Los Angeles, Calif. 90024

Federal Bldg., Room 363
511 NW Broadway
Portland, Ore. 97209

1068 16th St.
San Diego, Calif. 92101

1601 2nd Ave.
Seattle, Wash. 98101

MIDWESTERN REGION

1 North Wacker Drive
Room 322
Chicago, Ill. 60606

U.S. Post Office and
Courthouse Bldg.
Room 903-B
Cincinnati, O. 45202

Century Bldg., Room 644-1
36 S. Pennsylvania
Indianapolis, Ind. 46204

50 West Broad St.
Room 2650
Columbus, O. 43215

The only way to have a friend is to be a friend.

—Ralph Waldo Emerson
  1803–1882
  American poet and essayist

JOINING AND SHARING 9

Foster Grandparent Reverend James Johnston of Birmingham, Alabama shown here tutoring.

bursement for their expenses. Assignments are broad; they range from preschool guidance to assisting probation officers and driving school buses.

SCORE (Service Corps of Retired Executives)
Score brings retired business people with management expertise together with owners of small business and with community organizations that need management counseling. Though part of ACTION for budgetary, recruiting and communications aspects, SCORE is directed and administered by the Small Business Administration. Borrowers from SBA are among those who may receive counseling from SCORE volunteers.

Volunteering

The volunteers are organized into chapters, which number over 200. In addition to offering individual counseling, many chapters sponsor business workshops and seminars.

SCORE volunteers are reimbursed for out-of-pocket expenses, such as transportation costs.

Senior Companion Program

The Senior Companion Program is the newest that ACTION offers involving older Americans. Its purpose is to provide community-service opportunities to low-income persons over 60 for the benefit of others who need an extra measure of help in their daily living at home or in nursing homes and other institutions.

Volunteers receive annual stipends, thus aiding their own finances.

Foster Grandparent Program

Working in institutions for the mentally retarded, the emotionally disturbed, the physically handicapped, the dependent and the neglected, over 4,000 older Americans are providing needy children with friendship and personal attention frequently lacking in their own environments.

Low-income people over 65 are eligible to serve.

Before entering service, Foster Grandparents receive 40 hours of orientation in the work for which they have volunteered. Then they are assigned to an institution—a hospital, a day-care center, for example—to work with the staff, but with specific assignments to two foster grandchildren.

The program requires that the participant devote four hours a day, five days a week, dividing the time between two children. Although they may change diapers or feed their "grandchildren," the relationship goes well beyond, often to the formation of intimate relationships. A Foster Grandparent receives an annual stipend of $1,670, is reimbursed for transportation costs, has lunch on working days, and is given a complete physical examination at the beginning of each year.

The number of Foster Grandparents depends on the federal budget. In some regions, there are waiting lists.

For additional information on any of the volunteer agencies or for applications, contact the nearest ACTION Recruiting Office listed, or write, ACTION Washington, D.C. 20525. (When writing, precede address by ACTION Recruiting Office.)

JOINING AND SHARING 9

Foster Grandparent W.L. Showman of Winfield, Kansas helps build a dollhouse.

AMERICAN AGING ASSOCIATION

This relatively new association is engaged in encouraging research on why and how we age, with the central purpose of discovering more practical means for increasing our healthy productive life spans.

The organization conducts symposia and issues a newsletter, **Age News**, four times a year.

Membership is open to professionals in aging and to the general public. Regular dues are $5 a year; people over 65 may join at $2 a year.

For additional information:
*American Aging Association
c/o Denham Harman
University of Nebraska Medical Center
Omaha, Neb. 68105*

AMERICAN GERIATRICS SOCIETY

The society, with approximately 18,000 members, is a professional organization of medical people in the field of aging.

For additional information:
*American Geriatrics Society
10 Columbus Circle
New York, N.Y. 10019*

Professional organizations concerned with aging

THE NATIONAL COUNCIL ON THE AGING

The council is a private, nonprofit organization serving as a central resource for planning, information, technical consultation and materials on older people. It is one of the major professional organizations for practitioners in the field of aging.

Some of the programs and services of NCOA include:

- *Training and technical assistance*: Provides guidance and model programs for public and private agencies. Evaluates and develops training materials and programs and organizes workshops for professionals.
- *Institute of Industrial Gerontology*: Provides services for and assistance to labor, government agencies and universities on the problems and potentials of workers as they age.
- *National Institute of Senior Centers* (See SENIOR CENTERS in this chapter)
- *Public policy:* Monitors legislation, presents testimony and disseminates information on the aging to Congress, the administration and the public.
- *Original research:*
- *Library:* Contains comprehensive collection of books and materials on aging.
- *Publications:* Produces and publishes a variety of special books and periodicals, including the bimonthly **Perspective on Aging**; the quarterly **Industrial Gerontology**; **Memo**, the newsletter of the National Institute of Senior Centers; **Older Worker Specialist Newsletter**; and **Newsletter of the National Voluntary Organizations for Independent Living for the Aged**.
- *National Voluntary Organizations for Independent Living for the Aged*: With a membership of 154 organizations, NVOILA oversees the implementation of Operation Independence, designed to stimulate voluntary agencies in developing community alternatives to nursing homes.
- *The Center for Older Americans and the Arts*: A clearinghouse of ideas and program information. Offers technical assistance and consultation to arts managers, practitioners in aging, and other groups and individuals interested in developing arts programs with older persons.
- *National Media Resource Center on Aging* (See COMMUNICATING)

For additional information:

*The National Council on the Aging
Suite 504
1828 L St. NW
Washington, D.C. 20036*

NATIONAL CAUCUS ON THE BLACK AGED

NCBA, a relatively new organization, specializes in the problems of the black older person. Working in conjunction with the caucus is the National Center on the Black Aged, which offers assistance and consultation to professionals working with the elderly.

For additional information:
*The National Caucus on the Black Aged/National Center on the Black Aged
1725 DeSales St. NW
Washington, D.C. 20036*

INTERNATIONAL FEDERATION ON AGEING

The International Federation on Ageing was created in 1973 to exchange information for people working in the field and to serve as an advocate before regional and international organizations that establish policy affecting the world's elderly population. Membership includes voluntary organizations that either provide services for the aging or represent their interests.

IFA currently has 20 member organizations from 12 countries. A quarterly newsletter, **Ageing International**, published in English, French and German editions, gives news of research, services and other developments concerning aging around the world. Subscriptions are $5 a year.

For Newsletter subscriptions or other information, write:

*International Federation on Ageing
Suite 690
1909 K St. NW
Washington, D.C. 20049*

JOINING AND SHARING 9

THE GERONTOLOGICAL SOCIETY

The society, with approximately 2,800 members, is a professional association of physicians and others concerned with the aging process. It is especially active in promoting research and in contributing professional findings to legislative bodies.

For additional information:
*The Gerontological Society
1 Dupont Circle
Washington, D.C. 20036*

INVEST YOURSELF

This catalogue of volunteer service opportunities is published annually by the Commission on Voluntary Service and Action. Listings include several hundred specific projects, with approximately 26,000 opportunities. The commission also publishes a newsletter five times a year. The catalogue is $2 and the newsletter $2.50 for five issues.

Write:
*Commission on Voluntary Service and Action
Room 1700 A
475 Riverside Drive
New York, N.Y. 10027*

You will find that the mere resolve not to be useless, and the honest desire to help other people, will improve yourself.

—John Ruskin, 1819–1900
English essayist, critic and social reformer

COMMUNICATING 10

IDEAS, INFORMATION . . . AND HUMAN CONTACT

Though today we live longer, we live more alone as families and individuals become more mobile and tend to change residence. At the same time we have made marvelous strides in the technology of communication. The long-distance phone call is an affordable joy for those with families in other places. No matter how brief the conversation, we are together. Television brings the world into the living room—with entertainment, education, religion, news. The printed word has never been more available, with the new world of paperback books and the growth of public libraries bringing the wealth of magazines, newspapers and books together in one communal setting.

Communicating with others does not happen automatically, however. Frequently we have to work at it, searching out the best sources, and the best approaches.

Communicating need not cost money. In your own community, the library is probably the best resource. And today books are but the library centerpiece as closed-circuit television and video tapes add new elements.

U.S. GOVERNMENT PRINTING OFFICE

Some of the best low-cost information comes from the federal government. From nutrition booklets to consumer hints, USGPO—the U.S. Government Printing Office—distributes millions of publications each year.

Finding out what is available—and obtaining it—is frequently a challenge. Considering the volume of requests, don't expect personal service. And don't expect delivery in less than six weeks, though there are signs that service may improve. But you may receive some of the best informational values available if you follow these basic tips:

☐ Make certain you have the correct title and stock number

☐ Enclose a check or money order for the correct price

☐ Unless you can visit one of the GPO book stores, address your request to:
  USGPO
  Washington, D.C. 20402

A nearby USGPO regional bookstore may be a pleasant and worthwhile place to visit. The bookstores have extensive displays of publications, including such topics as nutrition,

USGPO BOOKSTORES

Room 102A, 2121 Bldg.
2121 8th Ave. N
Birmingham, Ala. 35203

Room 1015
Federal Office Bldg.
300 North Los Angeles St.
Los Angeles, Calif. 90012

Room 1023, Federal Office Bldg.
450 Golden Gate Ave.
San Francisco, Calif. 94102

Room 1421 Federal Bldg.
1961 Stout St.
Denver, Colo. 80202

Pueblo Industrial Park
Pueblo, Colo. 81001

710 North Capitol St.
Washington, D.C. 20402

1776 Pennsylvania Ave. NW
Washington, D.C. 20547

14th & E Sts. NW,
Room 1605
Washington, D.C. 20230

21st & C Sts. NW
First floor
Washington, D.C. 20520

Room 158, Federal Bldg.
400 West Bay St.
Jacksonville, Fla. 32202

Room 100, Federal Bldg.
275 Peachtree St. NW
Atlanta, Ga. 30303

Room 1463
Everett McKinley Dirksen Bldg.
219 South Dearborn St.
Chicago, Ill. 60604

Government publications and resources

Room G25
John F. Kennedy Federal Bldg.
Sudbury St.
Boston, Mass. 02203

Patrick V. McNamara Federal Bldg.
Suite 160
477 Michigan Ave.
Detroit, Mich. 48226

Room 144 Federal Office Bldg.
601 East 12th St.
Kansas City, Mo. 64106

Room 110
26 Federal Plaza
New York, N.Y. 10007

Federal Office Bldg.
201 Cleveland Ave. SW
Canton, O. 44702

1st Floor, Federal Office Bldg.
1240 East 9th St.
Cleveland O. 44114

Room 1214, Federal Office Bldg.
600 Arch St.
Philadelphia, Pa. 19106

Room 1C46, Federal Bldg.
U.S. Courthouse
1100 Commerce St.
Dallas, Tex. 75202

45 College Center
9319 Gulf Freeway
Houston, Tex. 77017

Room 194, Federal Office Bldg.
915 Second Ave.
Seattle, Wash. 98104

Room 190, Federal Bldg.
519 East Wisconsin Ave.
Milwaukee, Wis. 53202

KEEP YOUR MIND WINDING

Read Government Publications

consumer interests, the national parks and travel in other countries. Should you be interested in data on pending legislation or applications for contracts or grants, official government papers, including the Federal Register, are available.

A monthly catalogue of publications of interest to the general public is mailed free on request. In Pueblo, Colo., there is a GPO division that distributes publications on consumer affairs. It publishes its own catalogue; the current listing contains some 200 titles, many also available from the main GPO locations.

USGPO is not a publisher, but a printer and distributor. It handles only publications of other government agencies. Occasionally you will find that you or someone you know has been fortunate enough to obtain a copy of a publication at no cost directly from one of the agencies. Generally, however, the publications are obtained through the printing office at nominal cost. They are a great value.

Be persistent, clear, and patient—and your efforts with USGPO will be rewarded.

You may notice from time to time that a commercial publisher has reprinted one or several government pamphlets already distributed by USGPO. This is perfectly legal, since the material is in the public domain and not copyrighted. You may find that the commercial edition is more attractive. Because it is in regular bookstores, you can know beforehand what you are buying without going to a GPO bookstore. Besides, the publisher may have combined several pamphlets on the same theme, thus giving you a more economical purchase.

COMMUNICATING 10

FEDERAL INFORMATION CENTERS

Have you ever tried to get an answer to a simple question about our huge federal government and found yourself on a merry-go-round? Or, have you ever been a little unsure of the precise question you wanted to ask but knew the general problem? Everyone, at one time or another, needs information from the government—such as where to get a passport, how to apply for food stamps, find a list of National Parks, or get information on a particular program for older people.

The Federal Information Centers have been established to meet such needs. Operated jointly by the General Services Administration and the Civil Service Commission, the centers will answer your questions and direct you from a number of offices around the country, as listed.

ALABAMA
Birmingham: 322-8591 (this is a toll-free line to Atlanta)
Mobile: 438-1421 (this is a toll-free line to New Orleans)

ARIZONA
Phoenix: 261-3313
Tucson: 622-1511

ARKANSAS
Little Rock: 378-6177 (this is a toll-free line to Memphis)

CALIFORNIA
Los Angeles: 213/688-3800
Sacramento: 916/449-3344
San Diego: 714/293-6030
San Francisco: 415/556-6600
San Jose: 275-7422 (this is a toll-free line to San Francisco)

COLORADO
Colorado Springs: 471-9491 (this is a toll-free line to Denver)
Denver: 303/837-3602
Pueblo: 544-9523 (this is a toll-free line to Denver)

CONNECTICUT
Hartford: 527-2617 (this is a toll-free line to New York City)
New Haven: 624-4720 (this is a toll-free line to New York City

DISTRICT OF COLUMBIA
202/755-8660

FLORIDA
Fort Lauderdale: 522-8531 (this is a toll-free line to Miami)
Jacksonville: 354-4756 (this is a toll-free line to St. Petersburg)
St. Petersburg: 893-3495
Tampa: 229-7911 (this is a toll-free line to St. Petersburg)
West Palm Beach: 833-7566 (this is a toll-free line to Miami)

GEORGIA
Atlanta: 404/526-6891

HAWAII
Honolulu: 808/546-8620

ILLINOIS
Chicago: 312/353-4242

INDIANA
Indianapolis: 317/269-7373

IOWA
Des Moines: 282-9091 (this is toll-free line to Omaha)

Government publications and resources

FEDERAL INFORMATION CENTERS (continued)

KANSAS
Topeka: 232-7229 (this is a toll-free line to Kansas City, Mo.)
Wichita: 263-6931 (this is a toll-free line to Kansas City, Mo.)

KENTUCKY
Louisville: 502/582-6261

LOUISIANA
New Orleans: 504/589-6696

MARYLAND
Baltimore: 301/962-4980

MASSACHUSETTS
Boston: 617/223-7121

MICHIGAN
Detroit: 313/226-7016

MINNESOTA
Minneapolis: 612/725-2073

MISSOURI
Kansas City: 816/374-2466
St. Joseph: 233-8206 (this is a toll-free line to Kansas City, Mo.)
St. Louis: 314/425-4106

NEBRASKA
Omaha: 402/221-3353

NEW JERSEY
Newark: 201/645-3600
Trenton: 396-4400 (this is a toll-free line to Newark)

NEW MEXICO
Albuquerque: 505/766-3091
Santa Fe: 983-7743 (this is a toll-free line to Albuquerque)

NEW YORK
Albany: 463-4421 (this is a toll-free line to New York City)
Buffalo: 716/842-5770
New York City: 212/264-4464
Rochester: 546-5075 (this is a toll-free line to Buffalo)
Syracuse: 476-8545 (this is a toll-free line to Buffalo)

NORTH CAROLINA
Charlotte: 376-3600 (this is a toll-free line to Atlanta)

OHIO
Akron: 375-5475 (this is a toll-free line to Cleveland)
Cincinnati: 513/684-2801
Cleveland: 216/522-4040
Columbus: 221-1014 (this is a toll-free line to Cincinnati)
Dayton: 223-7377 (this is a toll-free line to Cincinnati)
Toledo: 244-8625 (this is a toll-free line to Cleveland)

OKLAHOMA
Oklahoma City: 405/231-4868
Tulsa: 584-4193 (this is a toll-free line to Oklahoma City)

OREGON
Portland: 503/221-2222

PENNSYLVANIA
Philadelphia: 215/597-7042
Pittsburgh: 412/644-3456
Scranton: 346-7081 (this is a toll-free line to Philadelphia)

RHODE ISLAND
Providence: 331-5565 (this is a toll-free line to Boston)

TENNESSEE
Chattanooga: 265-8231 (this is a toll-free line to Memphis)
Memphis: 901/534-3285

TEXAS
Austin: 472-5494 (this is a toll-free line to Houston)
Dallas: 749-2131 (this is a toll-free line to Fort Worth)
Fort Worth: 817/334-3624
Houston: 713/226-5711
San Antonio: 224-4471 (this is a toll-free line to Houston)

UTAH
Ogden: 399-1347 (this is a toll-free line to Salt Lake City)
Salt Lake City: 801/524-5353

WASHINGTON
Seattle: 206/442-0570
Tacoma: 383-5230 (this is a toll-free line to Seattle)

WISCONSIN
Milwaukee: (this is a toll-free line to Chicago)

If you prefer writing or are not within dialing distance of a Federal Information Center, write:

Federal Information Center
General Services Administration
Washington, D.C. 20405

COMMUNICATING   10

MAGAZINES

Magazines are marvelous sources of ideas, information and entertainment. Whether you buy them at the newsstand, receive them in the mail, share them with a friend or read them at the library, they are a great help in countless ways. We have selected several which we believe have special merit for older people. Some of them have always been familiar to you, for they are publications which know no age barriers. They may, however, be read differently by you at this stage of life. Others are specifically geared to older people. Subscriptions are frequently offered at considerable savings. Watch newspaper ads, mail offers and coupons in the magazines; you often will save a great deal.

Good Old Days

This is pure fun! The publication takes the readers for a nostalgic trip back to the "good old days." Whether or not they really *were* is an individual interpretation, but the magazine is filled with popular features from earlier in the century, including comics, advertisements and photos. The same publisher also puts out four seasonal issues.
Newsstand Price: 60¢
Subscription: $4/year (11 issues)

Good Old Days
Box 428
Seabrook, N.H. 03874

A LETTER FROM THE WHITE HOUSE

As longevity increases, many people are celebrating more of the important milestones. When properly advised, the President will send a special greeting on certain occasions:

- ☐ A birthday card with the President's official seal to people celebrating their 80th through 100th birthday
- ☐ A letter of congratulations with the President's personal signature to people celebrating their 101st or later birthdays
- ☐ A wedding anniversary card to couples celebrating their 50th through 69th anniversaries
- ☐ A personally signed letter to couples celebrating their 70th or greater anniversaries

Requests for greetings should be received at the White House 30 days in advance and must contain the full names, address, date and number of the birthday or anniversary.

Write to:
Mrs. Barbara Flynn
Room 17
Old Executive Office Bldg.
Washington, D.C. 20500

GRIT: "America's Greatest Family Newspaper"

A good "old-fashioned" newspaper is hard to find these days, but **Grit** seems to be one answer. Now in its 97th year of publication, this weekly tabloid sells for the newsstand price of 25¢. Not really a newspaper nor a scandal sheet, it is more a magazine published in newspaper format. A typical issue runs to 34 pages, with frequent items of interest to older people. Poetry, profiles of interesting personalities, both famous and not, features, philosophical inserts, cooking hints and outdoor news make for a well-edited, bright weekly. Available on some newsstands
Subscription: $4.75/half year
$9/year
$17/two years

Grit Publishing Company
Williamsport, Pa. 17701

Mature Years

Published by the United Methodist Church, this quarterly magazine deals with items of interest to older persons and with general features, health hints and articles of a religious nature. Subscription only: $3/year.

Mature Years
United Methodist Church
201 Eighth Ave. South
Nashville, Tenn. 37202

The happy spirit of a wedding anniversary as captured in this 1920's painting by Douglas Crockwell

COMMUNICATING 10

Retirement Living

This is one of the few commercial magazines—if not the only one—devoted to the interests of retired people exclusively. It is a monthly publication covering a broad range of subjects for older people, from finances to leisure to legislative news.
Subscription only: $7.95/year

Retirement Living
99 Garden St.
Marion, O. 43302

The magazine also publishes several retirement planning and adjustment guides, which are listed separately in various chapters of this book. The entire series, covering leisure, finance, the home, legal matters and health, may be obtained in kit form for $7.50 to subscribers to the magazine or $10 to nonsubscribers. The pamphlets are also available separately. Quantity discounts are offered to groups or to businesses that wish to use this material to help retiring employees.

Aging Tomorrow

This bimonthly newsletter gives a diversity of information on aging, including book reviews, new products, food hints and insights into people and experiences.
Subscription only: $6/year

Aging Tomorrow
Box 617-S
Cathedral Station
New York, N.Y. 10025

Second Spring

The purpose of this bimonthly is to create a positive and uplifting attitude among older persons. Articles deal with consumer affairs, productive people, nostalgia, and events in the San Francisco Bay area. (With the exception of those few latter pages, the magazine is broad enough for a national readership.)
Subscription only: $4/year

Second Spring Adult
Benevolent Association
121 Golden Gate Ave.
San Francisco, Calif. 94102

Modern Maturity

Each member of the American Association of Retired Persons receives this bimonthly magazine covering a broad variety of general features sharing information and philosophy.
Included with $3 annual membership

American Association of Retired Persons
215 Long Beach Blvd.
P.O. Box 2400
Long Beach, Calif. 90801

NRTA Journal

Issued bimonthly, this magazine is part of the annual membership in the National Retired Teachers Association. Features include a broad variety of articles of interest to the retired person—and the retired teacher in particular. Throughout each issue there is a pervasive atmosphere of experience and philosophy sharing.
Included with $3 annual membership

National Retired Teachers Association
215 Long Beach Blvd.
P.O. Box 2400
Long Beach, Calif. 90801

Magazines

Senior Power

This magazine, published six times a year, has a general religious theme throughout, in addition to news and hints and profiles of productive older people.
Subscription only: $2/per year.

*Senior Power
500 North Murray Road
Lee's Summit, Mo. 64063*

Aging

The Administration on Aging publishes its own monthly magazine. It features developments in the social-service aspects of aging. It is particularly useful if you are in a leadership position.
Subscription only: $5.05/year

*USGPO
Washington, D.C.*

Changing Times

Keeping up with the changing times is this monthly magazine's goal, as it covers dozens of areas of interest to daily life: money, gardening, self-reliance, shopping, consumerism.
Newsstand price: $1
Subscription: $9/year

*Changing Times
1729 H St. NW
Washington, D.C. 20006*

Dynamic Maturity

This is the official publication of AIM—Action for Independent Maturity—the retirement-preparation division of AARP-NRTA. The magazine, focused on preparation for retirement, includes articles on a broad variety of related concerns. Included with $3 annual membership

*Action for Independent Maturity
215 Long Beach Blvd.
P.O. Box 2400
Long Beach, Calif. 90801*

Yankee

A monthly magazine with a rather traditional and general approach, each issue has articles geared toward the New England lifestyle and traditions. It is heavy with advertisements for crafts and other items, as well as a popular "swappers" column.
Newsstand price: 75¢
Subscription: $7/year

*Yankee
Dublin, N.H. 03444*

Southern Living

Whether you live in the South or think sunny thoughts, this large magazine is for you. The monthly contents include regular features in the areas of travel and recreation, homes, gardening, food and entertaining.
Newsstand price: $1
Subscription: $10/year

*Southern Living
Box 523
Birmingham, Ala. 35201*

Sunset

This regional monthly magazine, like *Southern Living*, reflects the sunny climate in which it is published. It covers such areas as decorating and craft ideas, food and entertaining, homes, travel and gardening.
Newsstand price: 75¢
Subscription: $8/year for subscribers living in California, Washington, Arizona, Nevada, Idaho, Utah, Hawaii and Alaska. Subscriptions to other states are $11/year.

*Sunset
Willow and Middlefield Roads
Menlo Park, Calif. 94025*

COMMUNICATING 10

Handyman

This monthly should appeal to some women as well as men. It covers home maintenance and improvements, projects, gardening questions and answers, and the latest in new books and booklets on home repairs and improvements.
Newsstand price: 95¢
Subscription: $8.50/year

*The Handyman
235 East 45th St.
New York, N.Y. 10017*

Handy Andy

This pocket-size magazine covers a broad range of do-it-yourself information 10 months a year, with particular emphasis on home maintenance and special decorating projects.
Newsstand price: 95¢
Subscription: $7.95

*Handy Andy
80 New Bridge Road
Bergenfield, N.J. 07621*

Popular Mechanics

News of home workshops, crafts, photography, electronics, how-to projects. All these categories are covered in this monthly.
Newsstand price: 75¢
Subscription: $7/year

*Popular Mechanics
224 West 57th St.
New York, N.Y. 10019*

Money

Time-Life has done it again—a consumer magazine covering money management and just about everything to do with finances and daily living.
Newsstand price: $1
Subscription: $9.75/year

*Money
541 North Fairbanks Court
Chicago, Ill. 60611*

Craft Horizons

This bimonthly magazine, published by the American Crafts Council, covers contemporary craft trends, techniques, news of exhibitions, reviews of books and general features.
 Included with the $18 annual membership in the American Crafts Council.

*American Crafts Council
44 West 53rd St.
New York, N.Y. 10019*

Prime Time

This bimonthly is issued by and for older women. In addition to general features, there are book reviews and articles on problems and opportunities.
Subscription only: $7/year.

*Prime Time
420 West 46th St.
New York, N.Y. 10036*

Family Health

Published monthly, this magazine includes news and features on health developments, food and nutrition and scientific information as it relates to health.
Newsstand price: 75¢
Subscription: $5.97/year

*Family Health
149 Fifth Ave.
New York, N.Y. 10010*

The Mother Earth News

This bimonthly magazine has become the "bible" for self-reliant, basic living. Oriented toward nature and natural foods, it has a wealth of ideas for saving by doing for oneself and enjoying the process.
Newsstand price: $2
Subscription: $10/year

*The Mother Earth News
P.O. Box 70
Hendersonville, N.C. 28739*

Magazines

Better Homes and Gardens

This long-popular monthly covers more than the surface of the home and the garden; it goes more deeply, with features on money, health, food, travel and decorating.
Newsstand price: 75¢
Subscription: $8/year

*Better Homes and Gardens
Meredith Bldg.
1716 Locust St.
Des Moines, Iowa 50336*

House and Garden

Like the other "decorating" magazines, this goes well beyond the initial subjects and covers features on wine and food, beauty, health and travel. Monthly.
Newsstand price: $1
Subscription: $10

*House and Garden
350 Madison Ave.
New York, N.Y. 10017*

House Beautiful

This monthly includes features on crafts, shopping and food as well as decorating.
Newsstand price: $1
Subscription: $10/year

*House Beautiful
717 Fifth Ave.
New York, N.Y. 10022*

Plants Alive

Filled monthly with informative features on raising and selling plants and decorating your home with them.
Newsstand price: $1
Subscription: $9/year

*Plants Alive
5509 First Ave. South
Seattle, Wash. 98108*

Ladies' Home Journal

This veritable institution still provides, in monthly form, general features, fiction, and excellent articles on food, home sewing, health, and crafts—all with economy in mind.
Newsstand price: 75¢
Subscription: $5.94/year

*Ladies' Home Journal
641 Lexington Ave.
New York, N.Y. 10022*

McCall's

This monthly magazine includes, as always, general articles, fiction and features on health, beauty, food and home management.
Newsstand price: 75¢
Subscription: $6.95/year

*McCall's
230 Park Ave.
New York, N.Y. 10017*

COMMUNICATING   10

READING IN LARGE PRINT

There is a great deal available today for those who find it more comfortable reading large print than small. Here are several sources, both commercial and noncommercial:

National Association for Visually Handicapped
The nonprofit NAVH supplies large-type reading materials to people of all ages. Where reimbursement for material not to be returned is possible, it suggests $5 a volume, which covers average production costs, but payment is not required. Books to be returned may be borrowed without charge. Through the use of the "free matter for the blind" label, books are mailed without postal fees. Some of the books distributed have been reproduced by NAVH, while others are commercial products. Several catalogues are issued. The selections include a very broad array, with such titles as **Born Free**, **Portrait of Jennie**, **The Spy Who Came in From the Cold**, **The French Lieutenant's Woman**, **The Autobiography of Miss Jane Pittman** and **Love Story**. The lists are frequently changed with addition of current books as well as fiction classics and nonfiction.

Several publishers are engaged in reproducing either their own books into large type or serve as specialists for this service.

This is regular size print used in most news publications. To read it is a strain for people who have poor vision.

This is the size print used in the Large Type Weekly. See how much easier it is to read.

To ease handicaps

NAVH operates an information clearinghouse for large-type reading matter and can supply information or provide references to other sources.

NAVH also has several free publications which give useful background and help for the visually impaired:

- **Guide to Visual Aids and Illumination**. This booklet describes lighting conditions and devices for making the most of one's eyesight.
- **Seeing Clearly**. This bimonthly newsletter in large type gives news of developments in materials to aid those with visual impairments and has regular features describing new products and exchanging ideas and recipes. There is even a crossword puzzle. Write:

National Association for Visually Handicapped
305 East 24th St.
New York, N.Y. 10010

The Bible
The Bible is available for sale in several editions:

- **The Holy Bible**, King James Protestant Text, set in 15-point type, $14.98
Write:

Consolidated Book Publishers
1727 S. Indiana Ave.
Chicago, Ill. 60616

- **The New Testament of the Jerusalem Bible**, set in 20-point type, $12.95
Write:

Doubleday and Co., Inc.
501 Franklin Ave.
Garden City, N.Y. 11530

The Reader's Digest Large-Type Edition
Each month, more than half of the articles appearing in the **Digest** are reproduced in a special nonprofit edition in type twice the standard magazine size. The edition is 6" x 9" and contains 348 pages. An annual subscription costs $16.95. Write:

Ellen Parker
Reader's Digest
Pleasantville, N.Y. 10570

The New York Times Large-Type Weekly
This publication incorporates material from the Sunday edition of the newspaper, including a review of the week's major news events, columns, articles on business, the arts, entertainment, sports and family living, the crossword puzzle and TV highlights. **The Times** is considered a national newspaper, particularly in the scope of its Sunday edition.

A three-month subscription normally costs $11, but frequently new subscribers are offered discounts. Write:

The New York Times
Large-Type Weekly
P.O. Box 2570
Boulder, Colo. 80302

Large Type Crosswords The New York Times
crossword puzzles, edited by Margaret Farrar, are available in a book containing 50 puzzles with answers. $2.95.

Education and Library Department
Simon and Schuster, Inc.
1 West 39th St.
New York, N.Y. 10018

Publishers of Large-Type Reprints
Several commercial publishers of large-type reprints send catalogues on request:

G.K. Hall and Co.
70 Lincoln St.
Boston, Mass. 02111

Viking Press
625 Madison Ave.
New York, N.Y. 10022

Lanewood Press, Inc.
89 Franklin St.
Boston, Mass. 02110

Keith Jennison Large Type Editions
730 Fifth Ave.
New York, N.Y. 10019

Ulverscroft Large Print Books
Oscar Stiskin, U.S. Agent
Stamford, Conn. 06905

(Ulverscroft's distribution is mainly to libraries and institutions, though it will fill individual orders.)

G.K. Hall and Co. has a new venture, the Large Print Book Club. It offers members at least 30% off the regular prices. There are no minimum purchase requirements, and books are not sent unless ordered. Book offerings are described in **The Large Print Review**, which members receive. Write:

The Large Print Book Club
G. K. Hall and Co.
70 Lincoln St.
Boston, Mass. 02111

COMMUNICATING 10

SERVICES FOR SPECIAL NEEDS... FROM THE TELEPHONE COMPANY

The Bell System has a tradition of helping persons with physical impairments to communicate. Alexander Graham Bell was himself a teacher of the deaf. Many of the services in this booklet [Services for Special Needs] were specially developed by the Bell System to help those with hearing, sight, speech, or motion impairments. Standard services, such as the speakerphone and repertory dialers, meet special needs because of their design.

If you have a problem using the telephone, perhaps one of these services will solve it. Or we may be able to arrange a special combination of services.

The booklet is available at your local telephone company office.

To ease handicaps

THE LIBRARY OF CONGRESS

The huge Library of Congress has many services which it can make available to the blind and visually handicapped, bringing them the joys of reading despite their handicaps.

The library's Division for the Blind and Physically Handicapped regularly publishes the free reference circular, **Reading Materials in Large Type**, that provides sources on and descriptions of books for the blind and physically handicapped. Much material is distributed through the mail.

The free reference circular, **Volunteers Who Produce Books, Braille, Large Type Books,** is a geographical directory.

Write:
*The Division for the Blind and Physically Handicapped
Library of Congress
Washington, D.C. 20542*

TELETYPEWRITERS FOR THE DEAF

Until the Teletypewriter for the Deaf was invented in 1964, profoundly deaf people could not communicate via the telephone. This device using a typewriter keyboard makes it possible. Calls are placed through regular phone lines. Approximately 10,000 such devices are now in operation; over 400 are in schools, libraries and organizations serving the deaf.

For further information on the device and costs, contact:

*Teletypewriters for the Deaf, Inc.
P.O. Box 28332
Washington, D.C. 20013*

TALKING BOOKS

Your local library generally will have access to "talking books"—spoken recordings made by qualified volunteers. **Newsweek** magazine and the **Reader's Digest** are regularly issued in this form. Further information can be obtained from:

*Magazine Department
American Printing House for the Blind
P.O. Box 6435
Louisville, Ky. 40206*

HOWE PRESS OF THE PERKINS SCHOOL FOR THE BLIND

More than ever, blind people of all ages can find help in communicating through the broader range of material which has been converted into Braille and through new devices. For a complete listing of the variety of Howe items and books, write:

*Howe Press of the Perkins School for the Blind
Watertown, Mass. 02172*

THE BANKS POCKET BRAILLE WRITER

The late Dr. Alfred E. Banks of San Diego, blinded in World War I, invented the simple-to-operate, pocket-size Braille Writer. He turned the device over to the Lions Club of San Diego without retaining any profit rights for himself, provided that it be made available to all blind people at a cost of not more than $5. The writers actually cost $35 and are purchased individually by a Lions Club for presentation to a blind person who requests one. Your local Lions Club can assist in applying.

XAVIER SOCIETY FOR THE BLIND

The society provides an extensive lending library of Catholic and religious books in Braille. They are available on loan by mail for one month at no cost to the borrower.

For a catalogue, write:

*Xavier Society for the Blind
154 East 23rd St.
New York, N.Y. 10010*

COMMUNICATING 10

BE OK SELF-HELP AIDS

Some communicating aids from Fred Sammons:

Portable Phone Amplifier
Speaking and hearing on the phone when you have a hearing loss can be very frustrating at both ends of the conversation. This device attaches quickly and securely to any phone with an elastic band. Fingertip on/off volume control increases sound up to five times. The amplifier is battery operated and can be carried in pocket or purse.
Catalogue #BK-4119 $15.15

Drop-In Phone Amplifier
This phone amplifier is ideally suited for individuals who have difficulty holding the receiver to the ear—and who require louder reception or wish to share the conversation with others in the room. The solid-state appliance amplifies voices of all parties conversing on the phone. Volume is adjustable.
Catalogue #BK-41112 $24.39

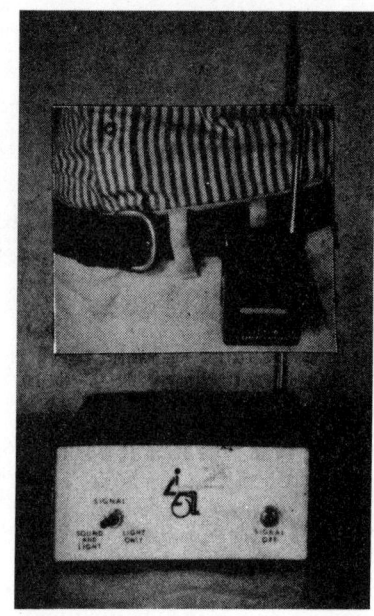

Little Companion Emergency Paging System
This system allows the person living alone to signal a neighbor up to four or five houses away when emergency aid is needed. It operates on a special citizens'-band frequency to transmit the signal from a cigarette-pack-size transmitter to an electrically powered receiver that flashes and beeps in response. Not for use in or near high-rise buildings.
Catalogue #BK-6357 $150

Reclining Viewer
Nothing seems so boring as being flat on your back—but sometimes it can't be helped. This device, made of lightweight, shatter-resistant plastic, has a cutout for the nose and can fit over eyeglasses. A 5½"-long mirror reflects the image and allows you to read or watch television in a reclining position. Can be cleaned easily with soap and water.
Catalogue #4089 $4.95

Order from:
*Fred Sammons, Inc.
Box 32
Brookfield, Ill. 60513*

GUIDELINES FOR A TELEPHONE REASSURANCE SERVICE

A telephone reassurance service is an organized volunteer program that calls people who live alone to check on their well-being. If the telephone is not answered at the appointed time, a neighbor, nurse, policeman or other designated person is dispatched to the residence.

This booklet of guidelines, reflecting 12 years of experience with a Michigan service, has been published

To ease handicaps
Helping those alone to keep in touch

by the Administration on Aging. This direct communication method is another of the ways to help people live alone at home more comfortably, and for older people to assist one another.

This booklet gives the interesting background of telephone reassurance and step-by-step instructions.

Free
Catalog #OHD 75-20200
USGPO
Washington, D.C. 20402

PHONE-CARE

Phone-Care is a device which enables persons living alone to signal for help when in trouble. The device consists of two units. The base unit, resting on the telephone, is set by the individual to activate a warning sound and flashing light at prescribed intervals. If the individual is well, he or she simply shuts the signal off manually. If the signal is not shut off after seven minutes, the unit will automatically place a prerecorded phone call for help to four or five previously chosen people. If the first number does not answer or is busy, the device automatically switches to the second and so on until there is an answer.

The other unit is a remote-control device so small it can be worn around the neck or carried in the pocket. It acts the same way as the phone-base system when the wearer is outside near the home.

The cost is $695, including installation.

Write:
National Phone Care, Inc.
3109 Hennepin Ave.
Minneapolis, Minn. 55408

LIFELINE

Lifeline is an electronic alarm system which can signal for help for the person alone in emergencies. The device, presently available only in the Boston area, consists of a timer and a coded beep transmitter connected to the telephone and emergency buttons which can be placed in any room. Wireless supplementary buttons can be attached to clothing.

When a button is pressed, the beeper sends a message to a central receiving station. From there, an operator calls for help according to prearranged instructions. If no one on the list responds, the police are then notified.

The device can signal help even if the person in trouble has not been able to press the button. The timer can be set so that if the person does not use the phone or at least lift the receiver within a prescribed interval—from one to 24 hours—the beeper will automatically call for help.

The service costs $75 for installation and $45 a month.

Write:
Lifeline Systems, Inc.
839 Beacon St.
Boston, Mass. 02215

EARLY ALERT PROGRAM

Early Alert is another example of enabling people in trouble to communicate. As part of a three-year experiment with the postal service in New York City, 10,000 older Manhattan and Bronx residents have their mailboxes marked with a red dot on the inside. If the mail carrier notes that such a box has not been emptied in two or three days, he reports to his supervisor, who notifies the coordinator of Early Alert. A designated relative or friend of the individual is then informed and help is dispatched either directly or through any of 1,200 participating agencies.

For further information on how the experiment is progressing, contact:

Mrs. Friedhield Milburn,
Director
Early Alert
250 Broadway
New York, N.Y. 10006

COMMUNICATING   10

STAMPS BY MAIL

Sending and receiving mail is one of the joys and necessities of everyday life. If you find it difficult getting to the post office, you can purchase stamps by mail and give your outgoing letters to the carrier when he calls.

The processing fee for stamps by mail is 40¢, in addition to the cost of the stamps. Ask your carrier to bring an order blank or pick one up next time you are in a post office.

LOTS OF MAIL

Some call it "junk mail," others welcome it.

Either way, we all receive a good deal of mail generated by those using mailing lists. If you want to be added to more lists, write to:

Direct Mail Marketing Association
6 East 43rd St.
New York, N.Y. 10017

If you want less of this type of mail, the association should be able to stop about 70% on your request.

If you are receiving mail that is pandering—or suggestive of "lower taste"—the local post office will stop it when you file the appropriate form. The central postal service, on the other hand, decides what is outright pornography and handles it according to rule.

CITIZEN BAND RADIOS

In the past year or two about six million hobbyists and serious users have acquired and installed CB radios. CB, basically a radiotelephone enabling you to communicate with other radios, can be an advantage if you are alone and need help not available by telephone. With CB, the person on the other end can be practically anywhere, in a car, in the garden, etc.

If you have special needs when you are alone, consider the possibilities of a CB radio. The models and prices vary. A good paperback reference is **The Official CB Book**, by Jon F. Thompson, published in 1976 and selling for $3.95.

THE NATIONAL MEDIA RESOURCE CENTER ON THE AGING

The Media Center represents a nationwide effort to develop greater public understanding of the diverse character of older persons and of their vast potential as a productive national resource. It tries to change the largely negative and inaccurate attitudes put forth by some of the communications media regarding older people and, through communication, to help older people form a positive view of themselves.

A good deal of the work of the center is accomplished through the existing programs of the National Council on the Aging (see JOINING AND SHARING chapter of this book), but it is also anxious to know of productive older people who can be examples to share with—and hopefully inspire—others. If you have interesting stories of such people or want additional information, write:

The National Media Resource Center on the Aging
National Council on the Aging
1828 L St. NW
Washington, D.C. 20036

SPREADING THE WORD . . .

Local government and volunteer agencies are providing more services than ever for older people. The big question is often how to spread the world. Concentrated and continuing media campaigns are part of the answer, but events are too. Consider, for example, the experience of Westchester County's **Senior Salute**. In one day, 4,000 older people came together to learn more

Helping those alone to keep in touch
Media resources

about the services available and to be entertained. As a result, many more people will now avail themselves of those services.
For more information, write:

Westchester County Office for the Aging
900 County Office Bldg.
Martine Ave.
White Plains, N.Y. 10601

OLD-TIME RADIO

Nostalgia is fun—and Grand Book, Inc., of New York has assembled a sizable catalogue of old-time radio programs on tapes, available for group or individual listening. This addition to the library of a senior center or organization can be in the form of audiotape cassettes, 8-track cartridges, or 7" open reels.

The selection, recorded from the originals, includes **Amos 'n' Andy**, the **Bob Hope Show**, **Edgar Bergen and Charlie McCarthy**, **Lux Radio Theatre**, **Fibber McGee and Molly**, and more.

The cassettes and 8-track tapes come in sets of two 90-minute tapes each at $12.95 the set. The open reels, running at 3¾ inches per second, cost $9.95 each.

A complete catalogue will be sent when a request is accompanied by a stamped, addressed envelope. Write:

Grand Book, Inc.
659 Grand St.
Brooklyn, N.Y. 11211

FREE LOAN FILMS... FROM ASSOCIATION-STERLING FILMS

If your group, small or large, can use films for information or stimulating discussion, Association-Sterling Films is in the business of providing them at no charge. Costs are borne by the producers and distributors, frequently manufacturers, government agencies and trade associations with a story to tell. The films rarely are commercial except for occasional references to products. They cover a wide range of subjects, including art, conservation, investment, health and safety, travel and community interests.

Your only obligation is to treat the film with care, return it promptly and pay the return postage.

All films are 16mm, in color and with sound.

Request the catalogue through the main office (below), which provides a list of the regional offices through which the films are distributed.

Association-Sterling Films
866 Third Avenue
New York, N.Y. 10022

THE NATIONAL RETIREMENT SHOW

If you are looking for an array of exhibits on retirement—from housing to leisure—a visit to the National Retirement Show should meet your needs. Set up like a convention exhibit, the show was organized twice in 1976 and will be scheduled again in major cities. If you would like to attend a future show, write:

The National Retirement Show Company
7th Floor West
527 Madison Ave.
New York, N.Y. 10022

COMMUNICATING   10

And some call it memories. In this 1920's painting by Douglas Crockwell, we are reminded of the lovely moments we cherish.

SOME CALL IT ORAL HISTORY

The modern and inexpensive audiocassette recorder suggests important uses.

Consider the possibilities, for example, of sitting down and recording—for your children and grandchildren, for today and tomorrow— some of your favorite thoughts . . . stories from your own childhood, something of the roots of the family, some of your own philosophies of life. In a sense, it can become your own precious talking memoir, sure to be a best-seller in the family.

Consider, too, how easy and personal an audiocassette "letter" to friends and relatives can be.

The tapes are erasable, the machines easy to operate and quite inexpensive, with good ones available in the $50–$150 price range.

History
Stories for children

STORIES AND POEMS TO READ TO YOUR GRANDCHILDREN
By Irma M. Kotler
Prince Communications,
415 Lexington Ave.
New York, N.Y. 10017

There is no scarcity of stories to read to grandchildren, and it is one of the distinct pleasures of being an older person. We do want to mention this very special collection not too many people have heard of—it is a delight. Written in a fashion reminiscent of the way stories were written when you were young, this book, printed in large type, with its talking animals, magic pencils and boys and girls, is meant to be read aloud.

WHEN YOU READ TO YOUNG CHILDREN

The pleasures of being a grandparent, aunt, uncle or volunteer include many hours of storytelling. A great deal of children's literature, however, contains negative or inaccurate stereotypes of what older people are like.

Dr. Thomas Ansello, associate director of the University of Maryland's Center on Aging, who recently completed a study documenting these stereotypes, has found some books that give a well-rounded, generally favorable and accurate portrayal of older people.

His list of recommendations includes:

Aaron and the Green Mountain Boys, by Patricia Gauch, Coward, McCann and Geoghegan, 1972, $4.69
Across the Meadow, by Ben Schecter, Doubleday
Angry Moon, by William Sleater, Little, Brown, 1970, $6.95
*The Big World and the Little House, by Ruth Krauss, Harper and Row, 1956
Fish for Supper, by M. B. Goffstein, Dial, 1976 $4.95
Grandpa, by Barbara Borack, Harper and Row, 1967, $4.95
Grandpa's Farm, by James Flora, Harcourt Brace Jovanovich, 1965, $6.95
*Jim and the Beanstalk, by Raymond Briggs, Coward, McCann and Geoghegan, 1970
Mandy's Grandmother, by Liesel Skorpen, Dial, 1975, $4.95
My Grandson Lew, by Charlotte Zolotow, Harper and Row, 1974, $4.95
A Story, A Story, by Gail Haley, Atheneum, 1970, $5.95
Tell Me a Mitzi, by Lore Segal, Farrar, Straus and Giroux, 1970, $4.95
William's Doll, by Charlotte Zolotow, Harper and Row, 1972, $4.95

*Generally out of print. We suggest you can find these, as well as the others, at your local public library.

RIGHTS AND LEGACIES 11

CLOSING HINTS

For over 200 years now, we have enjoyed and reconfirmed our rights as individuals in this country. But faced with some of the special problems of being older—or being a consumer, a member of a minority, a land owner, a tenant, etc.—we are confronted daily with problems, frustrations and threats.

Perhaps no stage of life is less prepared for than that final moment of passing. Much of what we have worked for and cherished during our lifetimes is part of the memories which we all leave. We can of course take some important steps that will simplify the material arrangements and the financial burdens of our heirs. In this concluding chapter, we offer several sources and some closing hints.

Federal and state activities

WHITE HOUSE CONFERENCE ON AGING

The following was adopted by the conference in 1961:

Rights of Senior Citizens

Each of our senior citizens, regardless of race, color or creed, is entitled to:
- ☐ The right to be useful
- ☐ The right to obtain employment, based on merit
- ☐ The right to freedom from want in old age
- ☐ The right to a fair share of the community's recreational, educational and medical resources
- ☐ The right to obtain decent housing suited to needs of later years
- ☐ The right to the moral and financial support of one's family so far as is consistent with the best interest of the family
- ☐ The right to live independently, as one chooses
- ☐ The right to live and die with dignity
- ☐ The right to access to all knowledge as available on how to improve the later years of life

Obligations of the Aging

The aging, by availing themselves of educational opportunities, should endeavor to assume the following obligations to the best of their ability:
- ☐ The obligation of each citizen to prepare himself to become and resolve to remain active, alert, capable, self-supporting, and useful so long as health and circumstances permit and to plan for ultimate retirement
- ☐ The obligation to learn and apply sound principles of physical and mental health
- ☐ The obligation to seek and develop potential avenues of service in the years after retirement
- ☐ The obligation to make available the benefits of his experience and knowledge
- ☐ The obligation to endeavor to make himself adaptable to the changes added years will bring
- ☐ The obligation to attempt to maintain such relationships, family, neighbors and friends as will make him a respected and valued counselor throughout his later years

RIGHTS AND LEGACIES   11

THE ADMINISTRATION ON AGING (AOA)

The work of the 1961 White House Conference on the Aging helped toward the passage of the Older Americans Act in 1965. Established as an operating entity of the Department of Health, Education and Welfare (HEW), AOA has been working toward more and better delivery of services for older people and advocacy of their rights.

With many goals, the work has just begun to bear fruit, and challenges lie ahead. Among the more important aspects of AOA's work: disbursement of funds for and coordination of state and area agencies on aging; administration of the hot-lunch program; research into various social aspects of the older population; the eventual cataloguing of information for dissemination to older people.

AOA works with other federal agencies in coordinating and advocating and with the Federal Council on the Aging, a 15-member body that advises the President on problems and policies.

The 10 official objectives of AOA are:
1. An adequate income in retirement in accordance with the American standard of living
2. The best possible physical and mental health which science can make available and without regard to economic status
3. Suitable housing, independently selected, designed and located with reference to special needs and available at costs which older people can afford
4. Full restorative services for those who require institutional care
5. Opportunity for employment with no discriminatory personnel practices because of age
6. Retirement in health, honor, and dignity—after years of contribution to the economy
7. Pursuit of meaningful activity within the widest range of civic, cultural and recreational opportunities
8. Efficient community services, including access to low-cost transportation, which provide social assistance in a coordinated manner and which are readily available when needed
9. Immediate benefit from proven research knowledge which can sustain and improve health and happiness
10. Freedom, independence, and the free exercise of in-

Federal and state activities

dividual initiative in planning and managing their own lives

Yes, there is a great deal of work lying ahead.

Write:
Administration on Aging
330 C St. SW
Washington, D.C. 20201

AOA's 10 REGIONAL OFFICES

REGION I:
Conn., Me., Mass, N.H., R.I., Vt.
J. F. Kennedy Federal Bldg.
Government Center
Boston, Mass. 02203
Phone: 617/223-6885

REGION II:
N.J., N.Y., Puerto Rico, Virgin Islands
26 Federal Plaza
Broadway and Lafayette St.
New York, N.Y. 10007
Phone: 212/264-4592

REGION III:
Del., D.C., Md., Pa., Va., W.Va.
P.O. Box 13716
3535 Market St.
Philadelphia, Pa. 19101
Phone: 215/597-6891

REGION IV:
Ala., Fla., Ga., Ky., Miss., N.C., S.C., Tenn.
50 Seventh St. NE, Room 326
Atlanta, Ga. 30323
Phone: 404/526-3482

REGION V:
Ill., Ind., Mich., Minn., Ohio, Wis.
300 S. Wacker Drive
Chicago, Ill. 60606
Phone: 312/353-4904

REGION VI;
Ark., La., N.Mex., Okla., Tex.
Fidelity Union Trust Tower Bldg.
1507 Pacific Ave.
Dallas, Tx. 75201
Phone: 214/749-7286

REGION VII:
Iowa, Kan., Mo., Neb.
601 East 12th St.
Kansas City, Mo. 64106
Phone: 816/374-2955

REGION VIII:
Colo., Mont., N.Dak., S.Dak., Utah, Wyo.
19th and Stout Sts.
Federal Office Bldg.
Denver, Colo. 80202
Phone: 303/837-2951

REGION IX:
Ariz., Calif., Hawaii, Nev., Samoa., Guam., Trust Territories
50 UN Plaza
San Francisco, Calif. 94102
Phone: 415/556-6003

REGION X:
Alaska, Idaho, Ore., Wash.
1321 Second Ave.
Seattle, Wash. 98101
Phone: 206/442-5341

RIGHTS AND LEGACIES 11

STATE AND AREA AGENCIES

ALABAMA:
Commission on Aging
740 Madison Ave.
Montgomery Ala. 36104
Phone: 205/832-6640

ALASKA:
Office on Aging
Juneau, Alaska 99811
Phone: 907/586-6153

AMERICAN SAMOA:
Government of American Samoa
Office of the Governor
Pago Pago, Samoa 96799

ARIZONA:
Bureau on Aging
543 East McDowell
Room 217
Phoenix, Ariz. 85004
Phone: 602/271-4446

ARKANSAS:
Office on Aging and Adult Services
7th and Gaines
P.O. Box 2179
Little Rock, Ark. 72202
Phone: 501/371-2441

CALIFORNIA:
Dept. of Aging
918 J St.
Sacramento, Calif. 95814
Phone: 916/322-3887

COLORADO:
Division of Services for the Aging
1575 Sherman St.
Denver, Colo. 80203
Phone: 303/892-2651

STATE AND AREA AGENCIES ON AGING

Stimulated and supported by the federal Administration on Aging, each state—and in turn over 600 areas within the states—has created an agency on aging. These various agencies are charged with a general function of coordinating the activities of all public and private agencies serving the older population.

Their overall community objectives are to enable older people to live in their own homes as long as they desire to do so and to provide opportunities that will help them improve the quality of their lives.

Although the primary purpose of the area agencies is to coordinate other bodies rather than offer specific services themselves, they may provide information and referral for older people needing transportation, housing, homemaker, medical or other assistance. If there is no other resource available, they may in some cases provide these services.

The area agencies are also the conduit for funds subcontracted to public and private agencies.

The state agencies coordinate the funds for the nutrition program which provides hot lunches at centers and home-delivered meals to hundreds of thousands of older people five days a week, thus affording not only nutrition but also the personal contact and social setting so important to all people.

Following are the addresses and telephone numbers of the state and equivalent agencies. (Information concerning area agencies can be obtained by contacting the state agencies or the public information offices of city or county governments.)

CONNECTICUT:
Dept. of Aging
90 Washington St.
Hartford, Conn. 06115
Phone: 203/566-2480

DELAWARE:
Division of Aging
2413 Lancaster Ave.
Wilmington, Del. 19805
Phone: 302/571-3481

DISTRICT OF COLUMBIA:
Office of Aging
1329 E St., NW
Washington, D.C. 20004
Phone: 202/638-2406

FLORIDA:
Division on Aging
1317 Winewood Blvd.
Tallahassee, Fla. 32301
Phone: 904/488-2650

GEORGIA:
Office of Aging
47 Trinity Ave. SW
Atlanta, Ga. 30334
Phone: 404/894-5341

GUAM:
Office of Aging
P.O. Box 2816
Agana, Guam 96910

State and area agencies

STATE AND AREA AGENCIES (continued)

HAWAII:
Commission on Aging
1149 Bethel Street
Honolulu, Hawaii 96813

IDAHO:
Office on Aging
Statehouse
Boise, Idaho 83720
Phone: 208/384-3833

ILLINOIS:
Dept. on Aging
2401 West Jefferson St.
Springfield, Ill. 62706
Phone: 217/782-5773

INDIANA:
Commission on the Aging and the Aged
215 North Senate Ave.
Indianapolis, Ind. 46202
Phone: 317/633-5948

IOWA:
Commission on the Aging
415 West 10th St.
Des Moines, Iowa 50319
Phone: 515/283-5187

KANSAS:
Services for the Aging Section
State Office Blvd.
Topeka, Kan. 66612
Phone: 913/296-3465

KENTUCKY:
Center for Aging and Community Development
403 Wapping St.
Frankfort, Ky. 40601
Phone: 502/564-6930

LOUISIANA:
Bureau of Aging Services
P.O. Box 44282, Capitol Sta.
Baton Rouge, La. 70804
Phone: 504/389-2171

MAINE:
Bureau of Maine's Elderly
State House
Augusta, Me. 04330
Phone: 207/622-6171
ask for 289-2561

MARYLAND:
Office on Aging
State Office Bldg.
301 East Preston St.
Baltimore, Md. 21201
Phone: 301/383-5064

MASSACHUSETTS:
Executive Office of Elder Affairs
State Office Bldg.
110 Tremont St.
Boston, Mass. 02109
Phone: 617/727-7750

MICHIGAN:
Offices of Services to the Aging
300 East Michigan
P.O. Box 30026
Lansing, Mich. 48913
Phone: 517/373-8230

MINNESOTA:
Governor's Citizens Council on Aging, Suite 204
7th & Robert St.
St. Paul, Minn. 55101
Phone: 612/296-2544

MISSISSIPPI:
Council on Aging
P.O. Box 5136, Fondren Sta.
510 George St.
Jackson, Miss. 39216
Phone: 601/354-6590

MISSOURI:
Office of Aging
Broadway State Office Bldg.
Jefferson City, Mo. 65101
Phone: 314/751-2075

MONTANA:
Aging Services Bureau
P.O. Box 1723
Helena, Mont. 58601
Phone: 406/449-3124

NEBRASKA:
Commission on Aging
State House Station 94784
300 S. 17th St.
Lincoln, Neb. 68509
Phone: 402/471-2307

NEVADA:
Division for Aging Services
505 East King St.
Carson City, Nev. 89701
Phone: 702/885-4210

NEW HAMPSHIRE:
Council on Aging
P.O. Box 786
14 Depot St.
Concord, N.H. 03301
Phone: 603/271-2751

NEW JERSEY:
Office on Aging
P.O. Box 2768
363 West State St.
Trenton, N.J. 98625
Phone: 609/292-4833

NEW MEXICO:
State Commission on Aging
Villagra Bldg.
408 Galisteo St.
Santa Fe, N. M. 87503
Phone: 505/827-5258

NEW YORK CITY:
Office for the Aging
Room 5036
2 World Trade Center
New York, N.Y. 10047
Phone: 212/488-6405

NEW YORK STATE:
Office for the Aging
Agency Bldg. #2
Empire State Plaza
Albany, N.Y. 10047
Phone: 518/474-5731

RIGHTS AND LEGACIES 11

STATE AND AREA AGENCIES *(continued)*

NORTH CAROLINA:
North Carolina Division for Aging
Administration Bldg.
213 Hillsborough St.
Raleigh, N.C. 27603
Phone: 919/733-3983

NORTH DAKOTA:
Aging Services
State Capitol Bldg.
Bismarck, N.D. 58505
Phone: 701/224-2577

OHIO:
Commission on Aging
50 West Broad St.
Columbus, O. 43216
Phone: 614/466-5500

OKLAHOMA:
Special Unit on Aging
P.O. Box 25352
Oklahoma City, Okla. 73125
Phone: 405/521-2281

OREGON:
Program on Aging
772 Commercial St. SE
Salem, Ore. 97310
Phone: 503/378-4728

PENNSYLVANIA:
Office for the Aging
Seventh and Forster Sts.
Harrisburg, Pa. 17120
Phone: 717/787-5350

PUERTO RICO:
Gericulture Commission
P.O. Box 11697
Santurce, P.R. 00908

RHODE ISLAND:
Division of Aging
150 Washington Court
Providence, R.I. 02903
Phone: 401/277-2858

SOUTH CAROLINA:
Commission on Aging
915 Main St.
Columbia, S.C. 29201
Phone: 803/758-2576

SOUTH DAKOTA:
Office on Aging
State Office Bldg.
Illinois St.
Pierre, S.D. 57501
Phone: 605/224-3656

TENNESSEE:
Commission on Aging
306 Gay St.
Nashville, Tenn. 37201
Phone: 615/741-2056

TEXAS:
Governor's Committee on Aging
Executive Office Bldg.
411 West 13th St.
Austin, Tex. 78703

TRUST TERRITORY OF THE PACIFIC:
Office of Aging
Saipan, Mariana Islands 96950

UTAH:
Division of Aging
345 South 6th East
Salt Lake City, Utah 84102
Phone: 801/328-6422

VERMONT:
Office on Aging
81 River St.
Montpelier, Vt. 05602
Phone: 802/828-3471

VIRGINIA:
Office on Aging
830 East Main St.
Richmond, Va. 23219
Phone: 804/786-7894

VIRGIN ISLANDS:
Commission on Aging
P.O. Box 539
Charlotte Amalie,
St. Thomas, Virgin Islands 00801

WASHINGTON:
Office on Aging
P.O. Box 1788
Olympia, Wash. 98504
Phone: 206/753-2502

WEST VIRGINIA:
Commission on Aging
State Capitol
Charleston, W.Va. 25305
Phone: 304/348-3317

WISCONSIN:
Division on Aging
1 West Wilson St.
Madison, Wis. 53703
Phone: 608/266-2536

WYOMING:
Aging Services
New State Office Bldg.
Cheyenne, Wyo. 82002
Phone: 307/777-7561

Federal and state activities
Legal aspects

YOU, THE LAW AND RETIREMENT

Lawyers have been important all your life, but—this booklet reminds you—financial losses incurred because of poor legal protection or misunderstanding of your rights will be much more difficult to recover from than at earlier ages, when income was generally higher. The booklet covers all aspects of life in relation to the law and gives some good general hints.

60¢
Catalogue #OHD 75-20800
USGPO
Washington, D.C. 20402

THE LAW . . . AND YOUR RETIREMENT

"Do you need a legal checkup?" asks this guidebook. Taking the point of view that a lawyer is "a legal doctor," it advocates using that professional to prevent legal troubles and to cure them if they do occur.

The booklet covers a large range of personal needs and problems which might require help and explains how to find a lawyer, what to do if you have no money to pay a fee, and how to use the lawyer's services most effectively.

$1.50 to current subscribers of the magazine, $2.25 to non-subscribers.

(See COMMUNICATING for other booklets in the series.)

Retirement Living Magazine
150 East 58th St.
New York, N.Y. 10022

THE FAMILY LEGAL ADVISER
Edited by Alice K. Helm
Crown, 1974, $9.95

While no substitute for the advice and services of an attorney, this is a thorough general reference and reminder on the law as it affects dozens of aspects of your daily life. In highly readable form, the book covers the law concerning marriage, citizenship, civil rights, wills, dying without a will, inheritance, incompetency, libel and slander, real estate, personal property, lost property, loans and credit, insurance, motor vehicles and crimes.

The book concludes with a glossary of common legal terms.

HELP

Legal help is there when you need it, even when you cannot afford to pay. If there is a legal aid society in your community, ask for its assistance when necessary. If you cannot locate one, write:

National Legal Aid and Defender Association
1155 East 60th St.
Chicago, Ill. 60037

Legal aspects

Some Closing Hints . . .

We are all interested in designating who will get what we can't take with us. This is equally true whether we have a large fortune or only a few personal belongings. Which way to achieve your intentions depends on a number of things: how much you are likely to leave; whether it is land or personal property; whether you own it alone or jointly with someone else; whom you may want to have it; the inheritance laws of your state; and the tax considerations. A lawyer can help you decide the best way for you.

Should you make a will?

By all means make one if you are in business or if you have promised to leave your estate in return for care and support. If there is any question of the division of property among relatives, friends and charities, the will becomes an important document.

If you do make a will or later revise one, have a lawyer do it. Do not buy a legal form and fill it in yourself. When used in a will, words can have a meaning quite different from common usage.

If you move to another state, find out if your will is still valid. Even if you do not move, your will should be reviewed from time to time, especially after a change in financial or family circumstances.

YOUR RETIREMENT LEGAL GUIDE

- What do you know about wills?
- How can you best plan your estate?
- Who will handle your affairs if illness strikes?
- How should you select an attorney?

These and dozens of other questions are answered in this thorough booklet from AARP-NRTA.

Free
AARP-NRTA
P.O. Box 2400
215 Long Beach Blvd.
Long Beach, Calif. 90801

PRACTICAL GUIDE FOR THE UNMARRIED COUPLE
By William L. Blaine and John Bishop
Two Continents Press, 1976, $7.95

Can the problems of loneliness and shortages of money be solved if people live in communes? Some already do, but certainly many others are living as couples without marrying in order to maximize their Social Security benefits.

Can two people simply live together as an unmarried couple without any problems? The authors answer this question with particular emphasis on the legal side. The book is important reading for those in that situation.

RIGHTS AND LEGACIES 11

HOW TO PREPARE FOR DEATH
By Yaffa Draznin
Hawthorn, 1977, $8.95

This blunt title frankly states that the sensitive and often ignored needs connected with one's death will be discussed. Topics included are preparation of wills, problems of estate planning, the question of cremation versus burial, the cost of funerals, and the steps to be taken immediately upon the death of a person close to you.

YOUR RETIREMENT WIDOWHOOD GUIDE

The loss of a spouse is a difficult experience, and coping becomes easier only with time—and communication with other people.

Perhaps the philosophy of this booklet is best summed up in the quote from Ethel Percy Andrus, AARP-NRTA founder:

Each of us has powers of which we are unaware, each of us has a circle of influence. Our limitations are the product of our own thinking and self-evaluation. If only we think, we can.

Free
AARP-NRTA
215 Long Beach Blvd.
P.O. Box 2400
Long Beach, Calif. 90801

Joint tenancy in personal property, such as bank accounts, stocks, bonds, cars, etc., frequently means that a surviving owner retains rights to all the property remaining upon the deaths of the other owners. Since this device can be tricky, be sure to get legal advice.

What if you allow the law to take its course? You can, if you want to. Each state provides laws which set forth who will get what when one of the residents dies without having made a valid will or having provided some other means of disposing of property.

Whether or not you make a will, it is a good idea to list your personal belongings such as jewelry, silverware and family heirlooms, and to put opposite each item the name and address of the person you want to have it. Such a list has no legal effect unless it is made part of your will. But if you do not make a will, you can still prepare such a list for the person (or persons) who by law will inherit what you leave. It is not legally binding but, chances are, your wishes will be followed.

It isn't all up to you.

There are some things about your estate that are beyond your control. Depending upon the laws of your state, your wife (or husband) may be entitled to a certain share of what you leave even without your consent.

If you owe money, your creditors can come in and ask to be paid first out of what you leave, before any of it is distributed to those you want to have it.

Certain benefits established by law, such as the lump sum Old Age, Survivors and Disability Insurance, must be paid to the person entitled under federal law and regulations. Other benefits, such as those under a private pension plan, may be just as specifically controlled, by the terms of the contract establishing the plan.

These things are beyond your personal control. It is well to be aware of them, however, so that you will not have false hopes or raise them in others.

Help over the hardest spot . . .

Most of us want to know that, when we die, the disposal of our remains—burial, cremation—and any religious ceremony or other memorial service will be carried out in a manner we consider fitting. If we let our wishes be known, in all likelihood they will be carried out. You might well leave your instructions with the person you have asked to look after things for you if you should be ill.

Legal aspects
Some final words

Your plans should include what you consider an appropriate price range for your funeral and for burial space or a marker, if you have not already provided these for yourself. If you do provide for your burial space ahead of time, be sure to take the same precautions that you would in any other real estate transaction.

If you wish cremation, be sure to let this be known. If you are not likely to be survived by close relatives who can give their consent to cremation, find out if there are forms you can sign now to authorize this for yourself.

For many people, making final plans brings peace of mind—a sense of comfort and security. Your plans will also bring comfort to those you leave behind. They will have much to do in the hours and days immediately following your death and they will be filled with many emotions. They will appreciate your thoughtfulness and guidance—they will feel better knowing that they are doing just what you wished done.

—Adapted from **You, the Law and Retirement**
HEW publication #OHD 75-20800

I have ever held it a maxim, never to do through another what it was possible for me to do myself.

—*Charles de Montesquieu, 1689–1755*
French philosopher

TEACH YOUR WIFE HOW TO BE A WIDOW
By the editors of U.S. News and World Report
U.S. News and World Report, P.O. Box 951, Hicksville, N.Y. 11802 $7.95

A practical, comprehensive approach to preparing your spouse for the legal and financial decisions she may have to make some day.

DONATING AN ORGAN

The use of organs for transplants, education and research is rapidly increasing as important new developments in the technology occur. Besides vast numbers of individual organs, approximately 7,000 bodies are needed annually for medical research and teaching. According to the Continental Association of Funeral and Memorial Societies, most Catholic, Protestant and Jewish religious authorities approve of or encourage donation. Orthodox Jewry is an exception, however.

The association provides, free of charge, a Uniform Donor Card which can be carried on the person at all times. For the card write:

Continental Association of Funeral and Memorial Societies
Suite 1100
1828 L St., NW
Washington, D.C. 20036

Additional information on certain organ transplants can be obtained from the following organizations:

The National Kidney Foundation
315 Park Ave. South
New York, N.Y. 10010

Eye Bank Association of America
1111 Tulane Ave.
New Orleans, La. 70112

Deafness Research Foundation (temporal bones)
366 Madison Ave.
New York, N.Y. 10016

Human Growth, Inc. (pituitary gland)
307 Fifth Ave.
New York, N.Y. 10016

RIGHTS AND LEGACIES

THE EUTHANASIA EDUCATIONAL COUNCIL

The council takes the position that supporting measures should not be used to prolong the lives of dying patients or those with terminal illness accompanied by intractable pain or irreversible brain damage. It opposes the prolongation of life by artificial means in these circumstances, but does favor administering sufficient medication to ease suffering, even though life may be shortened.

The council issues several publications dealing with its controversial positions. Write:

The Euthanasia Educational Council, Inc.
250 West 57th St.
New York, N.Y. 10019

CONTINENTAL ASSOCIATION OF FUNERAL AND MEMORIAL SOCIETIES

The continuing development of memorial societies reflects a movement toward simplicity, dignity and economy in funeral arrangements. Each local society deals with several aspects of death arrangements, including education, simple funerals and encouragement of organ transplants and body donations.

A small pamphlet titled **Funeral and Memorial Societies** explains their concepts and lists the local societies across the country.

An expanded explanation is given in a book called **A Manual of Death Education and Simple Burial**, by Ernest Morgan. It details not only the concepts of the memorial society, but gives particular attention to some of the emotional problems associated with death. One particularly interesting section deals with euthanasia—ending a life when there is no serious hope of recovery. The author, who is pro-euthanasia, includes a model "living will" for the purpose of declaring one's desire to be allowed to die in medically hopeless situations.

Morgan's book costs $1.50 and is available from:

Celo Press
Burnsville, N.C. 28714

For additional information and a free copy of the pamphlet, write:

Continental Association of Funeral and Memorial Societies
Suite 1100
1828 L St., NW
Washington, D.C. 20036

200

A FINAL WORD

Now I ask to see life as whole from youth to age; sustain me with faith that the best is yet to be. Many are the opportunities that await me. There are blessings that only the maturity of age can bring; there is a ripeness that experience alone can yield.

—From the prayer, "On Reaching the Age of Retirement," in **Gates of Prayer**, edited by Rabbi Chaim Stern. Copyright 1977 Central Conference of American Rabbis. Reprinted by permission.

INDEX

Aaron and the Green Mountain Boys (Gauch), 187
AARP (American Association of Retired Persons), 148
AARP-NRTA. *See* American Association of Retired Persons-National Retired Teachers Association.
About Aging: A Catalog of Films (Andrus Gerontology Center; catalogue), 24, 25
ACE (Active Executives), 159
ACI FILMS, Inc., 24
Across the Meadow (Schecter), 187
ACTION, 14, 159–63
Action for Independent Maturity (AIM), 43, 56, 82, 125, 146, 175
Active Executives (ACE), 159
ADA (American Dental Association), 74
A.D. Alpine, Inc., 104
Adams, Jeannette T., 47
Addison, Joseph, 144
Adler, Joan, 21
Administration on Aging (AOA)
  lunch programs of, 30, 153
  objectives and regional offices of, 190–91
  publications of, 14, 55, 182–83
Adult Education Association of the USA, 92
After a Coronary (AHA publication), 67
After 65: Resources for Self-Reliance (Public Affairs Pamphlets; publication), 18
Ageless Aging (Winter), 19
Agency on Aging, 112
Age News (American Aging Association; newsletter), 164
Aging International (IFA; newsletter), 165
Aging, general facts about, 12–19
Aging (AA; magazine), 175
Aging Eye: Facts on Eye Care for Older Persons, The (National Society for the Prevention of Blindness; booklet), 69

Aging Tomorrow (newsletter), 174
Agriculture, Department of (USDA)
  Extension Service of, 156
  Food Stamp Program of, 130
  publications of, 30, 34–36, 47, 108–9, 134
AHA (American Heart Association), 67
AHCA (American Health Care Association), 49, 51
Aicardi, Anna, 159
Aids
  communication, 181, 182
  health, 63–65
  hearing, 71
  safety, 89
  sewing, 109
  traveling, 122
  for the visually handicapped, 68–69
  See also Appliances.
AIM (Action for Independent Maturity), 43, 56, 82, 125, 146, 175
Aiming for Dynamic Maturity (AIM; booklet), 56
Alabama
  Federal Information Centers in, 170
  State agencies in, 192
Al-Anon Family Groups, 74
Alaska, state agencies in, 192
Albert Constantine and Son, Inc., 102
Alcoholics Anonymous, 74
Alcoholism, 74–75
Alcoholism (Metropolitan Life Insurance Co.; booklet), 62
Alford, Bea, 161
Allergies, 70–71
Allergy Foundation of America, 61, 70, 71
Allergy Research: An Introduction (National Institute of Allergy and Infectious Diseases; booklet), 70
Altrusa International, 155
AMA (American Medical Association), 17, 49, 52–53, 90,

141
Amazing Mrs. Pollifax, The (Gilman), 22
American Aging Association, 164
American Association of Homes for the Aging, 50, 51
American Association of Retired Persons (AARP), 146–48
American Association of Retired Persons-National Retired Teachers Association (AARP-NRTA)
  Driver Improvement Plan of, 89, 147
  programs of, 56, 146–48
  publications of, 146, 174
    on better aging, 18
    on consumerism, 136
    on crime prevention, 80, 82
    on financial matters, 124, 127, 141
    on health, 52, 56
    on home maintenance, 47
    on how to cope with death, 198
    on moving, 46
    on nutrition, 28
    on pets, 10
    on rights and legacies, 197
    on safety, 87
  travel discounts offered by, 113
American Cancer Society, 76–77
American Cancer Society: What It Is, What It Does, How It Began, Where It Is Going (American Cancer Society; pamphlet), 77
American College of Nursing Home Administrators, 51
American Crafts Council, 99, 176
American Dental Association (ADA), 74
American Digestive Disease Society, 78
American Foundation for the Blind, 68–69, 89
American Geriatrics Society, 164
American Health Care Association (AHCA), 49, 51
American Health Education Foundation, 58

American Heart Association (AHA), 67
American Heart Association Cookbook, The (Eshleman and Winston), 39–40
American Hospital Association, 61
American Medical Association (AMA), 17, 49, 52–53, 90, 141
American Movers Conference, 45
American Nurses' Association, 61
American Parkinson's Disease Foundation, 78
American Podiatry Association, 75
American Printing House for the Blind, 181
American Samoa, agencies on aging in, 192
America on the Rocks (film), 75
Amos 'n' Andy (radio program), 185
Amplifiers, portable and drop-in phone, 182
Ancowitz, Arthur, 66
Anderson, Joanne, 136
Andrus, Ethel Percy, 18, 52, 148, 198
Andrus Gerontology Center (University of Southern California), 24, 148
Angle of Repose (Stegner), 23
Angry Buyer's Complaint Directory, The (White, Yanker, and Steinberg), 136
Angry Moon (Sleater), 187
Ansello, Thomas, 187
Answering Your Questions About Cancer (American Cancer Society; pamphlet), 77
Antonia: A Portrait of a Woman (film), 26
AOA. See Administration on Aging.
Appliances
  gardening, 98
  for the visually handicapped, 69
  See also Aids.

Area agencies, 192–94
Are You Planning on Living . . . the Rest of Your Life? (Chicago Mayor's Commission for Senior Citizens; booklet), 20
Arizona
  Federal Information Centers in, 170
  state agencies in, 192
Arkansas
  Federal Information Center in, 170
  Green Thumb projects in, 143
  state agencies in, 192
Around the World Vegetarian Cookbook (Bayramian), 34
Arthritic's Cookbook, The (Dong and Banks), 40
Arthritis, 72–73
Arthritis: The Basic Facts (The Arthritis Foundation; pamphlet), 72
Arthritis Foundation, The, 40, 72–73
Arthritis Quackery (The Arthritis Foundation; pamphlet), 72
Arthur and Lillie (film), 26
Art of Age, The (film), 24–25
Association-Sterling Films, 185
Asthma, Climate and Weather (Allergy Foundation of America; booklet), 70
Atchley, Robert C., 21
Atlanta (Ga.)
  ACTION recruiting offices in, 159
  USGPO bookstores in, 168
At My Age (film), 27
Audiovisual Center (University of Iowa), 27
Audiovisual Center (University of Wisconsin), 24
Audio-visual Education Center (University of Michigan), 24, 25
Audio-Visual Services (Pennsylvania State University), 25
Autobiography of Miss Jane Pittman, The (film), 27
Autobiography of Miss Jane Pittman, The (Pittman; book), 178
Auto Consumer Action Panel, 131
Automobiles
  driver safety, 87, 89
  health and driving, 62
  insurance for, 140
  repairing and renting, 118
  travel by, 118
Auto Repair Frauds: How to Prevent Your Car from Driving You to the Poorhouse (Engle), 118
Autumn Leaves (National Federation of Grandmother Clubs of America; periodical), 151
Aylesworth, Florence, 159
Aylesworth, Rolland, 159

Baker, Karle Wilson, 23
Baltimore (Md.), Mature Temps in, 142
Baltimore Longitudinal Study of Aging, 16
Banks, Alfred E., 181
Banks, Jane, 40, 73
Banks pocket Braille writer, 181
Basic Baskets (Cary), 101
Basic Bibliography (Gray Panthers), 151
Basic Crafts Co., 99
Basketry, 101
Bath Book, The (G. Frazier and B. Frazier), 59
Bath-safety devices, 89
Bayramian, Mary, 34
Beauvoir, Simone de, 12
Beginner's Guide to Refinishing Furniture, A (Johnson Wax; booklet), 103
Bell, Alexander Graham, 180
Bellak, Leopold, 17
Bellow, Saul, 22
Bell System, 180
Beltone Electronics Corp., 71
Benet, Sula, 16
Be OK Self-Help Aids (Fred Sam-

205

mons, Inc.; catalogue), 63, 109, 182
Bergen Arts and Crafts (Bergen Arts and Crafts; catalogue), 100
Bernardin Home Canning Guide (Bernardin, Inc.; guide), 37
Berri, Claude, 22
Best Loved Poems of the American People (Felleman), 23
Best Years of Your Life, The (Bellak), 17
Better Business Bureau, 51, 138-39
  See also Council of Better Business Bureaus, Inc.
Better Health in Later Years (Public Affairs Pamphlets; publication), 61
Better Homes and Gardens (magazine), 177
Bible, 179
Big World and the Little House, The (Krauss), 187
Birmingham (Ala.), USGPO bookstores in, 168
Bishop, John, 197
Bittinger, Marvin L., 137
Blackhawk Films, Inc., 27
Blaine, William L., 197
Blessings of Love, The (film), 25
Blindness, 68–69
Blue Angel, The (film), 27
Bob Hope Show (radio program), 185
Bookbinding, 99
Book of Home Verse, The (Stevenson), 23
Bookstores, USGPO, 168–69
Borack, Barbara, 187
Born Free (Adamson), 178
Boston (Mass.)
  ACTION recruiting offices in, 159
  Mature Temps in, 142
  Telecheck service in, 66
  USGPO bookstores in, 169
Boundless Resource, The (Wirtz), 91

Bradford House, 103
Braille writer, 181
Brico, Antonia, 26
Brief Explanation of Medicare, A (Social Security Administration; booklet), 128
Briggs, Raymond, 187
Brookstone Company: Hard-to-Find Tools and Other Fine Things (Brookstone Co.; catalogue), 103
Brown, W. Jann, 39
Browning, Robert, 23
Butcher, Lee, 42
Butler, Robert N., 14, 16, 56
Buying and Financing a Mobile Home (HUD; pamphlet), 44
Buying Your House: A Complete Guide to Inspection and Evaluation (Davis and Walker), 44
California
  AOA office in, 191
  Federal Information Centers in, 170
  Green Thumb projects in, 143
  state agencies in, 192
Callahan, Dorothy, 39
Cancer, 76–77
Cancer Facts for Men (American Cancer Society; pamphlet), 77
Cancer Facts for Women (American Cancer Society; pamphlet), 77
Caning supplies, 101
Canning, 37
Canton (Ohio), USGPO bookstores in, 169
Can We Eat Well for Less? (National Dairy Council; booklet), 29
CAPS (Consumer Action Panels), 131
Car and Truck Renting and Leasing Association, 118
Cardiovascular system, 66–67
Care and Maintenance of Common Household and Office Plants (National Parks Service; booklet), 97
Carousel Films, Inc., 25
Carpet and Rug Industry Consumer Action Panel, 131
Cars. See Automobiles.
Carts, 98
Carver, W. F., 71
Cary, Mara, 101
Catalog of Kits, The (Feinman), 100
Catalogue of Publications and Films (National Society for the Prevention of Blindness, Inc.), 69
Cataract: What It Is and How It is Treated (National Society for the Prevention of Blindness; booklet), 69
CB radios (citizen band radios), 184
Celo Press, 200
Center for Older Americans and the Arts, 165
Central Arizona Film Cooperative (Arizona State University), 24
Ceramic equipment, 104
Chamber of Commerce, reporting nursing home complaints to, 51
Changing Times (magazine), 175
Chapel Hill (N.C.), ACTION recruiting offices in, 159
Chicago (Ill.)
  ACTION recruiting offices in, 161
  Mature Temps in, 142
  USGPO bookstores in, 168
Chicago Mayor's Commission for Senior Citizens, 20
Children's books, 187
Church (and synagogue) programs of AARP-NRTA, 147
Cider Press, 39
Cigarette Quiz (AHA publication), 67
Citizen band radios (CB radios), 184
Citizens for Better Care, 50

Citizen's Handbook: Program Options and Public Participation Under Title 20 of the Social Security Act, A (Social Security Administration; booklet), 129
Civil Service Commission, 170
Cleo Living Aids (company), 63
Cleveland (Ohio), USGPO bookstores in, 169
Clinical Physiology Branch of NIA, 16
Clothing, 108–10
    buying, 110
    repairing and sewing, 108-9
Clothing Can Burn (National Fire Protection Association; pamphlet), 84
Clothing Repairs (USDA; booklet), 108–9
Collected Poems of Dylan Thomas (Laughlin), 23
Colorado
    AOA office in, 191
    Federal Information Centers in, 170
    state agencies in, 192
Columbus (Ohio), ACTION recruiting offices in, 161
Comfort, Alex, 14
Coming of Age, The (de Beauvoir), 12
Commission on Voluntary Service and Action, 166
Committee on Aging (AMA), 52
Communal living, 155
Communication resources
    to combat loneliness, 183–84
    governmental, 168–71
    for the handicapped, 178–83
    magazines, newspapers and books, 172–79
        See also specific magazines newspapers, and books.
    media resources, 184–85
    stories to read one's grandchildren, 187
Community Concern for Senior Citizens, 139
Complaints, how to handle nursing home, 51

Complete Book of Dressmaking (MacTaggart), 108
Complete Guide to Home Canning, Preserving and Freezing (USDA), 37
Complete Home Owner's Guide: From Mortgage to Maintenance, The (Doyle), 46
Complete Retirement Planning Book, The (Dickinson), 20
Complete Sprouting Cookbook, The (Whyte), 35
Complete Yogurt Cookbook, The (Whyte), 35
Condominium Book: A Guide to Getting the Most for Your Money, The (Butcher), 42
Condominiums, 42–43
Congressmen, reporting nursing home complaints to, 51
Connecticut
    AOA office, 191
    Federal Information Centers in, 170
    state agencies in, 192
Consolidated Book Publishers, 179
Consumer Action Panels (CAPS), 131
Consumer Complaint Guide (Rosenbloom), 134
Consumer Federation of America, 137
Consumer Information Center, 133
Consumerism, 131–40
    AARP-NRTA information programs on, 147
Consumer News, Inc., 45
Consumer Product Safety Commission, 87, 133
Consumer Reports (magazine), 32, 137
Consumers Union, 32
Consumer Survival Book: How to Fight Inflation, The (Bittinger), 137
Consumer Survival Kit (Dorfman), 134
Consumer Tips on Bait and Switch (Better Business Bureau; booklet), 139
Consumer Tips on Buying by Mail (Better Business Bureau; booklet), 139
Consumer Tips on Guarantees and Warranties (Better Business Bureau; booklet), 139
Contessa Yarns (company), 107
Continental Association of Funeral and Memorial Societies, 199, 200
Continuing education, AARP-NRTA programs of, 146–47
Cook to Your Heart's Content (Brown, Liebowitz and Olness), 39
Cooking for One in the Senior Years (Cornell University publication), 29
Cooking for Two (USDA publication), 35
Cooper, Louise Field, 22
Cooperative Extension Service (USDA), 156
Cornell University, 29
Correspondence courses, 94
Cosmetic Allergy (Allergy Foundation of America; booklet), 70
Council of Better Business Bureaus, Inc., 48, 71, 84, 118, 139
Coupon Way to Lower Food Prices, The (Katz and Lee), 139
Courses, correspondence, 94
Craft Horizons (magazine), 99, 176
Crafts, 99–104
Crafts 'n Things (magazine), 101
Creative Crafts (magazine), 100
Credit Union National Association, 138
Crime prevention, 80–82
    AARP-NRTA program of, 147

Dahleberg, Charles Clay, 66
Dallas (Tex.)
    ACTION recruiting offices in,

159
Mature Temps in, 142
USGPO bookstores in, 169
Dana Productions (company), 26
Danger: Cigarettes (American Cancer Society; pamphlet), 77
Davis, Joseph C., 44
Deafness Research Foundation, 199
Death, coping with, 198–99
"Death of the Hired Man, The" (Frost), 23
Deeken, Alfons, 19
Delaware, state agencies in, 192
Dennenberg, Herbert S., 140
Dental care, 74
Dentures: What You Don't Know Can Hurt You (ADA; booklet), 74
Denver (Colo.)
  ACTION recruiting offices in, 159
  USGPO bookstores in, 168
Depression: Causes and Treatment (Public Affairs Pamphlets; publication), 61
Detroit (Mich.), USGPO bookstores in, 169
Dick Blick (company), 102
Dickinson, Peter A., 20, 56
Diet. See Nutrition.
Dietary Control of Cholesterol (Fleischmann's Margarine; booklet), 40
Diet for Living, A (Mayer), 28
Direct Mail Marketing Association, 184
Directory of Participating Physicians (Intermedic, Inc.), 121
Directory of State and Local Consumer Groups (Consumer Federation of America), 137
District of Columbia. See Washington (D.C.).
Diverticulosis (American Digestive Disease Society; pamphlet), 78
Dollhouses, building, 103

Dong, Collin H., 40, 73
"Do Not Go Gentle Into That Good Night" (Thomas), 23
Don't Do It Yourself (ADA booklet), 74
Don't Give Up on an Aging Parent (Galton), 58
Dorfman, John, 134
Doubleday and Co., Inc., 179
Doyle, John M., 46
Draznin, Yaffa, 198
Dreiser, Theodore, 27
Driver Improvement Program of AARP-NRTA, 89, 147
Driving. See Automobiles.
Drop-in phone amplifiers, 182
Drug Allergy (Allergy Foundation of America; booklet), 70
Drug Allergy (National Institute of Allergy and Infectious Diseases; booklet), 71
Drugs, 59
  allergies to, 70, 71
Drummond, Henry, 156
Durant, Ariel, 91
Durant, Will, 91
Dust Allergy (National Institute of Allergy and Infectious Diseases; booklet), 70
Dying Person and the Family, The (Public Affairs Pamphlets), 61
Dynamic fitness, defined, 55
Dynamic Maturity (AIM magazine), 175

Eating Right for Less (editors of Consumer Reports), 32
Eat Well but Wisely (AHA; publication), 67
Edgar Bergen and Charlie McCarthy (radio program), 185
Edna McConnell Clark Foundation, 15
Education
  AARP-NRTA continuing education programs, 146–47
  AARP-NRTA health education programs, 147

as leisure, 90–95
Education of Children for the New Era of Aging (AMA; booklet), 17
Edwards, Tryon, 13
Elderhostel program, 92–93
Eleven Principles of Effective, Organized Consumer Action (Consumer Federation of America; booklet), 137
EM Complaint Directory for Consumers (Credit Union National Association; booklet), 138
Emergencies
  health, 60–61
  paging system in cases of, 182
  while traveling, 120–21
Emergency Answering System (Medic Alert Foundation International), 60–61
Emerson, Ralph Waldo, 161
Employment, 141–43
Employment of Older People (AMA; pamphlet), 141
Energy, tips on saving, 132–33
Engle, Lyle Kenyon, 118
Eshleman, Ruthe, 39
Esophagitis/hiatal hernia (American Digestive Disease Society; pamphlet), 78
Esquire Films (company), 27
Essential Guide to Prescription Drugs, The (Long), 59
Estates, settlement of, 197–98
Estimating Your Social Security Retirement Check (Social Security Administration; booklet), 128
Euthanasia Educational Council, Inc., 200
Everybody's Money (Credit Union National Association), 138
Every Ten Seconds (Insurance Information Institute; pamphlet), 140
Everything You Can Get for Free . . . Or Almost for Free (C. Norback and P. Norback), 129
Exit: Escape from Fire Wherever

You Are (National Fire Prevention Association; pamphlet), 84
Extension Media Center (University of California at Berkeley), 24, 26
Eye Bank Association of America, 199
Eyesight. *See* Visually handicapped, the.

Facts About Health Insurance (Better Business Bureau; booklet), 139
Facts About Hearing Aids (Council of Better Business Bureau; booklet), 71
Facts About Organic Gardening (Cornell University; booklet), 29
Facts About Strokes (AHA publication), 67
Facts and Myths about Aging (NCOA; booklet), 15
Fads, Myths, Quacks—and Your Health (Public Affairs Pamphlets; publication), 61
Family Health (magazine), 176
Family Legal Adviser, The (Helm), 195
Family Register of Personal and Financial Papers, The (editors of *U.S. News and World Report*), 124
Farrar, Margaret, 179
Fat and Sodium Control Cookbook, The (Payne and Callahan), 39
FDA (Food and Drug Administration), 32, 132
Federal Alcohol and Tax Department, 101
Federal Council on the Aging, 190
Federal Energy Administration, 132–33
Federal Information Centers, 170–71
Federal Recreation Fee Program (National Park Service; folder), 117
Federal Register, 169
Federal Reserve System, 132
Federal Savings and Loan Association Insurance Corporation, 132
Federal Trade Commission (FTC), 132
Feerlick, Mary, 159
Feinman, Jeffrey, 100, 129
Feinman, Max L., 67
Felleman, Hazel, 23
Fibber McGee and Molly (radio program), 185
Fiction, 22–23
Film Dynamics (company), 24
Film Library (Oregon Division of Continuing Education), 25
Films on aging, 24–27
 on alcoholism, 75
 on crime prevention, 82
 free loan, 185
 on product safety, 87
Films, Inc., 25
Financial matters, 124–43
 consumer help, 131–40
 employment, 141–43
 making preparations for retirement, 124–26
 social security and government benefits, 128–30
 taxes, 127
Fire prevention, 84
Fire Prevention All Over Your Home (National Fire Protection Association; pamphlet), 84
First New England Catalogue, The (Hall), 100
Fish for Supper (Goffstein), 187
Fitness, 53–57
Fitness Challenge in the Later Years: An Exercise Program for Older Americans, The (AOA and President's Council on Physical Fitness and Sports), 55
Fleischmann's Margarine (company), 40
Floating thermometer, 63
Floor care (Johnson Wax; booklet), 47
Flora, James, 187
Florida
 Federal Information Centers in, 170
 Green Thumb projects in, 143
 state agencies in, 192
Flynn, Barbara, 172
Folding luggage carriers, 122
Food Allergy (Allergy Foundation of America; booklet), 70
Food Allergy (National Institute of Allergy and Infectious Diseases; booklet), 70
Food and Drug Administration (FDA), 32, 132
Food grinders, 37, 39
Food Guide for Older Folks (USDA; booklet), 30
Food Stamp Program, 130
Foot care, 75
Foote, Estelle, 108
Foot Health and Aging (American Podiatry Association; pamphlet), 75
"For Age Is Opportunity" (Longfellow), 23
For the People: A Consumer Action Handbook (Anderson), 136
Foster Grandparent Program, 159, 163
Four Steps to Weight Control (Metropolitan Life Insurance Co.; booklet), 62
Franklin, Benjamin, 32, 58, 144
Franklin, Marshall, 66
Frazier, Beverly, 62
Frazier, Gregory, 62
Fred Sammons, Inc., 63, 89, 109, 122, 182
Freedom from Backaches (Friedman and Galton), 65
French Lieutenant's Woman, The (book), 178
Fried, James F., 59
Friedman, Lawrence W., 65
Frost, Robert, 23
Fruit grinders, 39
FTC (Federal Trade Commis-

sion), 132
Funeral and Memorial Societies (Continental Association of Funeral and Memorial Societies; pamphlet), 200
Funeral arrangements, 198–200
Furniture Industry Consumer Action Panel, 131
Furniture refinishing, 103

Gallbladder (American Digestive Disease Society; pamphlet), 78
Galton, Lawrence, 58, 65
Games for the visually handicapped, 69
Garage Sale Manual, The (J. Young and J. Young), 140
Gardener's Catalogue, The (Rottenberg and Riker), 97
Gardening, 36, 96–98
Garden Way Home Fruit Grinder, 39
Garden Way Model cart, 98
Garden Way Research (company), 39, 98
Gates of Prayer (Stern), 201
Gauch, Patricia, 187
General medical care, 58–61
General Services Administration, 133, 170
Georgia
  AOA office in, 191
    Federal Information Centers in, 170
  state agencies in, 192
Georgia Center for Continuing Education, 20
Gerontological Film Collection (North Texas State University), 25
Gerontological Society, 166
Getting Older and Staying Younger (Stonecypher), 19
Getting Started in Stained Glass (Whittemore Durgin Glass; instruction sheet), 102
Giant playing cards, 109
Gifts to Make from Odds 'n Ends (Pack-O-Fun; manual), 101
Gilman, Dorothy, 22
G. K. Hall and Co., 179
Glassman, Judith, 99
Glaucoma (National Society for the Prevention of Blindness; booklet), 68
Goffstein, M. B., 187
Golden Age Passport, 117
Gomer's Guide (Lewis), 113
Good Age, A (Comfort), 14
Goodbye Mr. Chips (film), 27
Good Housekeeping Basic Gardening Techniques (editors of *Good Housekeeping*), 97
Good Housekeeping Guide to Fixing Things Around the House (M.D. Liles, R.M. Liles and Stukane), 48
Good Housekeeping New Complete Book of Needlecraft (Guild), 107
Good Old Days (magazine), 172
Government benefits, 128–30
Government Printing Office (USGPO)
  bookstores of, 168–69
  ordering publications from
    on clothes repair, 108
    on consumerism, 132
    on gardening, 97, 98
    on general facts about aging, 14
    on general facts about retirement, 20
    on health, 55, 74
    on home maintenance, 47
    on nursing homes, 50
    on nutrition, 30, 34–36
    on rights, 195
    on safety, 88
    on telephone communication, 182
Grand Book, Inc., 185
Grandpa (Borack), 187
Grandpa's Farm (Flora), 187
Graphic arts, sources of materials for, 102
Graphic Arts (Van Nostrand Reinhold; folder), 101
Gray Panthers, 150–51
Gray Panthers Brochure (Gray Panthers), 151
Greene, Graham, 22
Greenfield, Josh, 22
Green Thumb projects, 142–43
Green Winter: Celebration of Old Age (Maclay), 18
Greetings from the White House, 172
Greyhound Bus Lines, Inc., 122
Grieg, Edvard, 154
Griesel, Elma, 50
Grinders, 37, 39
Grit (newspaper), 172
Grit Publishing Company, 172
Growing Flowering Annuals (*House and Garden Bulletin*), 98
Growing Old: An Exploration of Our Treatment of and Resources for the Aging (G. Moss and W. Moss), 13
Growing Old and How to Cope With It (Deeken), 19
Growing Old in the Country of the Young (Percy and Mangel), 12
Growing Vegetables in the Home Garden (Wester), 36
Guam, agencies on aging in, 192
Gubrium, Jaber F., 50
Guidelines for a Telephone Reassurance Service (AOA; booklet), 182–83
Guide to Aging Programs for Synagogues, A (Synagogue Council of America), 155
Guide to Do-It-Yourself Packing, A (Moving and Storage Industry of New York; guide), 46
Guide to Home and Personal Security (AIM; guide), 82
Guide to Housing Security (AIM; guide), 43
Guide to Supplemental Security Income (Social Security Administration; booklet), 128

Guide to the Golden Years, A (Rusk), 17
Guide to Visual Aids and Illumination (National Association for the Visually Handicapped; booklet), 179
Guild, Vera P., 107

Haley, Gail, 187
Hall, Marie S., 100
Hammacher Schlemmer (company), 64
Handbook for the Asthmatic (Allergy Foundation of America; booklet), 70
Handbook of the Nutritional Contents of Food (Watt and Merrill), 29
Handicapped, the
 communication resources for, 178–83
 transportation services for, 122
 See also Hard-of-hearing, the; Visually handicapped, the.
Handle Yourself With Care: An Instructor's Guide for an Accident Prevention Course for Older Americans (USGPO publication), 88
Hand-weaving supplies, 107
Handy Andy (magazine), 176
Handyman (magazine), 176
Happy Baby Food Grinder, 37
Hard-of-hearing, the, 71
 communication resources for, 180–82
Harold and Maude (film), 27
Harrisville Designs (company), 108
Harry and Tonto (Greenfield and Mazursky), 22
Harvard Medical School, 58
Harvard Medical School Health Letter, 58
Hawaii
 Federal Information Centers in, 170
 state agencies in, 193
Hay Fever (Allergy Foundation of America; booklet), 70
Health (and illness), 52–79
 AARP-NRTA health education programs, 147
 alcoholism, 74–75
 allergies, 70–71
 arthritis, 72–73
 cancer, 76–77
 dental, 74
 digestive diseases, 78
 eyesight, 68–69
 fitness and, 53–56
 foot care, 75
 general medical care, 58–61
 health aids and homemakers' service, 62–66
 hearing problems, 71
 heart and cardiovascular system, 66–67
 medical emergencies while away, 120–21
 Parkinson's disease, 78
 special care and conditions, 61–68
Health, Education and Welfare, Department of (HEW), 50, 199
Health aids, 63–65
Health education programs of AARP-NRTA, 147
Health Foods: Facts and Fakes (*Public Affairs Pamphlets*; publication), 30
Hear Better with Your Hearing Aid (Carver), 71
Hearing Loss Handbook, The (Rosenthal), 71
Heart, the, 66–67
Heart Attack (AHA publication), 67
Heart Attack: How to Reduce Your Risk (AHA publication), 67
Heart Doctors' Heart Book, The (Franklin, Krauthamer, Tai and Pinchot), 66
Heart Quiz (AHA publication), 67
Helm, Alice K., 195
Help: the Useful Almanac (Rowse), 137
HEW (Health, Education and Welfare, Department of), 50, 199
History of the Gray Panthers Movement (Gray Panthers), 151
Holiday Home Exchange Bureau, Inc., 114
Hollenbeck, Frances, 159
Holmes, Oliver Wendell, Jr., 90
Holy Bible, 179
Home and Garden Bulletins, 30, 34–36, 98
Home canning, 37
Home Care (Johnson Wax; booklet), 47
Home Care Programs in Arthritis: A Manual for Patients (The Arthritis Foundation; booklet), 73
Home Fire Detection (National Fire Protection Association; pamphlet), 84
Home Handyman's Electricity and Electric Appliances Handbook (Adams), 47
Home health care, 63–66
Home Health Care and Convalescent Products (Sears Roebuck and Co.; catalogue), 63
Home Health Care Under Medicare (Social Security Administration; booklet), 128
Homemaker's Guide to Home Nursing (Schmidt), 64
Homemakers Services, 64–66
Homemakers Upjohn, 64
Homes
 buying and selling, 44–45
 fire prevention at, 84
 insurance for, 140
 maintenance and improvement of, 46–48
 moving from, 45–46
 safety at, 82
 tips on cleaning, 47
Home-Sew, Inc., 109
Hopeful Side of Cancer, The (American Cancer Society; pamphlet), 77
Horn, Linda, 50

House and Garden (magazine), 177
House Beautiful (magazine), 177
"House Call" (television program), 58
Housing, 42–44
    communal, 155
    See also Homes.
Housing and Urban Development, Department of (HUD), 43–45
Houston (Tex.), Mature Temps in, 142
Howe Press of the Perkins School for the Blind, 181
How Medicare Helps During a Hospital Stay (Social Security Administration; booklet), 128
How the Older Person Can Get the Most Out of Living (AMA publication), 53, 90
How to Beat the High Cost of Travel (editors of *U.S. News and World Report*), 113
How to Buy and Sell Real Estate for Financial Security (Irwin), 140–41
How to Buy Food for Economy and Quality (USDA; booklet), 30
How to Challenge Your Local Electric Utility (Consumer Federation of America; booklet), 137
How to Choose a Nursing Home: Shopping and Rating Guide (Institute of Gerontology of University of Michigan; booklet), 50
How to Cope with Crises (*Public Affairs Pamphlets*; publication), 61
How to Examine Your Breasts (American Cancer Society; pamphlet), 77
How to Form a Consumer Complaint Group (Consumer Federation of America; booklet), 137

How to Have a Garage Sale (Moving and Storage Industry of New York; pamphlet), 140
How to Keep Your Family Burglar Unhappy (Insurance Information Institute; pamphlet), 140
How to Live to Be 100 (Benet), 16–17
How to Make Your House Behave (Philbin), 46
How to Prepare for Death (Draznin), 198
How to Protect Yourself from Crime (Lipman), 81
How to Sell Your Home Without a Real Estate Broker (Kosnar), 44
How to Stop Smoking (AHA publication), 67
How We Can Reduce the Risks of Heart Attacks (AHA publication), 67
HUD (Department of Housing and Urban Development), 43–45
Human Growth, Inc., 199

IAMAT (International Association for Medical Assistance to Travelers), 120
Idaho, agencies on aging in, 193
IFA (International Federation on Ageing), 165
If You Have Angina (AHA publication), 67
If You Have a Complaint About Advertising (Better Business Bureau; booklet), 139
If You Want to Give Up Cigarettes (American Cancer Society; pamphlet), 77
I Have a Secret Cure for Cancer (American Cancer Society; pamphlet), 77
Ileitis and Colitis (American Digestive Disease Society; pamphlet), 78
Illinois

    AOA office in, 191
    Federal Information Centers in, 170
    Green Thumb projects in, 143
    state agencies in, 193
Illness. See Health (and illness).
Income. See Financial matters.
Indiana
    Federal Information Centers in, 170
    Green Thumb projects in, 143
    state agencies in, 193
Indianapolis (Ind.), ACTION recruiting offices in, 161
Industrial Gerontology Memo (NCOA; newsletter), 165
I Never Told Anybody: Teaching Poetry in a Nursing Home (Koch), 23
Inheritance, legal aspects of, 197–98
Insect Stings Can be Dangerous (Allergy Foundation of America; booklet), 70
Institute for Retired Professionals (IRP; New School for Social Research), 148
Institute of Gerontology (University of Michigan), 50
Institute of Industrial Gerontology, 165
Institutes of Lifetime Learning, 146
Insurance for the Home (Insurance Information Institute; pamphlet), 140
Intermedic, Inc., 121
Intermedic Overseas Health Information Service, 121
Internal Revenue Service (IRS), 127
International Association for Medical Assistance to Travelers (IAMAT), 120
International Federation on Aging (IFA), 165
International Senior Citizens Association (ISCA), 147
Introduction to Home Gardening (Cornell University; booklet), 29

Investigate Before You Invest (SEC; booklet), 133
Investments, 133
Invest Yourself (Commission on Voluntary Service and Action; catalogue), 166
Iowa
    Federal Information Centers in, 170
    state agencies in, 193
IRP (Institute for Retired Professionals; New School for Social Research), 148
IRS (Internal Revenue Service), 127
Irwin, Robert, 140
ISCA (International Senior Citizens Association), 147
ISCA News (ISCA; newsletter), 147
Israel, Joan, 15
Israel, Kenneth, 15
Is Your Home Insured for Today's Values? (Insurance Information Institute; pamphlet), 140
It's Your Move (Moving and Storage Industry of New York; booklet), 46

Jacksonville (Fla.), USGPO bookstores in, 168
Jaffe, Joseph, 66
JCAH (Joint Commission on Accreditation of Hospitals), 51
John Eastman Miniatures (company), 103
Johnson, G. Timothy, 58
Johnson Wax (company), 103
John XXIII (pope), 91
Joint Commission on Accreditation of Hospitals (JCAH), 51
Jonas, David J., 18
Jonas, Doris G., 18
Joy of Communication, The (film), 26
Kansas
    Federal Information Centers in, 171
    Green Thumb projects in, 143
    state agencies in, 193
Kansas City (Mo.), USGPO bookstores in, 169
Karpman, Harold L., 67
Katz, Carole, 139
Keith Jennison Large Type Editions (company), 179
Kelly Brothers Nurseries, Inc., 97
Kennedy, John F., 159
Kentucky
    Federal Information Centers in, 171
    Green Thumb projects in, 143
    state agencies in, 193
Kick-step stool, 89
Kilns, 104
Knopf, Olga, 19
Know How Catalog (N.Y. State College of Agriculture and Life Sciences; catalogue), 29
Koch, Kenneth, 23
Kosnar, Karl J., 44
Kotler, Irma M., 187
Krasker Memorial Film Library (Boston University), 24
Krauss, Ruth, 187
Krauthamer, Martin, 66

Labor, Department of, 14, 126, 142
Laboratory of Behavioral Sciences (NIA), 16
Laboratory of Cellular and Comparative Physiology (NIA), 16
Laboratory of Molecular Aging (NIA), 16
Ladies' Home Journal (magazine), 177
Lanewood Press, Inc., 179
Large Print Book Club, 179
Large Print Review (magazine), 179
Large Type Crosswords (*The New York Times*), 179
Large-type reading materials, 32, 50, 178–79
Last Angry Man, The (film), 27
Laughlin, James, 23
Law . . . and Your Retirement (Retirement Living Magazine; booklet), 195
Learning Corporation of America, 25
Leclerc Corporation, 107
Leclerc West, Inc., 107
Lee, Albert, 139
Legal aspects, 195–97
Legislative representation by AARP-NRTA, 146
Leisure
    crafts for, 99–104
    education for, 90–95
    gardening for, 97–98
    pets for, 109
    sewing for, 107–9
    sports and, 110
Leshan, Eda, 18
"Let Me Grow Lovely" (Baker), 23
Lewis, Gomer, 113
Lewis, Myrna, 56
Liberation from Agism; Two Essays (Gray Panthers), 151
Library of Congress, 181
Liebowitz, Daniel, 39
Lifeline, 183
Lifeline Systems, Inc., 183
Light on your Feet (Public Affairs Pamphlets), 61
Liles, Marcia D., 48
Liles, Robert M., 48
Lipman, Ira A., 81
List of Materials for the Public, A (AHA publication), 67
Little Companion Emergency Paging System, 182
Little Fish Goes a Long Way, A (National Marine Fisheries Service; booklet), 35
Live Longer—Control Your Blood Pressure (Feinman and Wilson), 67
Liver disease (American Digestive Disease Society; pamphlet), 78
Living and Dying at Murray Manor (Gubrium), 50
Living with a Heart Ailment (Public Affairs Pamphlets), 61
Living With Arthritis and Where to

Turn for Help (The Arthritis Foundation; booklet), 73
L. L. Bean, Inc., 110
Local representatives, reporting nursing home complaints to, 51
Locke, Sam, 67
Long, James W., 59
Longfellow, Henry Wadsworth, 23
Looking Ahead: A Woman's Guide to the Problems and Joys of Growing Older (Troll, J. Israel, and K. Israel), 15
Los Angeles (Calif.)
    ACTION recruiting offices in, 161
    Mature Temps in, 142
    USGPO bookstores in, 168
Lost Phoebe, The (film), 27
Louis Harris and Associates, 15
Louisiana
    Federal Information Centers in, 171
    state agencies in, 193
Love in the Later Years (Peterson and Payne), 56
Love Story (book), 178
Low-Sodium Diets Can Be Delicious (Fleischmann's Margarine; booklet), 40
Luger, Norton, 113
Luggage carriers, folding, 122
Lunch programs, 30, 153
Lux Radio Theatre (radio program), 185

MACAP Handbook for the Informed Consumer, 131
MACAP . . . Representing Consumers at the Highest Levels of Industry, 131
Macaroni Is Number One (National Macaroni Institute; booklet), 37
McCall's (magazine), 177
McGraw-Hill Films (company), 25
Maclay, Elise, 18
MacMillan Audio Brandon, 25

MacMillan Films (company), 27
MacTaggart, Ann, 108
Magazines, 172–77
    See also specific magazines.
Mail, receiving, 184
Maine, agencies on aging in, 193
Major Appliance Consumer Action Panel (MACAP), 131
Make It with Foam Egg Cartons (Pack-O-Fun; manual), 101
Making Cottage Cheese at Home (USDA; booklet), 34–35
Making Products Safer: What Consumers Can Do (Public Affairs Pamphlets; publication), 61
Male "Menopause" Crisis in the Middle Years (Public Affairs Pamphlets; publication), 61
Mandy's Grandmother (Skorpen), 187
Mangel, Charles, 12
Manpower Education Institute, 126
Manual for Patients with Parkinson's Disease, A (American Parkinson's Disease Foundation; pamphlet), 78
Manual of Death Education and Simple Burial, A (Morgan), 200
Manufactured Housing Institute, 44
Marcus Aurelius (Roman emperor), 155
Maryland
    Federal Information Centers in, 171
    state agencies in, 193
Mary Maxim (company), 107
Massachusetts
    AOA office in, 191
    Federal Information Centers in, 171
    state agencies in, 193
Mass Media Ministries, 24
Massow, Rosalind, 113
Mature Temps, 142, 148

Mature Years (magazine), 172
Maxwell, Toni, 161
Mayer, Arthur, 26
Mayer, Jean, 28
Mayer, Lillie, 26
Mazursky, Paul, 22
Meals on wheels programs, 32
Media Resources Center (Iowa State University), 26
Media resources for communication, 184–85
Medicaid agencies, reporting nursing home complaints to, 51
Medic Alert Foundation International, 60–61
Medicare Benefits in a Skilled Nursing Facility (Social Security Administration; booklet), 129
Medicine Your Doctor Prescribes: A Guide for Consumers, The (PMA), 59
Medox (organization), 66
Membership organizations, 144–54
Mender's Manual, The (Foote), 108
Menopause: The Experts Speak (NIA; booklet), 62
Merribee Needlecraft Company, 107
Merrill, Annabel L., 29
Metropolitan Life Insurance Co., 62
Miami (Fla.), Telecheck service in, 66
Michigan
    Federal information Centers in, 171
    Green Thumb projects in, 143
    state agencies in, 193
Midwest, the, ACTION recruiting offices in, 161
Milwaukee (Wisc.), USGPO bookstores in, 169
Minigardens for Vegetables (USDA; booklet), 36
Minnesota
    Federal Information Centers in, 171

Green Thumb projects in, 143
   state agencies in, 193
Mississippi, state agencies in, 193
Missouri
   AOA office in, 191
   Federal Information Centers in, 171
   Green Thumb projects in, 143
   state agencies in, 193
Mr. Sammler's Planet (Bellow), 22
Mitchell, S. Weir, 156
Mobile homes, 44
Modern American Poetry (Untermeyer), 23
Modern Maturity (AARP; magazine), 146, 174
Money (magazine), 176
Money . . . and Your Retirement (*Retirement Living Magazine*; booklet), 125
Money matters. *See* Financial matters.
Money-Saving Main Dishes (USDA; booklet), 34
Monopoly (game) for the visually handicapped, 69
Montana
   Green Thumb projects in, 143
   state agencies in, 193
Morehouse, Lawrence A., 55
More Sock Toys You Can Make (Pack-O-Fun; manual), 100
Morgan, Ernest, 200
Moss, Gordon, 13
Moss, Walter, 13
Mother Earth News, The (catalogue), 99, 176
Mother's Bookshelf (*Mother Earth News*; catalogue), 99
Moving, 45–46
Moving and Storage Industry of New York, 46, 140
Museum of Contemporary Crafts (NYC), 99
Musson, Noverre, 43
My Grandson Lew (Zolotow), 187
"My Lost Youth" (Longfellow), 23

Nader, Ralph, 150
National Association for the Visually Handicapped (NAVH), 178–79
National Association of Retired Federal Employees (NARFE), 145
National Audiovisual Center, 27, 75
National Caucus on the Black Aged (NCBA), 165
National Center for Voluntary Action (NCVA), 158
National Center on the Black Aged, 165
National Council for Homemaker–Home Health Aide Services, Inc., 65
National Council of Senior Citizens (NCSC), 145
National Council on the Aging (NCOA), 15, 153, 154, 165, 184
National Dairy Council, 29
National Directory of Retirement Residences: Best Places to Live When You Retire, The (Musson), 43
National Farmers Union, 142
National Federation of Grandmother Clubs of America, 151
National Fire Protection Association, 84
National Gallery of Art, 95
National Guide to Craft Supplies (Glassman), 99
National Home Study Council, 92
National Institute of Allergy and Infectious Diseases, 70–71
National Institute of Senior Centers (NISC), 153, 154, 165
National Institutes of Health (NIH), 16, 70–71, 74
National Institute on Aging (NIA), 14, 16–17, 62
National Institute on Alcohol Abuse and Drug Abuse, 74, 75
National Kidney Foundation, the, 199
National Legal Aid and Defender Association, 195
National Macaroni Institute, 37
National Marine Fisheries Service, 35
National Media Resource Center on Aging, 165, 184
National Park service, 97
   Golden Age Passport issued by, 117
National Phone Care, Inc., 183
National Retired Teachers Association (NRTA), 148, 174
National Retirement Show Company, 185
National Safety Council, 87, 89, 147
National Society for the Prevention of Blindness, Inc., 68–69
National Voluntary Organizations for Independent Living for the Aged (NVOILA), 165
Nature Crafts: Over 1500 Uses for Twigs, Leaves, Gourds, and More (Pack-O-Fun; manual), 101
NAVH (National Association for the Visually Handicapped), 178–79
NCBA (National Caucus on the Black Aged), 165
NCOA (National Council on Aging), 15, 153, 154, 165, 184
NCSC (National Council of Senior Citizens), 145
NCVA (National Center for Voluntary Action), 158
Nebraska
   Federal Information Centers in, 171
   Green Thumb projects in, 143
   stage agencies in, 193
Needlecraft (Van Nostrand Reinhold; folder), 101
Needle threaders, 109
Network, The (Gray Panthers;

newsletter), 151
Nevada, state agencies in, 193
Never Slip Safety Treads, 89
Newell Workshop (company), 101
New Facts About Older Americans (AOA; pamphlet), 14
New Hampshire, state agencies in, 193
New Hope for the Arthritic (Dong and Banks), 40, 73
New Hope for the Hard-of-Hearing (Beltone Electronics Corp.; booklet), 71
New Jersey
    Federal Information Centers in, 171
    Green Thumb projects in, 143
    state agencies in, 193
New Mexico
    Federal Information Centers in, 171
    state agencies in, 193
News bulletins (AARP-NRTA), 146
Newsletter of the National Voluntary Organizations for Independent Living for the Aged, 165
Newsweek (magazine), 181
New Testament of the Jerusalem Bible, 179
New York
    Federal Information Centers in, 171
    Green Thumb projects in, 143
    state agencies in, 193
New York City (N.Y.)
    ACTION recruiting offices in, 159
    AOA office in, 191
    Mature Temps in, 142
    state and local agencies in, 193
New York Times Guide to Continuing Education in America, The (Thompson), 95
New York Times Large-Type Weekly, The (newspaper), 179

NIA (National Institute on Aging), 14, 16–17, 62
NIH (National Institutes of Health), 16, 70–71, 74
Nilius Leclerc (company), 107
NISC (National Institute of Senior Centers), 153, 154, 165
Nonte, George C., Jr., 80
Norback, Craig, 129
Norback, Peter, 129
North Carolina
    Federal Information Centers in, 171
    state agencies in, 194
North Dakota
    Green Thumb projects in, 143
    state agencies in, 194
Northeast, the, ACTION recruiting offices in, 159
Novels, 22–23
Now is Forever (film), 24
Now It's Your Turn to Travel (Massow), 113
NRTA (National Retired Teachers Association), 146–48, 174
NRTA Journal 146, 174
Nursing homes, 42, 49–51
Nursing Homes: Citizen's Action Guide (Horn and Griesel), 50
Nutrition, 28–40
    cooking and growing, 32–37
    products and processes, 37–39
    special diets, 39–40
Nutrition Almanac (Nutrition Search, Inc.), 28
Nutrition Foundation, 29
Nutrition Search, Inc., 28
NVOILA (National Voluntary Organizations for Independent Living for the Aged), 165

Official CB Book, The (Thompson), 184
Ohio
    Federal Information Centers in, 171
    Green Thumb projects in, 143
    state agencies in, 194
Oklahoma
    Federal Information Centers in, 171
    Green Thumb projects in, 143
    state agencies in, 194
Oklahoma City (Okla.), Telecheck service in, 66
Old Age, Survivors and Disability Insurance, 198
Older Americans Month, 147
Older Americans Act (1965), 190
Older Americans Are a National Resource (AOA; booklet), 14
Older Worker Specialist Newsletter (NCOA), 165
Old Fashioned Woman (film), 25
Old-House Journal, The (magazine), 48
Old-House Journal Buyer's Guide (*Old-House Journal*), 48
Old Is What You Get: Dialogues on Aging by the Old and the Young (Shanks), 15
"Old Man's Winter Night, An" (Frost), 23
Old Woman, The (film), 24
Olmstead, Alan H., 21
Olness, Marlene, 39
On constipation and diarrhea (American Digestive Disease Society; pamphlet), 78
One Dragon Too Many (Cooper), 22
On gas and heartburn (American Digestive Disease Society; pamphlet), 78
On stomach trouble (American Digestive Disease Society; pamphlet), 78
Open Wide (American Cancer Society; pamphlet), 77
Operation Independence, 165
Oregon
    Federal Information Centers in, 171
    Green Thumb projects in, 143
    state agencies in, 194

Organ donations, 199
Organic fitness, defined, 55
Organic Gardening (magazine), 36
Osteoarthritis: A Handbook for Patients (The Arthritis Foundation; pamphlet), 73
Otten, Jane, 17

Pacifica Crafts (company), 104
Pacifica Potter's Wheels (Pacifica Crafts; catalogue), 104
Pack-O-Fun (magazine), 100–1
Paid Neighbor Service, 155
Pancreatitis (American Digestive Disease Society; pamphlet), 78
Parker, Ellen, 179
Pasta Primer (National Macaroni Institute; booklet), 37
Pathways to Living (American Health Education Foundation; newsletter), 58
Patterns for Better Living (U-Build Enterprises; catalogue), 102
Payne, Alma, 39
Payne, Barbara, 56
Payne, John Howard, 45
Peace Corps, 159, 161
Peace from Nervous Suffering (Weekes), 75
Pearl's Freighter Tips, Inc., 117
Peege (film), 26
Pennsylvania
    Federal Information Centers in, 171
    Green Thumb projects in, 143
    state agencies in, 194
Pennsylvania State University, correspondence courses of, 94
Pension plans, where to ask questions about, 126
Peptic/duodenal ulcer (American Digestive Disease Society; pamphlet), 78
Percy, Charles, 12
Perspective on Aging (NCOA), 165

Peterson, James A., 56
Pets, 109
Pharmaceuticals Manufacturers Association (PMA), 59
Pharmacy service of AARP-NRTA, 146
Philadelphia (Pa.)
    ACTION recruiting offices in, 159
    AOA office in, 191
    Mature Temps in, 142
    Telecheck service in, 66
    USGPO bookstores in, 169
Philbin, Tom, 46
Phoenix (Ariz.), Telecheck service in, 66
Phoenix Films (company), 26
Phone amplifiers, portable and drop-in, 182
Phone-Care (device), 183
Physical fitness, 53–56
Picasso, Pablo, 13
Picasso Is 90 (film), 25
Pinchot, Ann, 66
Planning for Your Successful Retirement (*Retirement Living Magazine*; booklet), 20
Plants Alive (magazine), 177
Playing cards, giant, 109
Plymouth Meeting (Pa.), Mature Temps in, 142
PMA (Pharmaceuticals Manufacturers Association), 59
Podiatrists' Services under Medicare (American Podiatry Association; pamphlet), 75
Poetry, 23
Popular Mechanics Complete Appliance Repair Manual, 46–47
Popular Mechanics (magazine), 176
Portable phone amplifiers, 182
Porter, Sylvia, 126
Portland (Ore.), ACTION recruiting offices in, 161
Portrait of Jennie (book), 178
Positive Approaches to Selecting Alternative Living Arrangements for the Elderly (Sandoz Pharmaceuticals; booklet), 49
Potter's wheels, 104
Pottery, 104
Pottery and Ceramics (Van Nostrand Reinhold Co.; folder), 101
Poultry in Family Meals (USDA; booklet), 34
Power of Years: The Wisdom of Ethel Percy Andrus (Andrus), 18
Practical Guide for the Unmarried Couple (Blaine and Bishop), 197
Preparing for Aging (Smith), 21
Preretirement Planning Center, 21
Preretirement Planning Guide (Preretirement Planning Center), 21
Prescription Drug Pricing: An Almost Total Absence of Competition (Consumer Federation of America), 137
Presidential greetings, 172
President's Committee on the Employment of the Handicapped, 61
President's Council on Physical Fitness and Sports, 55
Presque Isle Wine Cellars (company), 101
Preventing Crime Through Education (AARP-NRTA; booklet), 82
Prime Time (magazine), 176
Prime Time (radio program), 148
Product safety, 87–88
Professional organizations, 164–66
Protecting Yourself from Prostate Problems (Public Affairs Pamphlets; publication), 61
"Provide, Provide" (Frost), 23
Proxmire, William, 56
Psychological and emotional aspects of digestive disease

(American Digestive Disease Society; pamphlet), 78
Public Affairs Committee, 60
Public Affairs Pamphlets, 18, 30, 60, 61
Public Citizen, Inc., 150
Pueblo (Colo.), USGPO bookstores in, 168
Puerto Rico
  agencies on aging in, 194
  Green Thumb projects in, 143
Puner, Morton, 18
Pyramid Films (company), 26

Questions About Condominiums: What to Ask Before You Buy (HUD; booklet), 43
Questions and Answers Concerning Your Insured Savings (FDIC; booklet), 132
Questions and Answers to Allergy and Allergic Diseases (Allergy Foundation of America; booklet), 70
Quick Breads and Cookies (Cornell University; booklet), 29
Quiz, 13–14

"Rabbi Ben Ezra" (Browning), 23
Radio programs
  of AARP-NRTA, 148
  old-time, 185
Radios, CB, 184
Raft of Craft Ideas, A (Johnson wax; booklet), 103
Reader's Digest Large-Type Edition, The (magazine), 179
Reader's Digest (magazine), 181
Reading Materials in Large Type (Library of Congress; circular), 181
Read the Label, Set a better Table (FDA; pamphlet), 32, 132
Ready or Not . . . A Study Manual for Retirement (Manpower Education Institute; manual), 126
Real estate transactions, 140–41

Recipes for Fat-Controlled, Low Cholesterol Meals (AHA publication), 67
Reclining viewer, 182
Redo, Maria A., 139
Religious programs of AARP-NRTA, 147
Rentals
  car, 118
  film, 24–27
  television program, 20
Representatives, reporting nursing home complaints to, 51
Rescue Breathing to Save a Life (AHA publication), 67
Retired Professional Action Group, 150
Retired Senior Volunteer Program (RSVP), 159–62
Retirement, general facts on, 20–21
Retirement: A Medical Philosophy and Approach (AMA; booklet), 52–53
Retirement Book, The (Adler), 21
Retirement Life (NARFE; magazine), 145
Retirement Living (magazine), 174
Retirement Living Magazine, 20, 44, 125
  publications of
    on financial matters, 125
    on health, 53
    on leisure, 91
    on rights, 195
    on work in retirement, 142
Retirement Living Magazine's Guide to Leisure . . . and Your Retirement (Retirement Living Magazine; guide), 91
Rheumatoid Arthritis: A Handbook for Patients (The Arthritis Foundation; booklet), 72, 73
Rhode Island
  Federal Information Centers, 171
  state agencies in, 194

Rights and legacies, 188–201
  federal and state activities dealing with matters of, 189–94
  legal aspects of, 195–99
  state and area agencies dealing with, 192–94
Rights of Patients, The (*Public Affairs Pamphlets;* publication), 61
Right to Appeal Supplemental Security Income (Social Security Administration; booklet), 128
Riker, Tom, 97
Rochester (N.Y.), ACTION recruiting offices in, 159
Roosevelt, Franklin D., 90, 117
Rosenberg, Magda, 53
Rosenbloom, Joseph, 134
Rosenthal, Richard, 71
Rottenberg, Harvey, 97
Rowse, Arthur A., 137
RSVP (Retired Senior Volunteer Program), 159–62
Rug and Carpet Care (Johnson Wax; booklet), 47
Rusk, James, Jr., 17
Rx for Sound Teeth (NIH folder), 74

Safety
  crime prevention, 80–82
  driver, 87, 89
  fire prevention, 84
  product and home, 82–89
Safety of the Elderly Program Kit (National safety Council), 87
Safety in the Kitchen (Cornell University; booklet), 29
Salton Company, 35
San Diego (Calif.), ACTION recruiting offices in, 161
Sandoz Pharmaceuticals (company), 49
San Francisco (Calif.)
  ACTION recruiting offices in, 159
  Mature Temps in, 142
  USGPO bookstores in, 168

Sappington, Harriet, 91
Savings, 132
SBA (Small Business Administration), 162
SCAMP (Senior Citizen Areawide Motor Pool), 122
Schecter Ben, 187
Schifferes, Justus S., 58
Schmidt, Alice M., 64
Schultz, Mort, 46
SCORE (Service Corps of Retired Executives), 159, 162–63
Scrabble (game) for the visually handicapped, 69
Scrap crafts, 100–1
Sears Roebuck and Co., 63
Seattle (Wash.)
   ACTION recruiting offices in, 161
   USGPO bookstores in, 169
SEC (Securities Exchange Commission), 133
Second Spring (magazine), 174
Securities Exchange Commission (SEC), 133
Seed catalogues, 97
Seeing Clearly (National Association for the Visually Handicapped; newsletter), 179
Segal, Lore, 187
Selected Bibliography on Politics, Social Action and Advocacy (Gray Panthers), 151
Seminars, retirement planning, 125
Semplex of USA (company), 101
Senators, reporting nursing home complaints to, 51
Senior centers, 153–54
Senior Citizen News (NCSC; newspaper), 145
Senior Companion Program, 159, 163
Senior Olympics, 110
Senior Personnel Employment, 155
Senior Power (magazine), 175
Senior Power—And How to Use It (film), 82
Senior Salute, 184

Senior Sports (magazine), 110
Senior Sports International, 110
Sense in the Sun (American Cancer Society; pamphlet), 77
Service Corps of Retired Executives (SCORE), 159, 162–63
Services for Special Needs . . . From the Telephone Company (Bell System; booklet), 180
7 Hopeful Facts About Strokes (AHA publication), 67
751 Handy Hints (Pack-O-Fun; manual), 101
7 Warning signals of cancer, 76
Sewing, 107–9
Sewing machines, 109
Sewing Supplies (Home-Sew; catalogue), 109
Sex After Sixty: A Guide for Men and Women in their Later Years (Butler and Lewis), 56
Sex After Sixty-Five (Public Affairs Pamphlets; publication), 61
Shameless Old Lady, The (film), 27
Shanks, Ann Zane, 15
Shelley, Florence, 17
Sheltered Workshops for the Disabled, Inc., 63
Shopper's Guidebook, The (Dennenberg), 140
Shopper's Guide to Choosing a Mover, A (Yakovich), 45
Simon and Schuster, Inc., 179
Simple Home Repairs . . . Inside (USDA; pamphlet), 47
Sinusitis (National Institute of Allergy and Infectious Diseases; booklet), 70
Sixty-Plus and Fit Again: Exercises for Older Men and Women (Rosenberg), 53
Skin and Its Allergies, The (Allergy Foundation of America; booklet), 70
Skorpen, Liesel, 187

Sleater, William, 187
Small Business Administration (SBA), 162
Smith, Burt Kruger, 21
Social Security Administration, 128–29
   reporting nursing home complaints to, 51
Social Security benefits, 128–29
   work and, 142
Social Security IQ (Social Security Administration; booklet), 128
Sociology of Retirement, The (Atchley), 21
Soldner Pottery Equipment, Inc., 104
Someone Close Drinks Too Much (National Institute on Alcohol Abuse; pamphlet), 74
S.O.S. (*Save on shopping;* directory), 136
South, the, ACTION recruiting offices in, 159
South Carolina, agencies on aging in, 194
South Dakota
   Green Thumb projects in, 143
   state agencies in, 194
Southern Living (magazine), 175
Special diets, 39–40
Specialized programs, 155–56
Special medical care, 61–64
Spock, Benjamin, 58
Spy Who Came in From the Cold, The (LeCarré), 178
Stamps, U.S. Postal, 184
State (and area) agencies, 192–94
   reporting nursing home complaints to, 51
State (and local) representatives, reporting nursing home complaints to, 51
Stay Healthy: Learn About Uterine Cancer (American Cancer Society; pamphlet), 77
Stegner, Wallace, 23
Steinberg, Harry, 136

Stengel, Casey, 91
Stern, Chaim, 201
Stevenson, Burton, 23
Stewart Clay Co., 104
Stocking device, 63
Stonecypher, D. D., 19
Stool, kick-step, 89
Stories and Poems to Read to Your Grandchildren (Kotler), 187
Story, A Story, A (Haley), 187
Story of Health: A Catalog of Films and Publications, The (PMA; pamphlet), 59
Stress and Your Health (Metropolitan Life Insurance Co.; booklet), 62
Stringbean (film), 25
Stroke: A Doctor's Personal Story of His Recovery (Dahleberg and Jaffe), 66
Strokes and their Prevention (Ancowitz), 66
Stukane, Eileen, 48
Successful Aging (Knopf), 19
Summary of Benefits for Veterans with Military Service Before February 1, 1955, and Their Dependents (VA; pamphlet), 128
Sunglasses . . . know what you're getting and what they're really for (National Society for the Prevention of Blindness; booklet), 68
Sunset (magazine), 175
Sunset Boulevard (film), 27
Supplemental Security Income for the Aged, Blind, and Disabled (Social Security Administration; booklet), 129
Swift, Jonathan, 12
Sylvia Porter's Money Book (Porter), 126
Synagogue Council of America, 155

Tai, A. Razzak, 66
Take Care of Yourself: A Consumer's Guide to Medical Care (Vickery and Fried), 59
Talking books, 181
Tape recordings, 186
Tax-Aide program, 127, 147–48
Tax Facts for Older Americans (AARP-NRTA; guide), 127
Teach Your Wife How to Be a Widow (editors of *U.S. News and World Report*), 199
Telecheck, 66
Telephone reassurance service, 182–83
Telephone services for the handicapped, 180, 182–83
Teletypewriters for the Deaf, 181
Television and Your Eyes (National Society for the Prevention of Blindness; booklet), 68
Television programs, 20
Tell Me a Mitzi (Segal), 187
Tennessee
  Federal Information Centers in, 171
  state agencies in, 194
Texas
  AOA office in, 191
  Federal Information Centers in, 171
  Green Thumb projects in, 143
  state agencies in, 194
They're Your Teeth: You Can Keep Them (ADA; booklet), 74
Thinking About a Nursing Home? (AHCA; booklet), 49
Thomas, Dylan, 23
Thompson, Frances Coombs, 95
Thompson, Jon F., 184
  Jim and the Beanstalk (Briggs), 187
Threshold: The First Days of Retirement (Olmstead), 21
Tips and Cautions on Self-Moving (Moving and Storage Industry of New York; booklet), 46
Tips for Energy Savers (Federal Energy Administration; booklet), 132–33
Tips on Home Fire Protection (Council of Better Business Bureaus; pamphlet), 84
Tips on Home Improvement (Council of Better Business Bureaus; publication), 48
Tips on Moving (American Movers Conference; pamphlet), 45
Tips on Refunds and Exchanges (Better Business Bureau; booklet), 139
Tips on Renting a Car (Car and Truck Renting and Leasing Association; booklet), 118
Tips on Work-at-Home Schemes (Better Business Bureau; booklet), 139
Tools, 103
To Stop a thief: The Complete Guide to House, Apartment and Property Protection (Nonte), 80
Total Fitness in Thirty Minutes a Week (Morehouse), 55
To the Good Long Life (Puner), 18
To Your Health . . . In Your Second Fifty Years (National Dairy Council; booklet), 29
Travel (and transportation), 112–22
  by car, 118
  medical emergencies while traveling, 120–21
  travel arrangements, 113–17
Travel Clinical Record (IAMAT), 120
Travelers' Directory, 117
Trust Territory of the Pacific, agencies on aging in, 194
Truth about Aspirin for Arthritis, The (The Arthritis Foundation; booklet), 72
Truth About Diet and Arthritis,

The (The Arthritis Foundation; booklet), 72
Travels with My Aunt (Greene), 22
Troll, Lillian E., 15
Twain, Mark, 39
Two of Us, The (Berri), 22

U-build Enterprises (company), 102
Ulvercroft Large Print books (company), 179
Uniform Donor Card, 199
United Methodist Church, 172
U.S. Consumer Product Safety Commission, 87
U.S. Department of Agriculture Shopper's Guide (USDA), 134
U.S. Postal Service Inspection, 132–33
University Year for Action, 159
Untermeyer, Louis, 23
Up and Around, a Booklet to Aid the Stroke Patient in Activities of Daily Living (AHA publication), 67
Upjohn Co., 64
USDA. *See* Agriculture, Department of.
USGPO. *See* Government Printing Office.
Using Credit Wisely (Credit Union National Association; booklet), 138
Utah
    Federal Information Centers in, 171
    Green Thumb projects in, 143
    state agencies in, 194

VA (Veterans Administration), 128
Vacation Exchange Club, 114
Vacations for the Aging (program), 113
Van Nostrand Reinhold Co., 101
Varicose Veins (AHA publication), 67
Vermont, agencies on aging in, 194
Veterans Administration (VA), 128
Vickery, Donald M., 59
Viewer, reclining, 182
Vigor in Maturity (VIM), 56, 147
Viking Press, 179
VIM (Vigor in Maturity) 56, 147
Violin, The (film), 25
Virginia
    Green Thumb projects in, 143
    state agencies in, 194
Virgin Islands, agencies on aging in, 194
VISTA (Volunteers in Service to America), 159–61
Visual Aids Service (University of Illinois), 26
Visually handicapped, the, 68–69
    communication resources for, 178–79
    giant playing cards, 109
Voluntary Action Centers, 159–61
Voluntary Action Leadership (National Center for Voluntary Action; magazine), 158
Volunteering, 158–63
Volunteers in Service to America (VISTA), 159–61
Volunteers Who Produce Books, Braille, Large Type Books (Library of Congress; circular), 181

Walker, Claxton, 44
Washington
    AOA office in, 191
    Federal Information Centers in, 171
    state agencies in, 194
Washington (D.C.)
    ACTION recruiting offices in, 159
    agencies on aging in, 192
    Federal Information Centers in, 170
    Mature Temps in, 142
    Telecheck service in, 66
    USGPO bookstores in, 168
Watch Your Blood Pressure (*Public Affairs Pamphlets*; publication), 61
W. Atlee Burpee Co., 97
Watt, Bernice K., 29
Way to a Man's Heart, a Fat-Controlled, Low Cholesterol Meal Plan to Reduce the Risk of Heart Attack, The (AHA; publication), 67
Weaving, 101
Weaving and textiles (Van Nostrand Reinhold Co.; folder), 101
Weekend (film), 24
Weekes, Claire, 75
Welfare office, complaints about nursing homes reported to, 51
West, ACTION recruiting offices in the, 159, 161
Westchester County Office for the Aging, 185
Wester, Robert E., 36
West Virginia
    AOA office in, 191
    state agencies in, 194
We Want You to Know About Adverse Reactions to Medicines (FDA; pamphlet), 132
We Want You to Know About Impact-Resistant Eyeglass Lenses (FDA; pamphlet), 132
We Want You to Know About Labels on Medicines (FDA; pamphlet), 132
We Want You to Know About Microwave Oven Radiation (FDA; pamphlet), 132
We Want You to Know About Prescription Drugs (FDA; pamphlet), 132
We Want You to Know About Television Radiation (FDA; pamphlet), 132
What's Your IPQ (Insurance Protection Quotient)? (Insurance Information Institute; pamphlet), 140
What to Look for in a Nursing Home (AMA; pamphlet),

49, 53
What Truth in Lending Means to You (Federal Reserve; pamphlet), 132
What Uncle Sam Owes You (Feinman), 129
What We Know About Headaches (*Public Affairs Pamphlets;* publication), 61
What You Should Know About Health Care Before You Call a Doctor! (Johnson), 58
When Your Parents Grow Old (Often and Shelley), 17
Whisperers, The (film), 27
White, Jack, 136
White House Conference on Aging (1961), 189, 190
Whittemore Durgin Glass Company, 102
Why Survive? Being Old in America (Butler), 14
Whyte, Karen Cross, 35
Widowed persons service program of AARP-NRTA, 147
William Brose Productions, Inc., 82
William's Doll (Zolotow), 187
Wills, 197–98
Wilson, Joseleen, 67
Winco Products, 64
Winemaking supplies, 101
Winfield Company, Inc., 64
Winston, Mary, 39
Winter, Ruth, 19
Wirtz, Willard, 91
Wisconsin
　Federal Information Centers in, 171
　Green Thumb projects in, 143
　state agencies in, 194
Wise Home Buying (HUD; booklet), 45
Woman's Guide to Social Security, A (Social Security Administration; booklet), 129
Wonderful Crisis of Middle Age, The (LeShan), 18
Woodworking supplies, 102

Working in Retirement (*Retirement Living Magazine;* booklet), 142
World Climate Chart (IAMAT), 120
World Immunization and Malaria Risk Chart (IAMAT), 120
Wyoming, agencies on aging in, 194

Yakovich, Linda S., 45
Yankee (magazine), 175
Yanker, Gary, 136
You, the Law and Retirement (HEW; booklet), 195, 199
You and Your Health (Metropolitan Life Insurance Co.; booklet), 62
You Can Still Work and Get Social Security Checks (Social Security Administration; booklet), 129
Young, Jean, 140
Young, Jim, 140
Young Till We Die (D.G. Jonas and D.J. Jonas), 18
Your Blood Pressure (AHA; publication), 67
Your Diet: Health Is in the Balance (Nutrition Foundation; booklet), 29
Your Duties as Representative Payee (Social Security Administration; booklet), 129
Your Eyes: For a Lifetime of Sight (National Society for the Prevention of Blindness; booklet), 68
Your Health and Your Driving (Metropolitan Life Insurance Co.; booklet), 59
Your Money's Worth in Foods (USDA; booklet), 30
Your New Dentures (ADA; booklet), 74
Your Retirement Anti-Crime Guide (AARP-NRTA; booklet), 80
Your Retirement Consumer Guide (AARP-NRTA;

booklet), 136
Your Retirement Food Guide (AARP-NRTA; booklet), 28
Your Retirement Health Guide (AARP-NRTA; publication), 52
Your Retirement Home Repair Guide (AARP-NRTA; publication), 47
Your Retirement Job Guide (AARP-NRTA; booklet), 141
Your Retirement Legal Guide (AARP-NRTA; booklet), 197
Your Retirement Money Guide (AARP-NRTA; booklet), 124
Your Retirement Moving Guide (AARP-NRTA; booklet), 46
Your Retirement Pet Guide (AARP-NRTA; booklet), 109
Your Retirement Psychology Guide (AARP-NRTA; booklet), 52–53
Your Retirement Safety Guide (AARP-NRTA; booklet), 87
Your Retirement Tax Guide (AARP-NRTA; booklet), 127
Your Retirement Widowhood Guide (AARP-NRTA; booklet), 198
Your Right to Question the Decision on Your Hospital Insurance Claim)Social Security Administration; booklet), 128
Your Right to Question Your Medical Insurance Payment (Social Security Administration; booklet), 128
Your Second Life (Karpman and Locke), 67
Your Social Security (Social Security Administration; booklet), 128

Your Social Security Check . . . While You're Outside the United States (Social Security Administration; booklet), 128
Your Social Security Earnings Record (Social Security Administration; booklet), 128
Your Social Security Rights and Responsibilities (Social Security Administration; booklet), 128

Xavier Society for the Blind, 181

Zolotow, Charlotte, 187

ACKNOWLEDGMENTS

The author and graphic designer thank the following for their special efforts and permission to use the illustrative material in the book:

Chapter One
Page 12 (right): *Library of Congress*; Page 13: *Carousel Films, Inc.*; Page 14: *National Institute on Aging*; Page 16: *The Dial Press*; Page 17: *Atheneum Publishers*; Page 19 (left): *Bruce Buchenholz for Viking Press*; Page 25: *McGraw-Hill Films*; Page 26 (left): *Dana Productions*; (right): *Pyramid Films*; Page 27 (right): *American Film Institute*.

Chapter Two
Page 28 (left): *General Electric Company*; Page 30 (center): *Montgomery Ward and Company*; Page 31: *Library of Congress*; Page 33 (top): *Library of Congress*; Page 36 (right): *National Institute on Aging*; Page 38: *Library of Congress*; Page 41: *United States Brewers Association, Inc.*

Chapter Three
Page 42: *Dow Jones Books.*

Chapter Four
Page 57: *Library of Congress*; Page 61: *Medic Alert Foundation*; Page 63: *The Arthritis Foundation*; Page 69: *Society for the Prevention of Blindness*; Page 72: *The Arthritis Foundation*; Page 79: *Library of Congress.*

Chapter Five
Page 81: *Atheneum Publishers*; Pages 82–83: *William Brose Productions*; Page 85: *Library of Congress*; Page 86: *National Safety Council.*

Chapter Six
Page 90: *Library of Congress*; Page 93: *National Institute on Aging*; Page 94–95: *National Gallery of Art*; Page 96: *W. Atlee Burpee Company*; Page 98 (top): *Tom Goodell for Community Programs in the Arts and Sciences, St. Paul, Minnesota*; Pages 105–106: *Library of Congress*; Page 110 (right): *US Postal Service*; Page 111: *Florida Department of Commerce.*

Chapter Seven
Pages 112, 115: *Library of Congress*; Page 116: *Pan American World Airways*; Page 118 (left): *Montgomery Ward and Company*; Page 119: *Uniroyal, Inc.*; Page 123: *Joe McCary for the Montgomery County, Maryland Sentinel.*

Chapter Eight
Page 135: *Sears Roebuck and Company.*

Chapter Nine
Page 144: *National Council on the Aging*; Page 149: *National Institute on Aging*; Page 152: *United States Brewers Association, Inc.*; Page 153: *Joe McCary for the Montgomery County, Maryland Sentinel*; Page 154: *National Institute on Aging*; Page 155: *Synagogue Council of America*; Page 157: *Joe McCary for the Montgomery County, Maryland Sentinel*; Pages 160, 162, 164: *ACTION*; Page 167: *American Library Association.*

Chapter Ten
Page 173: *United States Brewers Association, Inc.*; Page 180: *Library of Congress*; Page 186: *United States Brewers Association, Inc.*; Page 187: *Prince Communications.*

Chapter Eleven
Page 196: *Library of Congress.*